During the eighteenth century British critics applied terms of gender to literature according to the belief that masculine values represented the best literature and feminine terms signified less important works or authors. Laura Runge contends however that the meaning of gendered terms like "manly" or "effeminate" changes over time, and that the language of eighteenth-century criticism cannot be fully understood without careful analysis of the gendered language of the era. She examines conventions in various fields of critical language – including Dryden's prose, the early novel, criticism by women and the developing aesthetic – to show how gendered epistemology shaped critical "truths." Her exploration of critical commonplaces, such as regarding the heroic and the sublime as masculine modes and the novel as a feminine genre, addresses issues central to eighteenth-century studies and still relevant today.

GENDER AND LANGUAGE IN BRITISH LITERARY CRITICISM
1660–1790

GENDER AND LANGUAGE IN BRITISH LITERARY CRITICISM
1660–1790

LAURA L. RUNGE

University of South Florida, St. Petersburg

CAMBRIDGE
UNIVERSITY PRESS

PUBLISHED BY THE PRESS SYNDICATE OF THE UNIVERSITY OF CAMBRIDGE
The Pitt Building, Trumpington Street, Cambridge CB2 1RP, United Kingdom

CAMBRIDGE UNIVERSITY PRESS
The Edinburgh Building, Cambridge CB2 2RU, United Kingdom
40 West 20th Street, New York, NY 10011–4211, USA
10 Stamford Road, Oakleigh, Melbourne 3166, Australia

© Laura L. Runge 1997

First published 1997

Printed in Great Britain at the University Press, Cambridge

Typeset in Baskerville 11/12½ [VN]

A catalogue record for this book is available from the British Library

Library of Congress cataloguing in publication data

Runge, Laura L.
Gender and language in British literary criticism, 1660–1790 / by Laura L. Runge.
p. cm.
Includes bibliographical references and index.
ISBN 0 521 57009 3 (hardback)
1. Criticism – Great Britain – History – 18th century. 2. English literature
– 18th century – History and criticism – Theory, etc.
3. English literature – Early modern, 1500–1700 – History and criticism – Theory, etc.
4. English literature – Women authors – History and criticism – Theory, etc.
5. Women and literature – Great Britain – History – 18th century.
6. Women and literature – Great Britain – History – 17th century.
7. Sex differences (Psychology) in literature – Terminology.
8. Language and languages – Sex differences – Terminology.
9. Criticism – Great Britain – History – 17th century.
10. Authorship – Sex differences – Terminology.
11. Criticism – Terminology. I. Title.
PR73.R86 1997
801'.95'0941–dc21
96–40456 CIP

ISBN 0 521 57009 3 hardback

Contents

Preface

A person unacquainted with literary studies asked me what literature I discuss in this book. To his surprise, I explained that I do not directly analyze literature. This is a theoretical work that posits a history of literary criticism in the eighteenth century to account for the way gendered knowledge shapes literary value. It obviously is not the only or, finally, the "true" history of literary criticism, but it offers an examination of conventions in critical language that tell a side of the story that has not yet been discussed. In doing so it complicates the understanding of the critical practice of the eighteenth century, which has implications for our own assumptions and commonplaces. I have structured the argument around several critical inheritances that inform the study of literature today. More importantly, however, the book opens up to inquiry the matrix of critical and gendered values through which eighteenth-century literature is produced. As such it re-signifies the critical vocabulary for analyzing those works, with particular attention to values or forms that have been denominated feminine.

The completion of this project is indebted to some dear friends and generous colleagues. I thank Martine Watson Brownley for her strong mentoring and support for my work. I am grateful to John Sitter for his judicious advice and instruction. The book gained much by the thoughtful readings and critical commentaries of Peggy DesAutels, Elisabeth Fraser, Bob Hall, Elizabeth Hirsh, Jo Parker, Ruth Whitney, James Winn, and most especially Carole Meyers. I also appreciate the comments of two anonymous readers from Cambridge, as well as the patient labor of my copyeditor Chris Lyall Grant. Parts of chapters 2 and 3 were previously published in different forms in *Essays in Literature* and *Eighteenth-Century Studies*, respectively. My greatest obligation and most pleasing to acquit is to Mark Gordon, to whom I dedicate this book.

CHAPTER I

Manly words on Mount Parnassus

Women we have often eagerly placed *near* the throne of literature:
if they seize it, forgetful of our fondness, we can hurl them from it.

Critical Review[1]

Eighteenth-century British writers metaphorically represent literary excellence as a throne or mountain, indicating a place of honor raised above the hordes of undistinguished writers. Exactly who gains access to that hallowed ground forms the subject of earnest debate throughout the period. The terms of the controversy reflect the configurations of power in critical authority, and the discourse of gender frequently supplies a language of definitive polarities.

In *The Battle of the Books* (*c.* 1697, 1704), Jonathan Swift memorably demonstrates the utility of gendered codes in the figure of Criticism, a composite of bestial and misogynist imagery who champions the Moderns over the Ancients in the contest for Mount Parnassus.

> The goddess herself had claws like a cat; her head, and ears, and voice, resembled those of an ass; her teeth fallen out before, her eyes turned inward, as if she looked only upon herself; her diet was the overflowing of her own gall; her spleen was so large, as to stand prominent, like a dug of the first rate; nor wanted excrescencies in form of teats, at which a crew of ugly monsters were greedily sucking.[2]

On the one hand, the image stimulates revulsion toward Criticism by distorting the creature's female body in beastly analogues with supernumeraries unmodestly exposed. On the other, Swift simultaneously invests her with pettiness, confirming feminine stereotypes of the goddess as vain and splenetic. By casting this new form of writing as vile coquette, Swift equates literary criticism with a frightening version of

---

[1] *Critical Review*, second series, vol. 5 (1792): 132.
[2] Jonathan Swift, *The Prose Works of Jonathan Swift, D.D.*, ed. Temple Scott, 12 vols. (London: G. Bell and Sons, Ltd., 1919), vol. I, p. 175.

I

his culture's most trivial character. Capitalizing on persistent anxieties surrounding female sexuality, Swift registers the threat of modern criticism and yet immediately neutralizes its force through implications of indecency and inferiority. In this way, Swift connects the illegitimacy of the goddess' reign with her grotesque femaleness; the success of the satire relies on the vilification of the feminine implicit in the organization of his society.

The sexuality of the creature becomes a greater focal point of fear in the description of Criticism's children, "Noise and Impudence, Dulness and Vanity, Positiveness, Pedantry, and Ill-manners," the result of an incestuous relationship with Ignorance, her father.[3] The den of Criticism, for Swift, is pointedly not the productive scene of writing; instead, he describes the activity as exaggerated gestation in which the offspring allegorize the omnipresence and vulgarity of modern judgment. Yet the goddess possesses an insidious power that lies in her exclusively female capacity to breed. The repulsive female body serves as a sign and a site for the cultural reproduction of monstrous falsehoods; conversely, the source of modern literary criticism is feminized and reviled as corrupt and uncontained. The allegory stigmatizes both the female body and modern criticism as dangerous cultural waste. The stakes in this debate become clear in Criticism's self-aggrandizing soliloquy, culminating in the preposterous claim: " 'Tis I who have deposed wit and knowledge from their empire over poetry, and advanced myself in their stead."[4] Swift represents the goddess herself as a pretender to the throne of poetry, advancing the modern errors of independence, complacency, and endless production. In ironic contrast, Swift upholds "wit and knowledge" as the founding authority of poetry, a position elaborated by the proponents for the Ancients. Thus, the language of gender invigorates Swift's polemic. Through the association with gross femininity, Swift impugns the critical output of his predominantly male contemporaries, engaging a semiotics of gender to convey a range of culturally specific meanings in defense of established literary authority.

Swift's personification highlights two relevant aspects of the history of literary criticism: first, the practice of criticism proliferated in the late seventeenth and eighteenth centuries, forming a part of a contested discussion about what was knowable, what was worth knowing, and who was authorized to know; and, second, gender was an explicit and fundamental part of that literary discourse. At the heart of the debate

---

[3] Ibid.   [4] Ibid., p. 176.

over Ancients and Moderns is the question of how one determines literary value. Throughout the long eighteenth century in Britain, the balance of this contest shifts from the classical to the modern, or what in retrospect we have labeled the Romantic. Ironically, by 1798 modified versions of the qualities that Swift attacks – autonomy, confidence, and excess – become the hallmarks of the Romantic poet. The proliferation of literary criticism during this period is in part fueled by the challenge to prevailing literary ideals and the persistent desire to protect established value from change.

At every point in this history, however, gender plays a complex and significant role. The language of gender enters the critical discussion of the Restoration and eighteenth century in numerous places, in metaphor or allegory, in models of hierarchy, in descriptive phrases, and prescriptive measures. At the most basic level, gender provides an everyday vocabulary through which the critic constructs literary distinctions. In these ways the discourse of gender informs, shapes, and, in part, enables early British literary judgment. Cultural designations of masculinity and femininity, which change over the course of this history, form part of a matrix of discourses through which this specialized literary knowledge is articulated. Assessments of literary value engage the hegemonic discourse in multiple and intricate ways. In short, gender is a constitutive element of eighteenth-century literary criticism.

Where they meet, neither literary value nor gender can be properly understood without reference to the other. The discussion of literary criticism and the consideration of gendered differences, both of which expand greatly during the eighteenth century, are at many points thoroughly bound together; thus Dryden labels Virgil "manly" and assumes his audience understands its significance. The *Spectator* contains essays on the beauties of *Paradise Lost* along with advice on ladies' hoop skirts, and John Bennett advises young girls to read Burke's *Philosophical Enquiry On the Sublime and the Beautiful* in order to acquire those very traits.[5] Because distinctions of literary worth are often articulated through cultural constructions of gender, the formal as well as the moral criteria of literature correspond with specific, historical gendered constructions. During the period 1660–1790, the reigning organization of society is patriarchal, by which I mean that the right to exercise all official forms of power – governmental, economic, legal, domestic, etc. – belongs first and foremost to the male subject and only to the female by default or

[5] John Bennett, *Letters to a Young Lady on a Variety of Useful and Interesting Subjects, Calculated to Improve the Heart, to Form the Manners, and Enlighten the Understanding*, ninth American edition (New York, 1827), p. 172.

exigency.[6] Literary criticism appropriates a wide range of patriarchal images and conventions in justification of its hierarchy of literature. Not surprisingly, as Virginia Woolf notes of a later period, "it is the masculine values that prevail."[7] The importance of "masculine" art always takes precedence over the "feminine," although the configuration shifts as the model of gender relations in society changes. Moreover, while the critical construction of gender admits some permutation over the course of a hundred and thirty years, the discourse regularly restricts certain privileges, like judgment and intellect, as masculine, effectively protecting them from female encroachment.

The prevalence of the word "manly" as a critical term of approbation and "effeminate" as a term of reproach testifies to the consistent privileging of "masculine" values over a category distinguished as not masculine, whether it is feminine or unmanly. Correspondingly, Addison praises "those rational and manly Beauties" of Milton, while Samuel Cobb discovers in Longinus "the expression of free, generous and manly spirit," and Joseph Warton describes Pope's genius for "solid and manly observations on life or learning."[8] Beyond signifying a sense of admiration for the writer, the term "manly" offers a rather nebulous meaning. These critics associate the word with a series of qualifiers that suggest different shades of import. Addison's phrasing modifies the "Divine Work" of *Paradise Lost* and suggests an intellectual and lyrical excellence achieved by the learned poet. Cobb's depiction of the sublime invokes an energetic, boundless male imagination, unrestrained by the chaste codes of behavior required of women. Warton indicates a worldliness in Pope's writing that might be beyond the scope of the poetic but is still dignified. In each example, the usage of "manly" evokes a world-view or experience that is gendered by a historical, social construction of the gentleman.

Despite its ambiguity, the word "manly" conveys a sense of universal masculine privilege that Fielding mocks in *Joseph Andrews* (1742). In a chapter entitled "A discourse between the poet and the player; of no other use in this history but to divert the reader," two thugs analyze

---

[6] See Michael McKeon's article, "Historicizing Patriarchy: The Emergence of Gender Difference in England, 1660–1760," for an analysis of the dynamic of male dominance in the societal shift from aristocratic to bourgeois manifestations of authority: *Eighteenth-Century Studies*, 28.3 (1995), 295–322.

[7] Virginia Woolf, *A Room of One's Own*. (San Diego, New York, and London: Harvest/HBJ, 1929), p. 77.

[8] Joseph Addison and Richard Steele, *The Spectator*, ed. Donald F. Bond, 5 vols. (Oxford: Clarendon Press, 1965), vol. III, p. 530; Cobb quoted in Samuel H. Monk, *The Sublime: A Study of Critical Theories in XVIII-Century England*, second edition (Ann Arbor: Michigan University Press, 1960), p. 27; Joseph Warton, *An Essay on the Writings and Genius of Pope* (London, 1756), p. 103.

drama while they kidnap the heroine. One says to the other: "for d——n me, if there are not manly Strokes, ay whole Scenes, in your last Tragedy, which at least equal *Shakespear*."9 Fielding's rustic scene invokes a patrician attitude toward criticism akin to Swift's, aligning the pretension to literary authority with a criminal use of masculine physical power. The application of the adjective "manly" in this context exposes its function as critical shorthand for literary status. Samuel Johnson, equally cynical about the use of critical cant, puts "manly" at the top of Dick Minim's list of epithets "of which he has never settled the meaning, but which are very commodiously applied to books which he has not read, or cannot understand."10 Here the term acts as an empty signifier, filling space in the bloated critical discourse. Both Fielding and Johnson attach an ironic consciousness to their construction of masculine critical authority that operates simultaneously with unqualified expressions of "manly" like Warton's. Such ridicule by mid-century critics indicates a pervasive reliance on the inaccurate word, but the positive connotations of "manly" were not questioned.

GROUNDING THE ARGUMENTS

The proliferation of literary criticism at the beginning of the eighteenth century in England resulted in part from the epistemological crisis of the seventeenth century, which valorized empirical knowledge. This widespread desire to evaluate literature in scientific, moral, national, and aesthetic ways represents just one of the areas in which society sought "truth." According to Michel Foucault, the objects of knowledge and the subjects who know become involved in numerous and varying power relationships when examination is intensified on a broad cultural level. By identifying the structure of knowledge – that is, how a culture gathers and validates knowledge – the "will to truth" illustrates one means of organization by which a society puts knowledge to work, and this arrangement is innately exclusive.

During this period, particularly in England, the establishment of truth takes on the ubiquitous forms of enumeration, measurement, and hierarchy: "a will to know which was prescribed . . . by the technical level

---

9 Henry Fielding, *Joseph Andrews*, ed. Martin C. Battestin (Middleton: Wesleyan University Press, 1967), p. 261.
10 Samuel Johnson, *The Idler and The Adventurer*, ed. W. J. Bate, John M. Bullitt, L. F. Powell, in *The Yale Edition of The Works of Samuel Johnson*, 16 vols. (New Haven: Yale University Press, 1963), vol. II, p. 192.

where knowledges had to be invested in *order* to be verifiable and useful."[11] In the early critical discourse, authors, readers, and works of art were scrutinized, categorized, and debated; systems of value were proposed, dismissed, and modified. The act of writing or speaking about literature assumed a certain authority, and despite (or, perhaps, because of) that century's keen awareness of the limitations of language, the critic became responsible for discerning truths about literature. Critical judgment involved the ability to distinguish specific qualities, and eighteenth-century critics apprehended these judgments through current models of difference, like gender, which involved a series of inherent power relationships.

As the inheritors of empirical discourse, eighteenth-century critics ground their literary truths in the language of objectivity, human nature, and reason. In order to be objective, writers attempt to recognize and evaluate the historical differences between various works. Thus, Pope assesses Homer's poetry in the context of his civilization in order to "regulate our present Opinion of them, by a View of that Age in which they were writ";[12] (in the process he produces a version of those epics imprinted with the unmistakable world-view of eighteenth-century Britain.[13]) For the less remote Dryden, Johnson demands that "to judge rightly of an author we must transport ourselves to his time, and examine what were the wants of his contemporaries, and what were his means of supplying them."[14] Ostensibly, this gesture removes the prejudices of a critic's entrenched perspective.

However, the discrimination of difference between the critic and the work generally gives way to the more satisfying recognition of sameness. Even though critics acknowledge some literary products as historically situated, most concur in dismissing idiosyncrasies in favor of timeless generalities, a set of privileged standards borrowed from the discourse on universal human nature. In the Western humanist tradition, influenced by Judeo-Christian origination myths, human nature is divinely ordained. Throughout this period, "nature" operates as an authoritative discourse, to borrow Bakhtin's term, because the idea refers to an honored, pre-established set of norms: "The authoritative word is located in a

[11] Michel Foucault, "The Order of Discourse," trans. Ian Mcleod, in Robert Young, ed., *Untying the Text, A Post-Structuralist Reader* (London: Routledge and Kegan Paul, 1981), p. 55 (my emphasis).
[12] Alexander Pope, trans., *The Iliad of Homer*, ed. Maynard Mack, vols. VII–VIII in *The Twickenham Edition of the Poems of Alexander Pope*, 10 vols. (London: Methuen, 1967), vol. VII, p. 28.
[13] For a discussion of the role gender plays in that translation, see Carolyn D. Williams, *Pope, Homer, and Manliness: Some Aspects of Eighteenth-Century Classical Learning* (London: Routledge, 1993).
[14] Johnson, *The Six Chief Lives from Johnson's Lives of the Poets with Macaulay's Life of Johnson*, ed. Matthew Arnold, reprint (New York: Russell and Russell, 1968), p. 176.

distanced zone, organically connected with a past that is felt to be hierarchically higher. It is, so to speak, the word of the fathers."[15] The concept of "human nature" provides the most widely accepted explanatory framework for all aspects of human experience. Consequently, "nature" underwrites the patriarchal system that enforces a hierarchical organization of gendered difference. As the ultimate ontological source of legitimation, the discourse of human nature authorizes the critic's assessment of generic difference and similarity and, furthermore, enables the rejection of representations that deviate from the standard representation of immutable human nature.

Because of its foundational status, human nature becomes the most fundamental knowledge for the critic. According to Johnson, "It ought to be the first endeavour of a writer ... to distinguish nature from custom, or that which is established, because it is right, from that which is right only because it is established."[16] Johnson admits the possibility that social constructions of taste, or custom, may hold sway in literary discourse, but he subjugates these contingencies to the superior power of universality. Johnson's faith in the centripetal force of human nature is axiomatic, for instance, in his successful projection of Shakespeare's fame – "Nothing can please many, and please long, but just representations of general nature."[17] By positing a continuity in humanity transcending time, Johnson's criticism simplifies the measure of literary worth to the reproduction of values consistent with that theoretical sameness. The critic's authority, therefore, rests on his or her ability to discern the dominant culture's version of "nature" – synonymous with right or truth – from fashion or other spurious forms of knowledge. As will become evident in the succeeding chapters, access to a full understanding of "human nature" is circumscribed according to gender.

The capacity for reason is a fundamental commonplace of Enlightenment discourses on human nature and the bottom line for literary judgment. Eighteenth-century literary discourse projects an ideal critical community of heterogeneous participants unified through the shared faculty of reason.[18] Addison explains the phenomenon in this way:

[15] Mikhail M. Bakhtin, *The Dialogic Imagination: Four Essays*, ed. Michael Holquist, trans. Caryl Emerson and Michael Holquist (Austin: University of Texas Press, 1981), p. 342.

[16] Quoted in Joseph Warton, *Essay on Pope*, p. 126.

[17] Johnson, *Johnson on Shakespeare*, vols. VII–VIII, ed. Arthur Sherbo, in *Works*, vol. VII, p. 61.

[18] For more detailed discussion of the constitution of the autonomous subject within this public literary discourse, see Laurie Finke, *Feminist Theory, Women's Writing*, Reading Women Writing Series (Ithaca: Cornell University Press, 1992), chapter 4, esp. pp. 112–113, and Terry Eagleton, *The Function of Criticism from the "Spectator" to Post-Structuralism* (London: Verso, 1984), especially chapter 1.

"Human Nature is the same in all reasonable Creatures; and whatever falls in with it, will meet with Admirers amongst Readers of all Qualities and Conditions."[19] The concept of universal human nature authorizes Addison, and other reasonable participants in the community, to extrapolate from his empirical point of view and to generalize about his fellow creatures. Reason thus serves as the commonality that binds all humans together; however, because not all members have equal shares of rationality, the faculty serves as a means to stratify individuals. Significantly, feminine "nature" is constructed as less rational than general human nature. Although theoretically available to all subjects in discourse, the criterion of reason acts as the practical means to limit access to "truth" and, hence, to qualify specific individuals to speak for others.

The appeals to objectivity, nature, and reason codify the critical task as orderly, stable, and to a certain extent democratic, but they also mask the historical limitations of the critic's authority. In particular, the universalizing tendencies of the discourse elide the extent to which criticism is structured by gender. In his unprecedented debunking of Pope's poetry in 1756, Joseph Warton praises Johnson's distinction between custom and nature as the "liberal and *manly* censure of critical bigotry."[20] Warton appeals to Johnson's authority to sanction his own innovative criticism, and he adopts the masculine term to enforce the propriety of his judgment. Warton's gesture aligns clear-sighted reason with the masculine identity, but more importantly, he suggests that changes in taste are negotiated in a masculine discourse. Gendered expressions in the critical discourse like Warton's expose the innately exclusive organization of knowledge that is necessary to establish the putatively neutral designation of truth.

Because I am interested in historicizing literary criticism as part of the unifying discourses of patriarchal hegemony, this analysis requires the tools that post-structuralist theories of discourse and power provide. By focusing on the level of language, these theories challenge the notion of "truth" as an objective, verifiable reality. Instead, "truth" becomes a linguistic construct whose referent is ultimately indeterminate among shifting significations. Discourse achieves a hegemonic status, nonetheless, through the impression that truth can be established and through the orchestration of power used to consolidate that impression. A single truth is posited only by the erasure of conflicting or alternative

---

[19] Addison, *The Spectator*, ed. Bond, vol. i, p. 297.
[20] Warton, *Essay on Pope*, pp. 126–127; my emphasis.

expressions, and such dominance is achieved when the truth coincides with or validates the experience of the ruling population. All discourses, as postulated by Foucault, serve as the vehicle through which power or knowledge is dispersed in society. Whereas humanist thought represents conventional language as the transparent medium for the transmission of information, Foucault's theories illustrate how the articulation of such knowledge functions as power and vice versa: "It is not possible for power to be exercised without knowledge, it is impossible for knowledge not to engender power."[21] By excluding all knowledge that fails to reify the autonomous subject, the humanist discourse represents truth or nature as a monolithic experience. Criticism operates in a similar manner. As a discourse invested in the identification of literary "truths," criticism erects authoritative structures through the definition of "right" principles and the displacement of contradictory views; in the interest of preserving a recognizable order, criticism tends to shape truths that are consistent with hegemonic values.

Like the notion of truth, the humanistic "self" is similarly revised as a site of linguistic construction in post-structuralist theories. The self, conceived as the autonomous author of meaning or truth, becomes the "subject," an identity shaped by a given matrix of complex, interactive discourses. The Western humanist tradition establishes the illusion of the autonomous self by privileging and universalizing the experience of the *masculine* elite through the exclusion and repression of alternative realities. Foucault's writings do not explicitly account for the differing effects that normative discourse has on male and female subjects, a failing noted in many feminist modifications of his theories.[22] While his analysis of the capillary forms of power in society exposes the mythical status of the authoritative self, it fails to recognize the gendered dimension of the fictive authority. Irene Diamond and Lee Quinby propose that "for feminists, the problem with humanism is not merely that it derives from illusory assumptions about an autonomous and universal self, but that this particular self is the domain of privileged white men."[23] In order to analyze the effects of gendered language in

---

[21] Michel Foucault, *Power/Knowledge: Selected Interviews and Other Writings, 1972–77*, ed. Colin Gordon (New York: Pantheon, 1980), p. 52.

[22] See Nancy Hartsock, "Foucault on Power: A Theory for Women?" in Linda J. Nicholson, ed., *Feminism/Postmodernism* (New York: Routledge, 1990), pp. 157–175; Linda Woodbridge, "A Strange, Eventful History: Notes on Feminism, Historicism, and Literary Study," *Exemplaria: A Journal of Theory in Medieval and Renaissance Studies* 2.2 (Fall 1990), and Irene Diamond and Lee Quinby, eds., *Feminism and Foucault: Reflections on Resistance* (Boston: Northeastern University Press, 1988).

[23] Diamond and Quinby, eds., *Feminism and Foucault*, p. xv.

literary criticism, it is important to realize that the construction of masculine privilege in discourse, which significantly bolsters the autonomous self, is achieved through the suppression of the feminine.

The mastery of the humanistic self is in part maintained through its separation from others, or a monolithic representation of the Other, whether designated in terms of race, culture, religion, class, gender, or any number of binary divisions. For this study, the perpetuation of a system of sexual difference in predetermined and ahistorical categories takes precedence. In order to avoid reproducing the humanistic binary of biologically determined sexes, it is helpful to envision gender as a semiotic process, drawing upon the theories of Foucault. Rather than view human sexuality as an unchanging, biological inevitability, Foucault argues that human bodies are constituted through historically specific matrices of signification.

Sexuality must not be thought of as a kind of natural given which power tries to hold in check, or as an obscure domain which knowledge tries gradually to uncover. It is the name that can be given to a historical construct: not a furtive reality that is difficult to grasp, but a great surface network in which the stimulation of bodies, the intensification of pleasures, the incitement to discourse, the formation of special knowledges, the strengthening of controls and resistances, are linked to one another, in accordance with a few major strategies of knowledge and power.[24]

As a matrix of signification, sexuality occupies "an especially dense transfer point for the relations of power."[25] Foucault resists, however, identifying any binary relationship as a stable construct of power; consequently his account of sexuality minimizes the historical consistency in the distribution of power between men and women.[26] Feminists like Joan W. Scott expand Foucault's ideas to focus specifically on the gendered dynamic in the discursive production of sexuality. She conceptualizes gender as a fundamental epistemological category informed by intersecting cultural languages: "gender is a constitutive element of social relationships based on perceived differences between the sexes, and gender is a primary way of signifying relationships of power."[27] Sexual difference is seen as socially constructed through manifold cultural forms of representation, and these signifying systems are not neutral but, rather,

---

[24] Foucault, *The History of Sexuality*, trans. Robert Hurley, 3 vols. (New York: Vintage Books, 1980), vol. 1, pp. 105–106.
[25] Ibid., p. 103.
[26] See in particular his "Rules of continual variations," ibid., p. 99.
[27] Scott, "Gender: A Useful Category of Historical Analysis," *American Historical Review*, 91 (December 1986), p. 1067.

incorporate a spectrum of political values. For Scott, gender operates as a "primary field within which or by means of which power is articulated."[28] As such, the language of gender – from the everyday expressions of gendered experience to the authoritative discourse of patriarchal law – contributes in a basic way to the organization of all social life.

In Restoration and eighteenth-century discourse, the widespread effect of gendered knowledge is evident on a fairly obvious linguistic level. Authors regularly characterize concepts or things as masculine and feminine by using gendered modifiers. Addison, for instance, recommends a "strong, steady masculine piety," and Joseph Warton praises a line for its "very strong and masculine sense," but Shaftesbury condemns "the effeminate kind or . . . the false tender, the pointed witticism, the disjointed thought," and Johnson derides the prevalence of "female phrases and fashionable barbarisms."[29] The writings of the period are also marked by a generous use of gendered personification, as in Dennis's claim that meter "may be said to be both the Father and the Child of Passion," or in Johnson's oppositional comparison: "I am not yet so lost in lexicography, as to forget that *words are the daughters of earth, and that things are the sons of heaven*."[30] By assigning gendered terms to otherwise neuter entities, criticism places these things in masculine and feminine realms, but it also changes the valence of meaning for these words and superimposes the cultural values associated with gender. And this is, at least in part, intentional.

The categories of gender provide a useful language for the eighteenth-century literary critic, because their discursive characters are discrete, binary, universal, and unchanging, which is not the same thing as saying that gendered categories are any one of those things. Through the consolidating forces of hegemony, gender *appears* to be stable throughout time, but it is actually constantly produced through a matrix of discourses situated in any given historical moment. The consistent subordination of women to men in patriarchal cultures contributes significantly to the "natural" and static appearance of gendered categories, which sanctions the use of gendered language in literary

---

[28] Ibid., p. 1069.
[29] Addison and Steele, *Spectator* (1711), ed. Bond, vol. II, p. 290; J. Warton, *Essay on Pope*, p. 85; Third Earl of Shaftesbury, Anthony Ashley Cooper, "Advice to an Author," in Scott Elledge, ed., *Eighteenth-Century Critical Essays*, 2 vols. (Ithaca: Cornell University Press, 1961), vol. I, p. 189; Johnson, *The Idler*, in *Works*, vol. II, p. 240.
[30] John Dennis, *The Critical Works of John Dennis*. ed. Edward Niles Hooker, 2 vols. (Baltimore: The Johns Hopkins University Press, 1939–1943), vol. I, p. 376; Johnson, preface, *A Dictionary of the English Language . . . In two Volumes* (London, 1755).

criticism. Nature, as we have seen, operates as an authoritative discourse for the eighteenth century in that it provides an unquestioned, universally recognized, vocabulary of "truth." Mimetic theories of art, which dominate literary criticism from the time of Ancient Greece through the eighteenth century, insist that art imitates nature. Praise for this mimesis often relies on the assumption of a universal and immutable human nature, and a uniform feature of this paradigm is the hierarchical division of the sexes. The gendered hierarchy of society thus serves as a "natural" metaphor for the description of literature because it is recognizable as a constant. The people might behead their king, as they did in 1649, and thus question the "natural" order of Sovereignty, but the right of male authority over women remained an apparent fixture of nature. The metaphor is widespread because it is simple – or simplified through the erasure of competing realities – and in the eighteenth-century bi-polar world, where "reality is made up of opposites," the contrast between masculine and feminine is highly effective.[31]

Gendered language imposes its own epistemological structure on the discourse of literary criticism, and, as Scott suggests, this imposition carries with it significations of power. Distinctions in literary criticism constituted through the language of gender assist or consolidate certain interests while they subjugate or erase others. With an emphasis on the ways in which various discourses dominate, produce, and reproduce knowledge, discursive theories, especially as translated through new historicist practice, tend to construct the subject as ultimately passive and determined by external forces. While recognizing the usefulness of gender as powerful discursive category, we need to avoid the conceptualization of a ubiquitous and totalizing hegemony that forecloses agency, resistance, and opportunities for change. Such lack of agency threatens to obviate the feminist goals of investigating and eradicating the systems of oppression at the intersections of class, race, gender, and sexuality.[32] Consequently, the feminist project of revisioning literary criticism does not end with the identification of different discourses involved in

---

[31] Earl Wasserman, "Johnson's *Rasselas*: Implicit Contexts," *Journal of English and Germanic Philology*, 74 (1975), p. 9.

[32] This criticism is not unique to Foucault but is also a frequently cited obstacle between the partnership of post-structuralism and feminist theory. For further discussion, see Catherine Belsey, "Constructing the Subject: Deconstructing the Text," in Judith Newton and Deborah Rosenfelt, eds., *Feminist Criticism and Social Change: Sex, Class, and Race in Literature and Culture* (New York, Methuen, 1985), pp. 45–64; Linda Alcoff, "Cultural Feminism versus Post-Structuralism: The Identity Crisis in Feminist Theory," *Signs: Journal of Women in Culture and Society*, 13.3 (Spring 1988), 405–436; Donna J. Haraway, *Simians, Cyborgs, and Women: The Reinvention of Nature* (New York: Routledge, 1991), pp. 183–201.

multiple power relationships. It is, on the contrary, essential to retain a sense of agency in order to resignify that discourse, in Judith Butler's sense of the word. Butler posits the usefulness of deconstructing universal categories like "woman" or "feminism" in order to reauthorize their meanings: "For if the term permits of a resignification, if its referent is not fixed, then possibilities for new configurations of the term become possible."[33] Rather than read this history of gendered literary criticism as moribund and complete – its meaning already determined – the process of thoughtfully reassessing the literary language of eighteenth-century discourse allows us to realign standards and reinterpret texts.

In "Patrolling the Borders" Walkowitz, Jehlen, and Chevigny propose two related models of historical change, which retain the subject's agency while remaining sensitive to the power of discourse. Through what Walkowitz calls "partial agency," we can understand the production of texts in society as the result of authorial agency; likewise, reading subjects are "active interpreters who resist the text, supplement it, displace pieces, and transform it."[34] The text itself, the cultural meaning it represents, is mutable and multiple; this plurality of meanings constitutes "discourse." Writing and reading subjects exercise partial agency and endure partial limitation within discursive constraints. Jehlen, on the other hand, focuses on agency at the level of discourse and sees the representation of cultural meaning in discourse as a process of construction and destruction. With partial agency exercised at the level of subject, the cultural discourse is in constant flux: "it has continually to recreate a coherence that continuously falls apart so that it can constitute a language of change."[35] Rather than define this process as politically neutral, Jehlen emphasizes the possibilities for disproportionate power relationships. All agents and all statements in discourse do not exert equal influence: "representations... gain power because of the spaces in which they are articulated and because of the political and social networks that are being organized around them. There are material resources that individuals and groups bring to bear, to push forward these representations ... Representations in turn help to forge political alliances, organized around those meanings."[36] Every utterance in discourse accrues power through the specific conditions under which it is pronounced.

[33] Judith Butler, "Contingent Foundations: Feminism and the Question of Postmodernism" in Butler, Seyla Benhabib, Drucilla Cornell, Nancy Fraser, *Feminist Contentions: A Philosophical Exchange*, intro. by Linda Nicholson (New York: Routledge, 1995), p. 50.
[34] Judith Walkowitz, Myra Jehlen, and Bell Chevigny, "Patrolling the Borders: Feminist Historiography and the New Historicism," *Radical History Review* 43 (Winter 1989), 28.
[35] Ibid., 40. [36] Ibid., 43.

The modes of inquiry introduced by Foucauldian analysis direct us toward a political diagnosis of various channels of knowledge in society. Specifically, they allow us to envision the ways in which articulations of gender constitute a field of power and knowledge within the establishment of literary values. The questions we ask – whose interest do these constructions of knowledge serve? What conditions promote these structures? What knowledge does this specific field of power produce? – clarify and restructure the dynamics of literary production on a broad cultural level. However, these tools tend to be most useful on that macroscopic level. The subjects within discourse may retain agency, and discourse may be active, but the microscopic points of articulation can only be understood in relationship to massive cultural formations of power, which are constantly shifting. Foucault conceptualizes power as a multitude of simultaneously immanent functions:

[I]t is the moving substrate of force relations which, by virtue of their inequality, constantly engender states of power, but the latter are always local and unstable. The omnipresence of power: not because it has the privilege of consolidating everything under its invincible unity, but because it is produced from one moment to the next, at every point, or rather in every relation from one point to another. Power is everywhere; not because it embraces everything, but because it comes from everywhere.[37]

Because of its state of perpetual change, the conception of power suggests the possibility of resistance or effective agency. But power is nonetheless omnipresent, and its monolithic stature hinders the meaningful interpretation of local articulations. Beyond recognizing the imprint of hegemony, our access to the meaning of texts is partial, transitory, and unstable. Moreover, conceptions of discourse as the vehicle of power and knowledge tend to objectify language and render it passive. Systemic shifts in power, only imperfectly reconstructed, are more significant factors in the constitution of meaning than, for instance, the intention of the author or the reader.

Bakhtin's linguistic theories of heteroglossia, dialogism, and unitary language provide a useful supplement to the analytic of power and knowledge by focusing on the contest of signification at the level of the individual statement. By envisioning language as a living entity that constantly changes, Bakhtin represents language and the people who use it as actively producing meaning, capable of signifying multiple political

---

[37] Foucault, *History of Sexuality*, vol. I, p. 93.

valences simultaneously.[38] For Bakhtin, all language is internally stratified, by geographical or nationalistic dialects, and, more importantly, by the ideological languages of social groups.[39] As such, language exists in a state of heteroglossia, or the strata of multiple languages, that overlap in a variety of ways:

> [A]ll languages of heteroglossia, whatever the principle underlying them and making each unique, are specific points of view on the world, forms for conceptualizing the world in words, specific world views, each characterized by its own objects, meanings and values. As such they all may be juxtaposed to one another, mutually supplement one another, contradict one another and be interrelated dialogically.[40]

Bakhtin uses the concept of dialogism to express the interaction of the multiple levels of language, whether intentional or unintentional. Every speech act enters into dialogue with the ideological perspectives that constitute it: "The living utterance, having taken meaning and shape at a particular historical moment in a socially specific environment, cannot fail to brush up against thousands of living dialogic threads, woven by socio-ideological consciousness around the given object of an utterance; it cannot fail to become an active participant in social dialogue."[41] This is the most liberating aspect of Bakhtin's treatment of language, for it recognizes the full potential of language to signify without suggesting an ultimate meaninglessness or relativistic free-play associated with some post-structuralist theories. In contrast to new historicist treatments of discourse as monolithic and deterministic, dialogism posits a language in which meaning can never be finally closed because it always relies in part on the epistemological framework of the receiver. The reader or auditor brings to the text a world-view that enters into the determination of meaning. Thus, dialogism presents the critic with greater possibilities for more complex readings than do more passive renderings of language.

While the concepts of heteroglossia and dialogism account for the conscious intentions and the incidental constructions of meaning, Bakhtin's philosophy does not propose that language is innocent of power. For Bakhtin, language is constantly changing in both centrifugal

---

[38] In adopting the rhetoric of Bakhtin I am taking my cue from Laurie Finke, who writes: "Bakhtin's notion of the dialogized word is useful to feminist critics precisely because it refuses to see the oppressed or marginalized as passive victims of their oppression; it returns to them a culturally specific agency and the power to participate in defining their struggles, in turning the oppressor's words against them" (*Feminist Theory*, p. 14).

[39] I have simplified here for the purpose of explanation. The stratifications of language are seemingly endless: see Bakhtin, *The Dialogic Imagination*, pp. 259–422.

[40] Ibid., p. 292.   [41] Ibid., p. 276.

and centripetal directions with every utterance. The centralizing forces of language tend toward the appearance of monologia or what he calls "unitary language":

A unitary language is not something given [dan] but is always in essence posited [zadan] – and at every moment of its linguistic life it is opposed to the realities of heteroglossia. But at the same time it makes its real presence felt as a force for overcoming this heteroglossia, imposing specific limits to it, guaranteeing a certain maximum of mutual understanding and crystalizing into a real, although still relative, unity – the unity of reigning conversational (everyday) and literary language, "correct language."[42]

Unitary language, in other words, acts as hegemony, or that which passes for truth but is actually the most powerful of several competing discourses. It is a useful concept for identifying the expression of a cultural intention or ideal, like masculine authority, that often appears in the language of truth or nature. Because unitary language appeals to the widest audience – and, consequently, is simplified – we can assume that the speaking and writing subject is aware of the unitary language of her culture; she is not, however, restricted to it. Rather, the subject within language chooses from the heteroglot languages available. However, because the stratifications correspond to specific ideological positions, not all languages are equally accessible. "Language is not a neutral medium that passes freely and easily into the private property of the speaker's intentions; it is populated – overpopulated – with the intentions of others."[43] The force with which a subject appropriates another person's language corresponds to the power that the speaking subject wields. Resistance to appropriation by another signifies the exclusivity of the language. For the present study, the unitary language of patriarchal society can be understood as the stratified language of gendered perspectives, with the feminine consequently marginalized or suppressed. Critics, male and female, appropriate gendered language and thus configure the value of literature in dialogic exchange with issues of gender.

   These post-structuralist theories enable me to postulate the relationships between the discourses of gender and literary criticism in the following way. The dialogue between the languages of gender and literary criticism produces a variety of effects, both liberating and oppressive, centrifugal and centripetal. Often by sheer reiteration, through which readers and writers come to recognize certain literary comments as standard, gendered formulations within literary criticism are granted a status of

---

[42] Ibid., p. 270.   [43] Ibid., p. 294.

"truth." The status of "truth" could be compounded by a variety of other circumstances, including the political, social, and material conditions through which each statement is produced. These utterances enter into a public discourse shared by the increasing numbers of literate consumers. Reading and writing subjects position themselves with respect to the established "truths"; each subject can choose to accept, produce, reproduce, or resist the hegemonic discourse. Furthermore, the meanings of individual statements are not always confined to the intentions of their authors; instead, a writer's language can engage in dialogic discourses of which he or she is unaware. Throughout history gendered "truths" in criticism change, illustrating that language is the site of struggle or, alternatively, that discourse is in constant flux. However, the "partial agency," described by Walkowitz, is circumscribed by the conditions of gender. Within a patriarchal society that enforces a gendered hierarchy of power, male subjects exercise greater influence and mobility; consequently, in discourse masculine values prevail over feminine.

IDENTIFYING THE PARAMETERS

Because eighteenth-century literary criticism often takes a form different from the professional, institutionalized criticism we now practice, it is appropriate to delineate how I am using the term here. As a discourse, criticism encompasses a wide variety of official and unofficial assertions, but in order to delimit my task I will be considering only those statements made in published form in English. The range covers all types of publications, from formal treatises on specific works, prefaces or dedicatory letters, essays in periodicals, conduct literature, satires, translations of modern and classic texts, to passages from poems and novels. These criteria – material published and in English – establish what I perceive as the minimal conditions of the public domain accessible by literate men and women of the middle and upper classes. I am interested in the hegemonic function of criticism, and criticism with these specifications seems to play a greater role in the formation of the cultural values passed on through higher education than, for instance, the unpublished diaries of private individuals. From the perspective of the late twentieth century, however, critical expressions in private writings can be read as a supplement to the public discourse in an effort to understand and perhaps resignify the literary "truths" we inherit from the eighteenth century. When such examples arise I incorporate them in my discussion, but the main argument pertains to published material.

The literariness of the criticism can be understood in its widest sense as referring to all writing that was perceived to have literary or aesthetic value. Consequently, romantic fiction and writing published in periodicals are considered along with epic and tragedy.

But literary criticism from this age is not restricted to texts; it often explicitly involves the reader and the writer. Throughout the eighteenth century literature is understood as a didactic tool, and, consequently, literary criticism takes as its proper object the printed word as well as the tastes and morals of the reading and writing subject. Because distinctions of gender often serve as the organizing principles in the prescription of literature, the constitution of the literary subject in criticism forms a significant part of this study.

To set boundaries to the language of gender is a more difficult task because this discourse is so thoroughly constituted through other discourses. As one of the fundamental structures of the organization of social life, gender permeates all areas of knowledge. I have used the term liberally to encompass any expression relating to gendered distinctions, whether abstract or concrete, fictional or experiential, prescriptive or descriptive, with the assumption that all utterances enter into dialogue with other speech acts, consequently affecting the cultural understandings of gender to some extent. Of course, not all expressions convey equal significance, and the power of gendered statements is contingent upon the material and ideological conditions through and in which they are articulated. Because I am interested in the interaction between statements on gender and literary criticism, the discourse of gender shares the same restrictions I have imposed on the selection of literary criticism, that it be material published in English. Again, the private correspondences of individuals will be cited when appropriate, but the majority of references to gendered discourse outside of literary criticism derives from literature, conduct manuals, didactic essays, and various educational, religious, and political tracts.

One specific feature of the Restoration and eighteenth-century discourse on gender greatly complicates the perception of gendered distinctions in literary criticism and therefore deserves more detailed scrutiny. Frequently when female subjects enter discourse as the audience or object – especially in the treatment of female authors – the rhetoric of gallantry inflects the critic's language through a variety of highly formalized verbal gestures. I would like to historicize the notion of gallantry by offering some preliminary statements here to be developed with further examples in the following chapters. For this discussion, the most relevant meaning of gallantry offered by Johnson is "courtship; refined address to women"; the term "gallantry," then, is in one sense synonymous with the term "courtship," whose origination is situated in the consolidation of a Renaissance court culture. According to Catherine Bates, "courtship" has semantic roots that refer simultaneously to the behavior of a courtier and the actions of a lover. Both rely on persuasive rhetoric to perform their role, which is understood essentially as flattery. Bates argues that at some point during the seventeenth century, "courtship" and "to court" lost their original aristocratic signification of being at court, and devolved into the exclusive amatory sense that they retain today.[44] During the eighteenth century, the language of courtship, or gallantry, was readily absorbed by the expanding bourgeois discourse and served as the dominant – but by no means only – pattern of communication between the sexes.

As a model for the interchange between men and women, the code of gallantry establishes an accepted set of expectations for social behavior: the gallant occupies an obsequious position, often the self-acclaimed "slave," and the mistress, like a monarch, receives his lofty terms of praise with passive acquiescence. From the start, however, these positions were conceived as roles with the potential for simultaneously false and genuine implications. Poets frequently manipulate the conventions to expose an underlying fabric of selfish motivation. Take, for instance, the lover of Marvell's "To His Coy Mistress," who proposes what he ought to do if there were "world enough and time":

> An hundred years should go to praise
> Thine Eyes, and on thy Forehead Gaze;
> Two hundred to adore each Breast,
> But thirty thousand to the rest;
> An Age at least to every part,
> And the last Age should show your Heart.
> For Lady you deserve this State;
> Nor would I love at lower rate.[45]

The remainder of the poem, however, focuses on the grim reality that they will die before such exalted wooing could come to pass. The exaggerated demands of gallantry quickly give way to satire, as the poet juxtaposes the idealized rhetoric of love with the frank desire for

---

[44] Catherine Bates, " 'Of Court it seemes': A Semantic Analysis of *Courtship* and *To Court*," *Journal of Medieval and Renaissance Studies*, 20.1 (Spring 1990), 22.
[45] Andrew Marvell, *The Poems and Letters of Andrew Marvell*, ed. H. M. Margoliouth, third edition, rev. Pierre Legouis, 2 vols. (Oxford: Clarendon Press, 1971), vol. 1, p. 28, lines 13–20.

sexual gratification. Bates suggests that in its original meaning "courtship" might have signified the genuine expression of admiration when articulated within an idealized court setting, but the predominant implication of the term was pejorative, "designating a mode of speech and behavior which was cunning, insincere, underhand, and even dangerous."[46] The negative associations of the word carry over into the representations of love, which are often transparently self-interested. The language of gallantry in the late seventeenth and eighteenth centuries constitutes an area of verbal play in which a highly ritualistic order belies a richly ambiguous signification. Marvell's deliberate misuse of tropes of praise suggests an awareness of the duplicity involved in gallant language. Aphra Behn's poetry also registers the significance of the roles in courtship, but she often represents the male's verbal skills as a superfluous part of seduction: "Forbear, fond Charming Youth, forbear, / Thy words of Melting Love: / Thy Eyes thy Language well may spare, / One Dart enough can move."[47] One of her less satisfied personae laments the falseness of her beloved's promise: "Inconstancy's the good supream / The rest is airy Notion, empty Dream!"[48] These poetic representations indicate that gallantry conveys a message to its audience, but its role is symbolic rather than denotative, acting as a gesture of intimacy, the final meaning of which is open to interpretation.

The practices of gallantry are historically linked with the increasing cultural insistence on female chastity and linguistic decorum. During the seventeenth century, cultural proscriptions against cruder forms of sexual expression began to regulate the acceptable vocabulary of love.[49] Women were denied a language to express personal desire, and undisguised expressions of male sexuality were deemed inappropriate.[50] The seemingly fatuous praise of women's beauty and virtue is coded in a

[46] Bates, " 'Of Court'," 43, 51, 45.

[47] *The Works of Aphra Behn*, ed. Janet Todd, 7 vols. (Columbus: Ohio State University Press, 1992–1996), vol. 1, "In Imitation of Horace," lines 13–16.

[48] Ibid., "To Alexis," lines 32–33.

[49] "The seventeenth century, then, was the beginning of an age of repression emblematic of what we call the bourgeois societies, an age which perhaps we still have not completely left behind. Calling sex by its name thereafter became more difficult and more costly . . ." (Foucault, *History of Sexuality*, vol. 1, p. 17).

[50] For discussion of the increased attention to female chastity and the control of language in the late seventeenth century, see Nancy Armstrong and Leonard Tennenhouse, eds., *The Ideology of Conduct: Essays on Literature and the History of Sexuality* (London: Methuen, 1987); Moira Ferguson, ed., *First Feminists, British Women Writers 1578–1799* (Indiana University Press, 1985); Angeline Goreau, ed., *The Whole Duty of a Woman: Female Writers in Seventeenth-Century England* (Garden City: Dial Press, 1985).

double language as the legitimate public speech of polite society and the thinly veiled vehicle of less-polite intentions.

The amatory conventions and their complicated dynamic of power were easily adopted into the published communication between men and women, both because the ostensibly positive terms of address were considered courteous and because the ritualistic flattery could not be construed as sincere. Writers like Dryden and Pope often exploit the tensions between convention and authenticity in their addresses to ladies. The dedicatory letter to *The Rape of the Lock* makes paradigmatic use of the formal relationship between men and women by positioning the author as the humble servant to the beautiful and highly esteemed patroness, Arabella Fermor. The letter's slick compliments to the ladies seem overly obsequious to the late-twentieth-century reader; however, Pope avoids appearing foolish by carefully manipulating gallant language to his advantage. He begins the letter: "It will be in vain to deny that I have some Regard for this Piece, since I Dedicate it to You," creating a parallel between the poem and the patroness that allows him to compliment both simultaneously.[51] This strategy mitigates the embarrassment of Pope's self-promotion at the same time as it fulfills the expectations for his patron's flattery. Through the artificial rhetoric of chivalry, Pope accomplishes two primary goals in scripting this letter to Fermor; he appeases her pride, wounded both in the actual event of losing her hair and in the poetical recreation of that story, and he justifies his expansion of the poem with the addition of odd machinery. He thanks her for consenting to have the story of her "Sex's little unguarded Follies" published, minimizing her shame through diminutives – as he does throughout the poem itself – and by characterizing her personal story as emblematic of women in general. He later assures her that "the Character of *Belinda*, as it is now manag'd, resembles You in nothing but in Beauty," distancing her from the poem but not from the compliment.[52] He explains the adaptation of Rosicrucian lore ostensibly for the benefit of Fermor and other female readers: "I know how disagreeable it is to make use of hard Words before a Lady; but 'tis so much the Concern of a Poet to have his Works understood, and particularly by your Sex, that You must give me leave to explain two or three difficult Terms."[53] Beneath the surface of his courtly rhetoric the voice of the pedagogue realigns the dynamic of power by asserting Pope's dominance in knowledge. Fermor operates as

---

[51] Alexander Pope, *The Rape of the Lock and Other Poems*, ed. Geoffrey Tillotson, *The Twickenham Edition of the Poems of Alexander Pope*, 10 vols. (London: Methuen and Co., 1940), vol. II, p. 142.
[52] Ibid., pp. 142, 143.   [53] Ibid., p. 142.

the purported dedicatee, but only at the cost of becoming a pupil. He closes with an encomium on her beauty and virtue and a restatement of his humble position: "If this Poem had as many Graces as there are in Your Person, or in Your Mind, yet I could never hope it should pass thro' the World half so Uncensured as You have done."[54] The conventions of gallantry protect the poet from accusations of vanity while they allow him to praise his own work, and they preserve the reputation of the patroness from indiscretion while they permit her public fame. Pope's symbolic use of ritualistic language conveys sincerity in the general sense of compliment but ultimately succeeds in its ends through polite ambiguity.

Whether in its usage in representations of love or its appearance in the public discourse between men and women, the language of gallantry was perceived as disingenuous. Still, the form persisted as a pattern of communication between the sexes and gained wider recognition as it passed into civil bourgeois society. We might consider, therefore, what was at stake in these conventions, and whose interests they served. *Webster's Unabridged Dictionary* offers two distinct definitions of "gallantry," both of which conform to late-seventeenth-century notions of polite male behavior: "dashing courage" and "courtly attention to women." Semantically, the word incorporates a paradoxical dualism of power and powerlessness, courage and obsequiousness, but within the Restoration court society these tensions might be resolved in the coincident roles of soldier and courtier. Outside of the court, the contradictions can be understood if we see acts of courage defining the manhood that is qualified to pay court to a lady. The fawning behavior ascribed to male courting might seem inconsistent with male authority in that culture, but the external and internal structures of patriarchy secured men from any material loss of power. Any cost to male pride is greatly stemmed by the conventionality and short duration of his subservience. Like Pope's explanation of "hard words" to Fermor, gallant forms of flattery sometimes involve condescension that perversely consolidates the speaker's authority over his audience. In the ambiance of Enlightenment philosophies, the protection and care of dependents, including women, children, servants, and animals, come to be seen increasingly as a mark of civilization and progress. If a gentleman could not justify his temporary subordination to female beauty and charm by the ends he hoped to gain, he could defend his generous attention to women as the actions of a benevolent patriarch.

[54] Ibid., p. 143.

The temporary or intermittent elevation in status women enjoy via these channels of flattery evidently had great appeal to otherwise disenfranchised women. Repeatedly, the warnings against this particular form of vanity sound from the didactic or polemic literature of the period, especially when the specious praise of a lover affects the woman's choice of marriage partner. Lady Mary Chudleigh closes her exhortation "To the Ladies" with the advice: "Then shun, oh! shun that wretched state, [marriage] / And all your fawning flatterers hate. / Value your-selves, and men despise: / You must be proud, if you'll be wise."[55] More playfully, Mary Davys charges her readers: "When you grow weary of Flattery, and begin to listen to matrimonial Addresses, chuse a Man with fine Sense, as well as a fine wigg."[56] Mary Astell, who sharply criticized the institution of marriage, recognized that the practice of gallantry served to protect women who were vulnerable in society: "Women, it's true, ought to be treated with Civility; for since a little Ceremony and out-side Respect is all their Guard, all the privilege that's allow'd them it were barbarous to deprive them of it."[57] The danger of gallantry, Astell declares, lies in how seriously one takes it:

She must be a Fool with a witness, who can believe a Man, Proud and Vain as he is, will lay his boasted Authority, the Dignity and Prerogative of his Sex, one Moment at her Feet, but in prospect of taking it up again to more advantage; he may call himself her Slave a few days, but it is only to make her his all the rest of his Life.[58]

As the ritualistic language of gallantry translates into generalized social practices, the attitude carries with it some material advantages for women who are increasingly denied economic independence. By representing men as responsible for women, the language of gallantry provides women with an appealing rationale for passivity.

Unlike Astell, who accepts the compliments of gallantry as a form of female advantage, Mary Wollstonecraft condemns the inflated praise of courtship because of its debilitating effect on female character.

My own sex, I hope, will excuse me, if I treat them like rational creatures, instead of flattering their *fascinating* graces, and viewing them as if they were in a

---

[55] Lady Mary Chudleigh, "To the Ladies," in *The Norton Anthology of Literature by Women, The Tradition in English*, ed. Sandra M. Gilbert and Susan Gubar (New York: W.W. Norton, 1985), lines 21–24.

[56] Mary Davys, *The Reform'd Coquet*, reprint, ed. Michael F. Shugrue, intro. Josephine Grieder, *Foundations of the Novel* (New York: Garland Publishing, 1973), p. viii.

[57] Mary Astell, *The First Feminist: "Reflections Upon Marriage" and Other Writings by Mary Astell*, ed. Bridget Hill (Aldershot: Gower/Maurice Temple Smith, 1986), p. 100.

[58] Ibid.

state of perpetual childhood, unable to stand alone. I earnestly wish to point out in what true dignity and human happiness consists – I wish to persuade women to endeavour to acquire strength, both of mind and body, and to convince them that the soft phrases, susceptibility of heart, delicacy of sentiment, and refinement of taste, are almost synonymous with epithets of weakness, and that those beings who are only the objects of pity and that kind of love, which has been termed its sister, will soon become objects of contempt.[59]

Wollstonecraft employs her strongest rhetoric to counteract the persuasiveness of gallantry, "those pretty feminine phrases, which the men condescendingly use to soften our slavish dependence."[60] In this passage she addresses women who to a certain extent believe the flattery of their admirers and happily abet the self-deception that they enjoy power over men. She exposes the illusion of female mastery that is ambiguously encoded in the language of gallantry by emphasizing how the seductive forms of language actually infantilize women and circumscribe their agency. Her arguments in *The Vindication of the Rights of Woman* identify the forms of heterosexual romance as a primary ruse to ensure patriarchal power and female subordination. Wollstonecraft's impassioned response to gallantry testifies to its enduring presence; the public's cool reception of her *Rights of Woman* indicates the extent to which the British were invested in those social forms.

Likewise, the consistent use of gallant language in the criticism of female authors indicates its pervasiveness in culture. It is important to recognize that these glib compliments operate symbolically in discourse not only, or even fundamentally, as praise, but in a host of ways less salutary for women. In the discussions of Dryden, fiction, and the aesthetic which follow, I will analyze the ways in which gallantry inflects the language of the critic and yields a pronounced tension in the evaluation of women and feminine attributes of literature.

POSITING THE HISTORIES

The examination of literary criticism and gendered discourse involves two separate strands of cultural authority, each embodying its own contests to establish "truth," and each employing language as the site of inherent struggle for signification. During the period from 1660 to 1790, the classical model of literary excellence, with its adaptation of rules from

[59] Mary Wollstonecraft, *The Works of Mary Wollstonecraft*, ed. Janet Todd and Marilyn Butler, 7 vols. (New York: New York University Press, 1989), vol. v, p. 75.
[60] Ibid.

the Ancients, a preference for heroic genres like epic and tragedy, and the instigation of innumerable imitations, is in competition with a modern model of literary ideals, based on the subjective response of the autonomous individual, the innovation of lyric genres, and a conscious reinvention of literary language. While one discourse looks toward the old and established authorities and the other locates its source in the present and the new, both tend to act as unifying languages, competing, as it were, for the highest place on Mount Parnassus. To simplify the representation of truth, exponents for one side of the debate establish their legitimacy through strategies that discredit or silence the opposing ideas, as Swift does in the *Battle of the Books*. Gendered language figures in these contests as one language among several used to differentiate and stratify. However, the language of eighteenth-century criticism is not always so polemical but, rather, embodies the perspectives of both the old and the new in moderation. Gender continues to operate therein as a pervasive epistemological structure.

The discourse of gender during this period is also the site of a major contest in signification. To borrow Thomas Laqueur's terms, the transition is from the social category of gender toward an ontological category.[61] In the former category, males and females are viewed as essentially similar in kind but different in their degree of common attributes, like strength and intellect. Laqueur argues that in seventeenth-century thought a one-sex model dominates, in which the female body is understood as the biological inverse of the male. The elaborations of gender, however, are further entrenched in systems of class differentiation, as Michael McKeon has demonstrated.[62] In the older one-sex model, the subject's identity corresponds to his or her place in a social organization regulated by external signs of status attached to kinship lines. Gender is understood as one of several social properties, including rank and family, that designate the subject's proper behavior. The alternative view, gaining hegemonic status by the middle of the eighteenth century posits a difference of kind between the sexes, and roots that distinction in a new recognition of biological uniqueness. As the order of society shifts from aristocratic notions of inherited authority to the bourgeois articulations of ethical autonomy, social identity relies

---

[61] Thomas Laqueur, *Making Sex: Bodies and Gender from the Greeks to Freud* (Cambridge: Harvard University Press, 1990), especially chapters 3 and 4. See also Ruth H. Bloch, who argues that English culture from the Renaissance through the Restoration viewed men and women as essentially similar creatures, whose differences were a matter of degree: "Untangling the Roots of Modern Sex Roles: A Survey of Four Centuries of Change," *Signs* 4.2 (1978), 238.

[62] McKeon, "Historicizing Patriarchy," esp. pp. 300–307.

more firmly on the verifiable distinctions of sex than on the variable degrees of inner worth. Thus gender comes to be figured in the purportedly immutable categories of male and female, public and private. These antagonistic conceptions of gender – social versus ontological – appear in discourse as unitary languages, invoking universal "nature" as the unquestioned authority. Like the struggle in the discourse of criticism, the language of gender often incorporates both orientations simultaneously.

At issue in this study is the history of significant change in the discourses of gender and literary criticism and the insights that can be gained by viewing each in sight of the other, or, more specifically, each as a component language of the other. The separate histories of these two discourses continue to be a source of scholarly debate, but little attempt has been made to consider these cultural changes in relation to each other.[63] The discourse of criticism, not surprisingly, takes from the language of gender its struggle for a unitary vision of gendered relations, and, consequently, mirrors the epistemological changes occurring in British conceptions of gender. When gendered categories are constituted as similar in kind, gendered distinctions become a product of cultivation, a negotiation of quantitative differences. Gendered characteristics easily translate into metaphoric qualities because these traits do not appear to have an inherent attachment to a biological identity. Neither sex owns intrinsic characteristics because they act as the large and small – or the perfect and flawed, normal and inverted – versions of the same model. Restoration critics habitually use gendered language in their literary metaphors, applying masculine and feminine epithets without regard to the sex of their objects. Dryden, whose literary criticism becomes in many ways the foundation for succeeding generations of critics, adopts a critical model of polite, gendered relations based on the ideal of male heroism and female refinement. In Dryden's view, the best literature combines both masculine and feminine attributes, the masculine being bold, heroic, strong, heady, charismatic, verbal; the feminine being soft, smooth, regular, pleasing, soothing, sweet-sounding, loving, simple.

---

[63] As an indication of the many types of literary scholarship that focus on the history of gender, see Catherine Gallagher, *Nobody's Story: The Vanishing Acts of Women Writers in the Marketplace, 1670–1820* (Berkeley: University of California Press, 1994); Felicity Nussbaum, *The Autobiographical Subject: Gender and Ideology in Eighteenth-Century England* (Baltimore: The Johns Hopkins University Press, 1989); Kathryn Shevelow, *Women and Print Culture: The Construction of Femininity in the Early Periodical* (London: Routledge, 1989). Examples of scholarship on the critical theory of the period include Monk, *The Sublime*; M. H. Abram, *The Mirror and the Lamp: Romantic Theory and the Critical Tradition* (Oxford: Oxford University Press, 1953), and, more recently, James Engell, *Forming the Critical Mind: Dryden to Coleridge* (Cambridge: Harvard University Press, 1989).

Neither style should repress the other, although it is clear that the masculine style possesses intrinsic virtue, whereas the feminine has only contingent value. The language of gender in the earlier criticism tends to emphasize a one-sex model and a free play between gendered tropes and referents.

Criticism from the middle years of my study incorporates the struggle between gendered models. The coexistence of equally compelling orientations threatens a sense of order, and yields the impulse to instruct through advice in the periodicals of John Dunton, Joseph Addison and Richard Steele, Eliza Haywood, and others. The critical discourse accommodates the need to instruct and entertain by crystallizing its literary inheritance into formulaic tableaus, whether the omnipresent "Art of Poetry" or the equally pervasive "rules." For John Dennis, who delineated the categories of "greater poetry" and "less poetry" in his *Grounds of Criticism in Poetry* (1704), rules were the key to an orderly understanding of literature: "If [poetry] is an art, it follows that it must propose an end to itself and afterwards lay down proper means for the attaining that end, for this is undeniable, that there are proper means for the attaining of every end, and those proper means in poetry we call the rules."[64] Characteristically, the term "manly" enjoys widespread popularity in critical usage, reflecting the critical discourse's insistence on masculine authority and investment in patriarchal hierarchy, which remains consistent in both gendered models.

Comparatively little attention is paid to the reading subject and the psychological effects of style until the mid-century. This later shift in attention indicates new priorities in the ends and means of criticism. In addition to judging a work of art according to rules established by precedent, mid-century critics theorize and interpret the spirit of composition and the readers' response. The radical subjectivity of the reader becomes a focus of continuing didacticism, and critical discourse reveals a new commitment to controlling the reading subject and the act of reading. In the process, criticism constitutes this reader as a specifically gendered subject. As the cultural construction of biologically determined sexual difference gains dominance in discourse, it shapes the relationship between gendered characteristics in criticism by positing separate and mutually exclusive gendered categories. The masculine, now characterized by sublime flights of imagination, cannot be harnessed to the retiring feminine and still be effective. On the one hand, the

[64] Elledge, ed., *Eighteenth-Century Critical Essays*, vol. 1, pp. 101–102.

balance shifts from a doctrine of virtue to an emphasis on pleasure, and the masculine writer fares better if he does not compromise; critics begin to look favorably on those who forsake the rules and follow genius. On the other hand, the beautiful and moral realm is celebrated in gallant terms as the pseudo-literary field of women. In both the discourses of gender and of literary criticism, the old epistemological structures persist at some level throughout the period, but we can detect a major increase in the cultural importance of the new ideas after mid-century.

One congruity between the competing models of gender is male dominance; indeed the persistence of the gendered hierarchy greatly aids the appearance of sexual difference as natural and unchanging. A similar uniformity runs through literary criticism; that is, despite the evidence that gender in criticism reflects a variety of permutations, certain critical faculties remain the exclusive prerogative of men, namely judgment, imagination or invention, and intellect. Additionally, "strength" acts as a masculine qualifier, indicating the degree of those faculties requisite for excellence. Meaning intensity, activity, and speed, the term "strength" connotes powers of the mind or qualities of language, but it also possesses an associative relationship to the physical superiority of men and, hence, reinforces the masculine exclusivity of the qualities it modifies. Based on examples from the classics and modern literature, eighteenth-century critical discourse negotiates literary excellence through this set of literary standards; Oliver Goldsmith's 1758 "poetical scale" offers a relevant comparison. Goldsmith measures the fame of eleven British poets according to the qualities of "Genius," "Judgment," "Learning," and "Versification."[65] Disqualifying the last category because it seems too variable – Pope and Shakespeare share the highest score – Goldsmith's scale isolates the importance of the three privileged faculties. In positing a set of definitive literary qualities, I want to suggest that these signify the broad categories through which the critical discourse assigned merit.

A proficiency in judgment is the mark of a good author and, incidentally, the most fundamental skill of the critic, and it generally involves the ability to make reasonable distinctions. Judgment assumes a certain level of objectivity, which is often opposed to emotional sensibility, and these become sex-specific traits by the end of the eighteenth century. In fact, of the three culturally appointed privileges

[65] Oliver Goldsmith, *Literary Magazine* (January 1758), quoted in Mark Van Doren, *John Dryden: A Study of His Poetry*, third edition (Bloomington: Indiana University Press, 1960), p. 248.

masking as inherently masculine qualities, judgment is most vehemently regulated. By imagination I mean a comprehensive sense of invention and creativity related to Dryden's nimble spaniel springing the hunted quarry.[66] Imagination is often constructed in opposition to judgment, following Locke. For example, Burke defines the imagination as "a sort of creative power of its own; either in representing at pleasure the images of things in the order and manner in which they were received by the senses, or in combining those images in a new manner, and according to a different order." Judgment, in contrast, "is for the greater part employed in throwing stumbling blocks in the way of imagination, in dissipating the scenes of its enchantment, and in tying us down to the disagreeable yoke of our reason."[67] The imagination finds similarities, while the judgment discerns differences. The discourse of the mid-century tends to conflate imagination with the category of genius, thereby granting the faculty a greater capacity for originality. Especially by the late eighteenth century, critical discourse grants women the capacity for imagination more than the other qualities, but female imagination tends to be cast as unintellectual and ephemeral, and it is, in any event, a contested ownership. The category of intellect encompasses erudition and facility of understanding, and it is most specifically related to the education of a gentleman. Because women gain access to some education during the period, the *degree* and *subject* of learning often act as gender-divides in the determination of literary excellence. As the best attributes of the poet and, significantly, the basic requirements of the critic, judgment, imagination, and intellect constitute definitive literary qualities, and eighteenth-century discourse preserved these privileges for male subjects.

This is not to say that all women were barred from the attainment of these attributes, but that literary discourse labeled them as masculine. Critics often identify the masculine values of women's poetry with mild surprise. Theophilus Cibber in his *Lives of the Poets* (1753) quotes Dryden's letter to Elizabeth Thomas in which he represents her poems as the exception to feminine standards: "They were I thought too good to be a woman's; some of my friends to whom I read them, were of the same opinion. It is not very gallant I must confess to say this of the fair sex; but, most certain it is, they generally write with more softness than

---

[66] John Dryden, *John Dryden: Of Dramatic Poesy and Other Critical Essays*, ed. George Watson, second edition, 2 vols. (London: Dent, and New York: Dutton, 1968), vol. I, p. 98.
[67] Edmund Burke, *A Philosophical Enquiry into the Origin of our Ideas of the Sublime and Beautiful*, ed. J. T. Boulton (London: Routledge and Kegan Paul, 1958), pp. 16, 25.

strength."[68] In an effort at a genuine compliment – one assumes – Dryden separates Thomas from her sex and aligns her work with the implicitly superior league of male poets.[69] After establishing her distinction from other women, he is free to condemn the weakness of female poetry in general. Cibber likewise evaluates the poetry of Katherine Philips by standards that assert the masculinity of intellect and strength: "Mrs. Philips' poetry has not harmony of versification, or amourous tenderness to recommend it, but it has a force of thinking, which few poets of the other sex can exceed, and if it is without graces, it has yet a great deal of strength."[70] Following a sense of gendered decorum, Cibber defends Philips' lack of "femininity" by emphasizing her excellence in qualities that are considered masculine. In both examples, the category of strength, which here signifies intellectual toughness as well as verbal force, is primarily identified with male subjectivity. Throughout the discourse of criticism, judgment, imagination, and intellect form a cluster of male privileges, modified by a degree of strength. The terms are so entirely secured to masculine identity that the gendered association does not change even when women practice these skills; rather, female authors risk becoming "unsex'd."

It follows that women who entered into published discourse meet with skepticism of their judgment, imagination, and intellect. To forestall accusations of impropriety, ineptitude, or even dishonesty, female authors frequently explain their unique relationship to those otherwise masculine rights. Aphra Behn's famous plea in the preface to *The Luckey Chance* illustrates the case: "All I ask, is the Priviledge for my Masculine Part the Poet in me, (if any such you will allow me) to tread in those successful Paths my Predecessors have so long thriv'd in, to take those Measures that both the Ancient and Modern Writers have set me."[71] Behn's linguistic manipulation of critical categories of gender is complex. She encodes as masculine her profession as a poet and, significantly, the tradition of classical and contemporary writers whom she emulates. Her rhetorical stance as petitioner puts into doubt her ability to earn a place beside those male poets, but her use of the possessive case – "my Masculine part" – anticipates and mitigates the

[68] Theophilus Cibber, *The Lives of the Poets of Great Britain and Ireland* (1753), reprint (Hildesheim: Georg Olms Verlagsbuchhandlung, 1968), p. 156.
[69] Joanna Lipking reads Dryden's compliments as conventional forms of praise, a point that confirms the prevalence of such gendered conceptions of literary value; see "Fair Originals: Women Poets in Male Commendatory Poems," *Eighteenth-Century Life* 12 (May 1988), 58–60.
[70] Cibber, *Lives of the Poets*, p. 157.
[71] Behn, *The Luckey Chance* (1687) in *The Works of Aphra Behn*, ed. Todd, vol. VII, p. 217.

disjunction between the female speaker and the male role. Grammatically, she already possesses that masculine category. She immediately reopens the question, however, by giving her critics the power to judge whether or not she is indeed a poet: "(if any such you will allow me)." Her deference in this late preface, unlike her earlier polemics, signals the power such literary designations of gender ultimately have over her self-representation.

Eighteenth-century critical discourse bandies about the name of "poet" and its ideal double, the "critic," with a zeal that exposes the culture's high investment in the terms. Different views as to what constitutes a poet-critic enter into heated debate, but the question of a poet-critic's qualification generally hinges on his easy familiarity with the classics. Evidence of an author's education is frequently requisite for his elevated status. Shakespeare is, of course, the famous exception, but the passionate defenses and attacks on his learning throughout the century testify to the importance of the standard.[72] The Scriblerian writers represent the newly literate populace as a threat to the classically constituted "republic of letters." In *The Dunciad* Pope pillories the prolific critics, Lewis Theobald and John Dennis, by representing their scholarship as absurd pedantry. Likewise, in his parody of the failed poet turned critic, Swift mocks his contemporaries' desire for quick success through superficial education:

> Get Scraps of *Horace* from your Friends,
> And have them at your Fingers Ends.
> Learn *Aristotle's* Rules by Rote,
> And at all Hazards boldly quote:
> Judicious *Rymer* oft review:
> Wise *Dennis*, and profound *Bossu*.
> Read all the *Prefaces* of *Dryden*,
> For these our Criticks much confide in . . .[73]

Swift implies that such mechanical processing of secondary literary information fails to develop the reason that a solid education in the classics would provide. These satiric representations of the critic as pointedly uncritical presuppose the necessity of the critic's judgment and intellect. The fundamentals implied by Swift and Pope are not inconsistent with statements made by writers from opposing orientations. Addison, who aimed to educate the critical masses, laments the woeful lack of taste

---

[72] See pp. 140–141.
[73] Swift, "On Poetry: A Rhapsody," in *The Poems of Jonathan Swift*, ed. Harold Williams, second edition, 3 vols. (Oxford: Clarendon Press, 1958), vol. II, lines 245–252.

among men: "it is our misfortune that some who set up for professed critics among us are so stupid that they do not know how to put ten words together with elegance or common propriety, and withal so illiterate that they have no taste of the learned languages and therefore criticize upon old authors only at second hand."[74] Though seemingly from different perspectives, Addison and Swift and Pope agree on an informed appreciation of the classics, a requirement that distinguishes the critic from spurious pretenders to knowledge.

Critical discourse tends to derive all three of the definitive literary qualities from a traditional education in classical and modern literature; and, if not derivative of the gentleman's education, the related skills are authorized by that study. The gendered dynamic in the discussion of classical literature, consequently, affects our understanding of the construction of literary values. During the eighteenth century, women and men from the non-landed classes received education in greater numbers than before, but knowledge of the classics remained a definite class and gender marker throughout the period. A number of factors complicate this generalization, including the changing practices in the standard education of men, the availability of translations of Greek and Latin texts, and the visibility of a handful of female virtuosos, such as Elizabeth Elstob, Sarah Fielding, and Elizabeth Carter. Seventeenth- and eighteenth-century pedagogy often included mental and physical discipline of the type immortalized in stories about Dryden's teacher, Busby.[75] Though Locke's influential treatise, *Some Thoughts Concerning Education* (1693), de-emphasized corporal punishment in favor of internalized forms of coercion, the personal reminiscences of writers throughout the period relate the attainment of classical knowledge as a painful rite of passage. The rigors of masculine education, whether in the forced repetitions of declensions or the beatings for poor performance, promoted a mental firmness that conflicted with constructions of female delicacy and passivity. Furthermore, the classics were perceived to be the culture's greatest purveyor of masculine values. Boys were encouraged to learn proper martial and civic behaviors through their representations in Homer and Virgil especially.[76] In both the methods of instruction and the ideological value of the literature, the *mythos* of the classics incorporated a distinct machismo.

The number of translations, however, introduced this masculine

---

[74] Addison and Steele, *Spectator*, no. 592 (1714), in Elledge, ed., *Eighteenth-Century Critical Essays*, vol. I, p. 77.
[75] See James A. Winn, *John Dryden and His World* (New Haven: Yale University Press, 1987), pp. 34–57.
[76] C. Williams, *Pope, Homer and Manliness*, p. 38.

literature to an audience who could not read Greek or Latin. In the suppressed preface to her poems, Anne Finch announces with shaky bravado:

I am . . . sensible, that Poetry has been of late so explain'd, the laws of itt being putt into familiar languages, that even those of my sex, (if they will be so presumptuous as to write) are very accountable for their transgressions against them. For what rule of Aristotle, or Horace is there, that has not been given us by Rapin, Despreaux, D'acier, my Lord Roscommon, etc.?[77]

Her apparent acquisition of this specialized knowledge does not engender self-confidence, however. Her defense incorporates a rather poor parody of the cultural voice that prohibits women from writing – "if they will be so presumptuous." The remonstration underscores rather than undermines the cultural proscription of female authorship.[78]

Nonetheless, changing attitudes toward female education, enhanced by Locke's philosophy and the civilizing discourse of Addison and Steele, created limited possibilities for some women to learn the ancient languages. Certain exceptional women enjoyed the ability to read the classics in their original tongue and even translate them for others, but these privileges were circumscribed by heavy social pressures against the display of female erudition. Significantly, most of these learned women advised other women to avoid the kind of education they received, suggesting that despite their own success, the classics remained a male prerogative.[79] This collective denunciation corresponds with Fénelon's influential opinion that women might take up Latin "only for what it is worth" and under the conditions that they "might renounce all vain Curiosity, might conceal that which they know, and might seek nothing hereby, but their own Improvement."[80] In other words, he grants "permission" on the grounds that women give up all the privileges of power contingent upon learning the language.

The cultural antagonism toward female learning magnifies the sense

---

[77] *Selected Poems of Anne Finch Countess of Winchilsea*, ed. Katherine M. Rogers (New York: Frederick Ungar Publishing Co., 1979), p. 11.
[78] See Charles H. Hinnant, *The Poetry of Anne Finch: An Essay in Interpretation* (Newark: University of Delaware Press, 1994), especially chapter 3.
[79] For more on women's education, see Beth Kowaleski-Wallace, "Milton's Daughters: The Education of Eighteenth-Century Women Writers," *Feminist Studies* 12.2 (Summer 1986), 275–293; Miriam Leranbaum, "'Mistresses of Orthodoxy': Education in the Lives and Writings of Late Eighteenth-Century English Women Writers," *Proceedings of the American Philosophical Society* 121.4 (August 1977), 281–301; Sylvia Myers, "Learning, Virtue and the Term 'Bluestocking'," *Studies in Eighteenth-Century Culture* 15 (1986), 279–288; Sheryl O'Donnell, "Mr. Locke and the Ladies: The Indelible Words on the Tabula Rasa," *Studies in Eighteenth-Century Culture* 8 (1979), 151–164.
[80] Quoted in Leranbaum, "Mistresses of Orthodoxy," p. 283.

of masculine privilege and poses a significant obstacle to women who aim to develop the faculties of judgment, imagination, and intellect. Among other difficulties, the educated lady needed to deflect negative stereotypes. The satiric representations that populate Western literature generally show her as slovenly, lascivious, bilious, and given to drink.[81] Lady Mary Wortley Montagu's advice to her granddaughter exemplifies the seriousness of the liability: it is, she writes, "absolutely necessary . . . to conceal whatever learning she attains with as much solicitude as she would hide crookedness or lameness."[82] One pervasive fear associated with female learning is that educated women will ignore their domestic duties. Lady Pennington writes in her *Unfortunate Mother's Advice to her Absent Daughters*: "It has been objected to all female learning, beyond that of household economy, that it tends only to fill the minds of the sex with a conceited vanity, which sets them above their proper business – occasions an indifference, if not total neglect of, their family affairs – and serves only to render them useless wives, and impertinent companions."[83] Even the liberal promoters of female education like Steele and Richardson stop short of allowing women as much learning as their husbands.[84] In its best construction, women's education should be limited and subordinate to male interests; in its worst, female learning signifies the collapse of civil and moral order. Although a classical education was remotely possible for some women, pervasive prejudices effectively prevented a woman's easy familiarity with the Ancients and, consequently, disqualified her from the socially constituted role of the critic.

The definitive literary qualities – judgment, imagination, and intellect – do not embody overtly gendered characteristics; it is only when we historicize the development of these concepts and read them in context with other cultural practices like education that the gendered dynamic clearly emerges. Likewise, certain literary values, which might otherwise appear gender-neutral, incorporate characteristics consistent with specific constructions of masculine identity from the eighteenth century. For instance, Dryden's use of "admirable" denotes, among other things,

[81] For a survey of satires on the learned lady in comedy, see Myra Reynolds, *The Learned Lady in England 1650–1760* (Boston and New York: Houghton Mifflin, 1920) chapter 5.

[82] Montagu, quoted in Jean Hunter, "The 18th-Century Englishwoman: According to the *Gentleman's Magazine*," in Paul Fritz and Richard Morton, eds., *Woman in the 18th Century and Other Essays* (Toronto: Samuel Steves Hakkert & Co., 1976), p. 79.

[83] Quoted in *Eighteenth-Century Women: An Anthology*, ed. Bridget Hill (London: George Allen & Unwin, 1984), p. 56.

[84] See Hilda L. Smith, *Reason's Disciples: Seventeenth-Century English Feminists* (Urbana: University of Illinois Press, 1982), p. 43; Rae Blanchard, "Richard Steele and the Status of Women," *Studies in Philology* 26 (1929), 325–355.

masculinity. To be admirable is to inspire awe through power or greatness, and admiration constitutes the primary end of heroic genres, which are intrinsically related to Restoration notions of manhood and authority. Consequently, "masculinity," specifically understood in the Restoration ethic of heroism and not, for instance, a self-controlled, Shaftesburian maleness, forms an aspect of Dryden's understanding of the "admirable." The investigation of gender in literary criticism ultimately reveals that certain literature is valued for its correspondence with the masculine identity current in society, or conversely, that dominant views of masculinity find expression in literature, which criticism thereafter valorizes.

Moreover, the intersection between criticism and gender in the eighteenth century produces effects on the gendered subjects in discourse, namely writers and readers. The discourse of gender constitutes an area of knowledge separate from literary discourse, but the statements about gender made within criticism reflect the social constructions of behavior and vice versa. The multiple articulations of the conceptions of gender affect the actual production and reception of literature. Because gender is a normative way of discerning differences among works of literature, literary criticism operates in the reciprocal capacities of description and prescription. Thus, women and men are designated as authors and readers in specific ways authorized by criticism.

For example, according to the Augustan or neoclassical hierarchy of literature, the Pindaric ode is beyond the reach of the female pen because it ranks among the most complex of genres. Critics describe the Pindaric, along with the epic and tragedy, with masculine epithets. William Congreve celebrates its "difficulty in the contrivance," and Dennis places it among the "greater poetry . . . by which a poet justly and reasonably excites passion."[85] In part, the genre's classical foundation immediately sets it among the privileged masculine accomplishments, but critics represent the Pindaric in gendered terms specific to their culture. In "On Lyric Poetry" (1728) Edward Young draws the analogy explicitly: "Judgment, indeed, that masculine power of the mind, in ode, as in all compositions, should bear the supreme sway; and a beautiful imagination, as its mistress, should be subdued to its dominion. Hence, and hence only, can proceed the fairest offspring of the human mind."[86] Young invokes the gendered hierarchy of his society by comparing the powers of judgment with absolute male authority and the creative and

---

[85] Elledge, ed., *Eighteenth-Century Critical Essays*, vol. 1, p. 146, 105.   [86] Ibid., p. 412.

unruly force of imagination with the dominated but lovely female. His literary recommendation incorporates the explicit heterosexual dynamic that establishes the feminine as adjunctive and subordinate to masculine productivity.

Rather than see these literary constructions as directly responsible for the poetic output in the century, we can recognize that these critics share cultural assumptions about gendered roles that influence female writers as well. Not surprisingly, the Pindaric ode does not predominate among the literary genres in women's writing, despite the fact that women tend more toward lyric poetry. Dorothy Mermin writes of Katherine Philips, Aphra Behn, and Anne Finch that they "generally avoid the solemnity of iambic pentameter, formal odes or epics, exalted diction, or (with a few significant exceptions), classical allusions. They prefer a lyric, occasional poetry, relatively simple narrative forms such as the fable, and understated, conversational tones, and small and ordinary themes."[87] Jane Barker, an accomplished poet and novelist of the early eighteenth century, justifies the standard from a female perspective. One of her women characters reports of Pindarics: "I neither love to read nor hear that kind of Verse. Methinks, it is to the Ear like Virginal Jacks to the Eye; being all of irregular Jumps, and Starts, sudden disappointments, and long-expected Periods, which deprives the Mind of that Musick, wherewith the good Sense would gratify it, if in other Measures."[88] In this evaluation, the revered complexity of the ode becomes "irregular Jumps, and Starts," while the "difficulty in contrivance" is lamented for its lack of musicality. Barker's assessment of the Pindaric, like the male-authored examples, implicitly invokes a gendered separation of literary tastes.

RESIGNIFYING THE DISCOURSE

As I have indicated, the interaction between the language of criticism and the language of gender is widespread and the implications are far reaching. In isolating parts of those discourses in which the interaction between gender and criticism is particularly pronounced, I have been necessarily selective. This project is intended to be representative rather than comprehensive. An examination of the works of recognized critics like Joseph Addison and Samuel Johnson might fulfill the expectations of a conventional narrative of this history, but disproportionate attention to

---

[87] Mermin, "Women Becoming Poets: Katherine Philips, Aphra Behn, Anne Finch," *ELH* 57.2 (1990), 336.

[88] Jane Barker, *A Patchwork Screen* (London, 1723), p. 7. I thank Kathy King for providing this reference.

"major figures" would skew the focus of this book and undermine the contention that literary criticism from the eighteenth century needs to be reassessed. Instead of replicating the patterns of interest instituted through anthologies and previous scholarly work, the analysis here records the movements in taste on a number of different levels of literary criticism, from the most powerful authorities to the least considered, and from the most prestigious genres and authors to the fledgling enterprise of the novel. The discussion of these literary changes centers on the ways in which aesthetic discourse embraces the cultural formulations of power, namely adopting the prevalent notions of gender to explain and defend literary standards. Moreover, I have organized my discussion around specific literary commonplaces that we have acquired from eighteenth-century discourse that establish their "truth" status through unifying discourses of patriarchy.

In order to elucidate the gendered dynamic in the structure of certain literary inheritances, I have borrowed from Laurie Finke a methodology that she calls "the politics of complexity." Incorporating the philosophies of language from Bakhtin and the feminist evaluations of science from Donna Haraway and N. Katherine Hayles, Finke proposes a strategy to reveal "the messiness behind the illusion of unified narratives about the world by restoring information – what I shall call noise – previously marginalized and excluded by those narratives. It attempts to expose the 'ficticity' – or the constructed nature – of facts."[89] Rather than being discovered or self-evident, facts are constructed by minimizing or erasing the multiple and heterogeneous opinions that precede the acceptance of a certain truth. A "fact" comes into existence as indisputable only after conflicting ideas are suppressed and forgotten. Consequently, returning the "fact" to its history involves the recovery of a variety of arguments, interpretations, and competing interests.

In terms of literary value, a certain set of "facts" can be represented by the canon, or the group of texts that informed people generally consider important. The concept of the canon is notoriously hard to define, but our understanding of it can be contained within the limits set by concrete lists from publishers, syllabi, standardized tests, and other institutional practices. Once recognized as significant, the canon itself simplifies the notion of literary value; a text is either of a certain quality and therefore in the canon, or it is not. The fact of canonization tends to mystify the historical conditions that produce the criteria of literary judgment and,

[89] Finke, *Feminist Theory, Women's Writing*, p. 7–8.

hence, to mask the political discourses through which literary values are established. Recent debates over the validity of the canon identify how literary judgments involve privilege. Elizabeth Fox-Genovese suggests that the feminist challenge at the curricular level "exposed the extent to which the canon represents a series of choices – choices made by the powerful to justify and perpetuate their own power."[90] Eighteenth-century critical discourse, which marks the beginning of the institutionalization of criticism in systems of higher education, decreed what literature was worthy or unworthy of notice, and these decisions served specific interests. This book demonstrates how the discourse of gender operates as one of the fundamental languages of power in literary distinctions.

By attempting to restore these critical commonplaces to the complexity of their historical production, I cannot claim to be finally uncovering or revealing the "true" meaning of eighteenth-century literary criticism. On the contrary, my position is interested in and informed by the political grounding of feminist goals. In revisioning this history, I am paying particular attention to the dialogue between critical values and cultural expressions of gender that has been unnoticed or distorted in previous scholarship. And while this study attempts to understand eighteenth-century texts in the terms of their historical production, the vantage point is necessarily shaped by late twentieth-century conceptions, particularly by the deconstruction of patriarchal systems of gender differentiation. Furthermore, the purpose of this study is to resignify the meaning of certain elements of eighteenth-century literary discourse for today's students. These goals may appear to defy traditional standards of critical objectivity or historical veracity. Allow me to forestall such criticism by reference to recent feminist critiques of knowledge by Donna Haraway. Rather than undermine the validity of the present study, the acknowledged – and inevitable – partiality of my narrative situates and limits the claims I make, establishing the grounds of their viability. As Haraway puts it: "Only the pose of disinterested objectivity makes 'concrete objectivity' impossible."[91] By analyzing eighteenth-century literary criticism through the languages of feminist literary criticism and discourse theories of the late twentieth century, the present study offers a fuller understanding of specific instances where historical concepts of gender shaped literary value and vice versa.

---

[90] Elizabeth Fox-Genovese, "The Feminist Challenge to the Canon," *National Forum* 69.3 (Summer 1989), 34.

[91] Donna Haraway, *Primate Visions: Gender, Race, and Nature in the World of Modern Science* (London: Routledge, 1989) p. 13.

The book investigates four areas of critical commonplaces from eighteenth-century British criticism and historicizes them with particular attention to the complexity of the gendered discourse that enabled them. The discussion begins with an examination of the heroic, a literary category more or less privileged throughout the period. Dryden, considered by some the manliest of English poets, constructs a discourse of literary value in which the masculine heroic is valorized as the greatest possible achievement. We have traditionally viewed the period as most clearly invested in these masculine interests, but the heroic values of the Restoration based on male extremes of valor and virtue are actually tempered by feminine lyricism.

The chapter on fiction examines the paradox that though the new genre of the novel is overtly feminized, canonical representation suggests that only men write good novels. Through examination of the gendered strategies in the criticism of early fiction, I argue that the feminized novel is not granted the status of great literature, in part because it is controlled or denigrated by male authority.

In my discussion of female critics, I complicate the widespread perceptions that there are no female critics before Virginia Woolf, and that the "woman critic" invokes a homogenous analytical voice in opposition to the male. The voices of female critics from the era are not silent but silenced; they in fact invent differing strategies to overcome the discursive prejudices against female judgment.

In the final chapter, the notion of the sublime as the authoritative aesthetic discourse of the mid- to late-eighteenth century comes under scrutiny as the dialectical double of the beautiful. Presenting the greatest challenge to Augustan ideals of literary excellence, the masculine sublime gains its apparent authority and stability only through the definition and suppression of the feminized beautiful. Each chapter situates these critical "truths" within the discourses of their production in order to highlight the power relation between the masculine and the feminine that informs them.

CHAPTER 2

Dryden's gendered balance and the Augustan ideal

In 1679 John Dryden compares Shakespeare's "masculine," "bolder," and "fiery" genius with Fletcher's "more soft and womanish" creativity, employing the language of gender to set two male literary figures into hierarchical antithesis.[1] The example typifies one of several uses Dryden makes of gendered language as a component of his critical vocabulary, illustrating the understanding of gender as a social category to which he ascribes certain measures of worth. Dryden's criticism is pivotal in this study because its dialogism between gendered discourse and literary value is diverse and conspicuous, and because it plays an enormously influential role in the development of criticism in eighteenth-century British literature. In the century following his life, Dryden's critical writings generated numerous imitations, and his privileging of heroic literature and harmonious versification set enduring standards of taste.[2] In his varied applications of gendered language, Dryden relies on the ideals of male heroism and female refinement, specific configurations of gender in Restoration discourse; these social categories correspond with a model of polite gendered relations that informs Dryden's poetic. Dryden joins the masculine flights of imagination with the sweetness and smoothness of feminine prosody to produce what becomes the Augustan golden mean.

Given the vitality of the gendered dynamic in Dryden's criticism, it is significant that the dominant view of his critical ideal – and of Dryden himself – largely ignores the feminine aspects of his conceptions. Dryden's integrated sense of gender relations as a system of balance and

---

[1] *John Dryden: Of Dramatic Poesy and Other Critical Essays*, ed. George Watson, second edition, 2 vols. (London: Dent and New York: Dutton, 1968) vol. 1, p. 247; hereafter, Watson.

[2] For a recent treatment of Dryden's role in the foundation of critical practice, see Earl Miner and Jennifer Brady, eds., *Literary Transmission and Authority: Dryden and Other Writers*, Cambridge Studies in Eighteenth-Century Literature and Thought (Cambridge: Cambridge University Press, 1993), esp. Miner's introduction, pp. 1–26.

exchange between masculine and feminine qualities retains a hierarchy of masculine privilege, but it nonetheless maintains that both categories contribute to literary excellence. As part of the process of transmission through the patriarchal organization of knowledge, Dryden's ideas underwent a pronounced masculinization; consequently, a conventional understanding of heroic literature and of Dryden's language still fails to register the importance of the feminine, which either falls out of the equation altogether, or is relegated to an opposing category, incommensurate with literary value. Historically, the suppression or trivialization of feminine literary values is facilitated by the emergent modernism in the mid-eighteenth century that embraces an ontological understanding of gendered difference; this is discussed in more detail in chapters 4 and 5. In this chapter, I approach and revise the masculinization of Dryden and his criticism in two ways, by examining the gendered construction of Dryden in several important critical studies, and, more importantly, by analyzing the gendered language of his criticism in its historical context. My aim, following the example of Laurie Finke, is to complicate the "fact" of his masculinity by returning the "noise" of its original discourses, which later becomes simplified or suppressed.[3]

The tendency to masculinize Dryden can be traced to Samuel Johnson's fortuitous label for his predecessor, "the father of English criticism." While the patronymic honors Dryden's genuine literary achievement in establishing the principles and methods of polite criticism, the gendered language ties this practice to a masculine role of authority and respect. Unlike later critics, Johnson does not over-simplify Dryden's writing by restricting him to a single gendered perspective; in fact, within a few paragraphs of conferring the masculine title, Johnson compares Dryden's criticism with "the majesty of a Queen."[4] Despite its regal connotations, however, the latter phrase is rarely cited when Dryden's reputation in criticism is invoked. Rather more prominently, the image of the founding patriarch imparts a sense of hegemonic privilege associated with masculine power and originality. Thus Dryden's historical signification comes to be marked by a masculine seminality and not a feminine grandeur.

A similar process occurs in the critical assessment of Dryden's writing

---

[3] See Laurie Finke, *Feminist Theory, Women's Writing*, Reading Women Writing Series (Ithaca: Cornell University Press, 1992), pp. 1–28.

[4] Samuel Johnson, *The Six Chief Lives from Johnson's Lives of the Poets with Macaulay's Life of Johnson*, ed. Matthew Arnold, reprint (New York: Russell and Russell, 1968), pp. 175, 178. Greg Clingham suggests that Johnson recognizes the "androgynous nature of Dryden's mind" in "Another and the Same: Johnson's Dryden," in Miner and Brady, eds., *Literary Transmission and Authority*, pp. 121–159.

style. Gerard Manley Hopkins, for instance, designates Dryden "the most masculine of our poets; his style and his rhythms lay the strongest stress of all our literature on the naked thew and sinew of the English Language."[5] Conveying a sense of admiration, Hopkins imputes to Dryden's poetry an extreme masculinity that apparently relates to the capable manipulation of sound. Hopkins' gendering of style and rhythm contrasts with Dryden's own expression of poetic balance between masculine and feminine qualities, a simplification that suppresses the feminine. This masculinization gains widespread acceptance, as indicated by J. Atkins' praise for Dryden's prose: "he develops a style, masculine, vivid and pliant, eminently suitable for critical discussion and everywhere readable by reason of its liveliness and charm."[6] Whereas Dryden tempers a masculine sense of loftiness and boldness with feminine delicacy and ornament, Atkins drops the feminine qualifiers and characterizes the delight of Dryden's criticism as entirely consistent with masculine assets. The application of gendered terms in the evaluation of Dryden is not surprising, since his own critical vocabulary exhibits pronounced dialogism with the language of gender; however, the absence of the feminine in this partial list of examples demonstrates the unifying force of patriarchal discourse in criticism, which denies or represses information when it jeopardizes the monolithic representation of hegemonic authority.

The pervasive use of masculine terms in the criticism of Dryden has more serious implications in the influential writings of Sir Walter Scott and Mark Van Doren. At the beginning of the nineteenth century, Scott's biography and collected works of Dryden attempt to recover the reputation of the former Poet Laureate during an age that valorized subjective aesthetic qualities and lyricism over the harshness of satire and heroic style. An obtrusive use of masculine qualifiers forms one part of his strategy. For example, Scott credits Dryden with improving the meter of satire, the significance of which he underscores by investing it with masculine power: "he gave them varied tone, correct rhyme and masculine energy, all which had hitherto been strangers to the English satire." Scott defends his somewhat anachronistic taste in Dryden's satire by emphasizing its virility. In response to the poetic standards of his era, Scott identifies the emotional force of Dryden's poetry, but again

---

[5] Gerard Manley Hopkins, *The Letters of Gerard Manley Hopkins to Robert Bridges*, ed. Claude Colleer Abott (London: Oxford University Press, 1955), p. 265.
[6] J. W. H. Atkins, *English Literary Criticism: Seventeenth and Eighteenth Centuries* (London: Methuen, 1951), p. 52.

he reinforces the "manliness" of his expressions. The evaluation of Dryden's intimate poem to Congreve stresses its strong philosophical reason and noble pathos: "the interest is excited by means of masculine and exalted passion, not of those which arise from the mere delicate sensibilities of our nature." Scott asserts a distinct hierarchy between the dignified source of emotion considered masculine and the involuntary affective response that, by contrast, is feminized. He elaborates by explaining that Dryden's depiction of love appeals to the sensitive character of "bearded men" and not to an audience of "youths and maidens." Here, the formulation of the feminine serves as a counter to Dryden's success and, consequently, an inferior or non-literary achievement.

Scott's use of dialogized terms, or constructions stratified by the language of gendered perspectives, is most problematic when the gendered associations obscure or subsume his critical precision. In one instance, he uses a gendered assessment to describe Dryden's occasional poetry; the elegies and odes, Scott claims, are "marked strongly by masculine character," by which we can deduce that he means grave, argumentative reason rather than tenderness. In another example, he implies that Dryden's ability to break away from stifling literary conventions is a gendered trait: "[i]t was reserved to Dryden manfully to claim and vindicate the freedom of a just translation."[7] These evaluations substitute gendered characteristics for literary ones and reinforce the historically contingent concept of rational yet bold masculinity as a purportedly natural and understood category of literary achievement. Through the use of gendered language, Scott's critical appraisal of Dryden exaggerates his masculinity and simplifies the more integral gendered structures underlying Dryden's poetics, and it simultaneously reproduces a gendered ideology that associates the definitive literary qualities of intellect and judgment with a specifically masculine character.

An even more pronounced masculinization is evident in Mark Van Doren's important study, first published in 1920, which, with T. S. Eliot's essays, is largely responsible for reviving a scholarly interest in Dryden's writings during the early twentieth century. Employing a variety of analogies, Van Doren aligns the powerful suggestiveness of Dryden's poetry with male sexuality. Van Doren asserts, with Johnson and Scott, that Dryden refines the English poetic line, and this development has virile significance: "Verse is not everything, but to assume that it is

---

[7] Sir Walter Scott, *The Life of Dryden*, ed. Bernard Kreissman (Lincoln: University of Nebraska Press, 1963), pp. 239, 409, 431, 434.

nothing is to ignore a primary source of pleasure and power, and in the end is to emasculate poetry."[8] By describing verse – or the melody of poetry – in the language of masculinity, Van Doren appeals to members of his audience, whose modern aesthetic de-emphasizes euphonic sound, in order to persuade them that they are missing something vital. Unlike Van Doren's contemporaries and the Tennysonian poets they despised, Dryden exploits the potential of *vigorous* sound. The source of our attraction to Dryden, Van Doren claims, lies in his ability to produce pleasure through utter strength.

> He attended to the craft of sound . . . with a man's interest in the muscle, the sinew, and the nerve of a poem that must be both heard and understood as saying something . . . The statement is what interests us, but there is a final pleasure in listening again to the way the lines move. They move in melody, which is everywhere in Dryden, and masculine.[9]

Like Scott, Van Doren credits the masculinity of Dryden's writing to its intellectual force, but he also insists that the harmony is masculine. Not only does Van Doren repress the feminine aspects of prosody prominent in Dryden's criticism, but additionally he constructs an isolated economy of masculine desire and pleasure to explain and sustain Dryden's work. Furthermore, the poetry's eminent masculinity becomes the signal feature in the rationale for recovering Dryden's work. By implying that Dryden conveys a gendered essence that viscerally affects its modern audience, Van Doren's criticism posits a universal understanding of manliness as a vehicle for continuity in poetic value. Unlike Scott's rejection of the feminine as unliterary, Van Doren denies utterly the presence of femininity in Dryden's poetry.

The twentieth-century concentration on Dryden's uniform masculinity motivates James Winn's recent reassessment of Dryden's writing. Winn is unique in privileging the sexual dynamic that permeates Dryden's work, and he provides a much-needed "corrective" view of Dryden's more feminine attributes: "the musical lyricism of his line, the visual splendor of his imagery, the precious moments when he recognizes his own emotional and sexual frailty."[10] Although Winn focuses primarily on the role of sexual passion in Dryden's creative process, several of his observations contribute to our understanding of Dryden's critical

[8] Mark Van Doren, *John Dryden: A Study of His Poetry*, third edition (Bloomington: Indiana University Press, 1960), p. viii.
[9] Ibid., pp. viii–ix.
[10] James Anderson Winn, *"When Beauty Fires the Blood": Love and the Arts in the Age of Dryden* (Ann Arbor: University of Michigan Press, 1992), p. 435.

appropriation of gendered language. In particular, Winn argues that a "subtle and refined association linking men with reason, women with pleasure features frequently in [Dryden's] comparisons of the arts, where the allegedly rational appeal of poetry allows him to define it as a masculine art, superior to the more sensuous, bodily, and feminine arts of music and painting."[11]

Winn perceives dichotomies in Dryden's critical writings in terms of masculine art versus feminine nature, or male reason versus female sensuality, but his focus on Dryden's intentions and idiosyncrasies regarding sexuality sometimes leads to misapprehensions in the history of gender. The study is valuable for the attention it draws to Dryden's gendered complexity, but it is limited by the binary categories Winn imposes, and by a concept of gender that tends toward universal assumptions rather than historical contingency. Throughout, Winn seems overly concerned about what he calls "the curious fluidity of gender values in Dryden's work," or his tendency to apply masculine qualifiers to female subjects and vice versa.[12] He is, for instance, unresolved as to why Dryden characterizes Hastings with masculine *and* feminine imagery by calling him Ganymede, Venus, and the phoenix. Likewise, he is intrigued by Dryden's combination of sexual descriptions in his tributes to Cromwell and the Duchess of Newcastle.[13]

He attempts to explain "the trope of shifting sexuality," or the "unconventional or ambiguous sexuality," by appealing to personal details of the individuals described, but such fluid constructions are actually characteristic of the period.[14] Much scholarship of the past twenty years focuses on the changing gendered roles of the Restoration and the eighteenth century.[15] Invoking Angellica's self-consciously gendered sign from *The Rover*, Janet Todd argues that Restoration notions of gender were understood to be artificial and constructed,

---

[11] Ibid., p. 9.   [12] Ibid., pp. 53–54.   [13] Ibid., pp. 37–40.   [14] Ibid., pp. 61, 65.
[15] The following have been instrumental in opening up the inquiry: Lawrence Stone, *The Family, Sex, and Marriage in England 1500–1800* (New York: Harper and Row, 1977); Susan Moller Okin, "Women and the Making of the Sentimental Family," *Philosophy and Public Affairs* 11.1 (1982), 65–88; Joan Kelly, *Women, History and Theory: The Essays of Joan Kelly* (Chicago: University of Chicago Press, 1984); Thomas Laqueur, *Making Sex: Bodies and Gender from the Greeks to Freud* (Cambridge: Harvard University Press, 1990). Relevant discussions can also be found in Moira Ferguson, *First Feminists, British Women Writers 1578–1799* (Bloomington: Indiana University Press, 1985); Angeline Goreau, ed., *The Whole Duty of a Woman: Female Writers in Seventeenth-Century England* (Garden City: Dial Press, 1985); Ellen Pollak, *The Poetics of Sexual Myth: Gender Ideology in the Verse of Swift and Pope* (Chicago: University of Chicago Press, 1985); Jane Spencer, *The Rise of the Woman Novelist: From Aphra Behn to Jane Austen* (Oxford: Basil Blackwell, 1986); Felicity Nussbaum, *The Autobiographical Subject: Gender and Ideology in Eighteenth-Century England* (Baltimore: The Johns Hopkins University Press, 1989).

especially in contrast to mid- and late-eighteenth-century sexuality.[16] From 1660 to 1790, the dominant discursive construction of gender changed from a difference in degree to one of kind, or from a social understanding of sexual difference to an ontological one. While both models of gendered difference coexisted in society, one model tended to prevail, and within the Restoration that paradigm was the difference in degree. In other words, the sexes were perceived to be fundamentally similar in kind and distinguished by the relative degree to which each sex possessed specific characteristics.[17] The traits that distinguished men from women were roles or cultivated, learned behaviors. As such, masculinity or femininity could be appropriated by any person regardless of sex, and gender-crossing, literalized by the frequent cross-dressing of stage actors, was permissible. While the categories of "masculine" and "feminine" began to stabilize along biological lines toward the last years of the seventeenth century, the gendered codes continued to be applied across sexes.[18] Dryden's ability to portray his patroness with masculine virtues or his dead schoolmate with feminine softness attests to the understanding of gender as a role, as a sign indicating specific characteristics that are not restricted to biological sex.

The understanding of gender as an artificial, learned code facilitates the widespread use of gendered language to describe otherwise neuter entities, the most important for our purposes being literature. Thomas Sprat, for instance, postulates that "there is a kind of variety of Sexes in Poetry as well as in Mankind: that as the peculiar excellence of the Feminine Kind is smoothnesse and beauty, so strength is the chief praise of the Masculine."[19] Sprat's comparison evokes a semiotic conception of gender, where the signs of masculine and feminine are attached to a specific field of knowledge that readily applies to a person or a poem. Within the context of a patriarchal culture, these gendered categories also convey meanings of power, and the gendered comparison almost

[16] Janet Todd, *The Sign of Angellica: Women, Writing and Fiction 1660–1800* (New York: Columbia University Press, 1989), pp. 3–5.
[17] See Michael McKeon, "Historicizing Patriarchy: The Emergence of Gender Difference in England, 1660–1760," *Eighteenth-Century Studies* 28:3 (1995), 295–322; Laqueur, *Making Sex*; Ruth H. Bloch, "Untangling the Roots of Modern Sex Roles: A Survey of Four Centuries of Change," *Signs* 4.2 (1978), 237–252.
[18] This semiotic understanding of gender is particularly evident in the periodical literature: see Kathryn Shevelow, *Women and Print Culture: The Construction of Femininity in the Early Periodical* (London: Routledge, 1989).
[19] Thomas Sprat, "An account of the Life and Writing of Mr. Abraham Cowley: Written to Mr. M. Clifford" (1668), in J. E. Spingarn, ed., *Critical Essays of the Seventeenth Century,* second edition, 3 vols. (Bloomington: Indiana University Press, 1963), vol. II (1650–1685), p. 129.

always implies that the category of the masculine is more significant than the feminine. Sprat uses the hierarchical measure here to extenuate the roughness of Cowley's verse by emphasizing the more substantial achievement of his poetic strength and downplaying smooth metrics as feminine.

The sex of the poet does not necessarily determine the application of gendered terms in criticism, nor are the gendered categories mutually exclusive. A poet, male or female, could combine feminine prosody and masculine strength. In praising the verse of Katherine Philips, Abraham Cowley imagines an ideal union of the sexes:

> 'Tis solid, and 'tis manly all,
> Or rather, 'tis Angelical:
>> For, as in Angels, we
>> Do in thy Verses see
> Both improv'd Sexes eminently meet;
> They are than Man more Strong, and more than Woman Sweet.[20]

In a compliment of poetic androgyny, Cowley identifies both masculine substance and feminine sweetness – a specific quality of harmonious prosody – in Philips' poetry. The conventional practice of praising a female author with masculine terms illustrates the culture's inclination toward semiotic rather than biological distinctions of gender.[21] Likewise, the epistolary pupil of Dryden, Elizabeth Thomas, ascribes a combination of masculine and feminine qualities to Dryden's credit: "With Worlds of Words *He* did our Speech Refine, / And Manly strength with Modern softness join."[22] Thomas adopts the conventionally gendered categories, but somewhat alters the expected balance by labeling "softness" modern instead of female. Her change increases the alliterative smoothness of the line, but she may also aim to protect the masculine reputation of her mentor from the negative associations of femininity. While gendered codes might modify male or female subjects, they continue to carry specific cultural significations, and femininity connotes potential weakness.

The heroic discourses of the Restoration constitute masculinity as part of a matrix of values including martial prowess, reverence for the epic,

---

[20] Abraham Cowley's "Upon Mrs. K. Philips her Poems" in Katherine Philips, *Poems* (1667), facsimile, intro. Travis Dupriest (Delmar, New York: Scholars' Facsimiles & Reprints, 1992).

[21] For references to the conventionality, see Joanna Lipking, "Fair Originals: Women Poets in Male Commendatory Poems," *Eighteenth-Century Life* 12 (May 1988), 58–72; Jacqueline Pearson, *The Prostituted Muse: Images of Women and Women Dramatists 1642–1737* (New York: Harvester-Wheatsheaf, 1988), esp. pp. 1–8.

[22] Elizabeth Thomas in *Luctus Britannici; or, The Tears of the British Muse; for the Death of John Dryden* (1700), quoted in Winn, *"When Beauty Fires the Blood,"* p. 433.

and ardent nationalism. Gendered distinctions of masculine strength
and feminine softness play a central role in the seventeenth-century
discussion of the superiority of the English language, an intense discourse
of linguistic chauvinism in which Dryden participated.[23] During a time
when the purity of the French language set the linguistic standard, the
British attempted to bolster national confidence by recasting a macho
image for their admittedly unrefined tongue. According to Sklar, "English-
language advocates sought to promote English as a language worthy of
national pride, one that could be perceived, moreover, as competitive
within an international linguistic community that had long held it in
contempt. Representing English as a 'manly' language was a key strategy
in this undertaking."[24] The campaign was predicated on the rationale
that rough, sonorous words were strong, masculine, and, therefore,
superior to the feminine, mellifluous words of Romance languages. The
English language, unlike the French or Italian, descended from the
hardy Germanic tribes of the rugged north, who invested the language
with its qualities of strength and substance. Dryden described French,
refined as it had become by his time, as "infeebled": "That, like pure
Gold, it bends at ev'ry touch." Whereas "Our sturdy Teuton, yet will Art
obey, / More fit for manly thought, and strengthen'd with Allay."[25]
Dryden designates the two functions of language – capacity for sound
and for thought – in gendered terms, denigrating the weak sophistication
of the French as feminine. His support for the heroic potential of English
– its ability to convey "manly thought" – is consistent with the cultural
project of advancing his national language.

Dryden's linguistic and literary nationalism reaches its highest
expression in his promotion of the epic, a critical position grounded in
patriarchal ideology and conveyed through explicitly gendered language.
In his dedication to the *Aeneis* (1697) he claims that "A heroic poem, truly
such, is undoubtedly the greatest work which the soul of man is capable
to perform."[26] With its celebration of martial values and national
identity, the epic is the most significant public literary form. Unable to

[23] For information on Dryden's involvement in several proposals for a British Academy to refine the English language, see O. F. Emerson, "John Dryden and a British Academy," *Proceedings of the British Academy* 10 (1921–1923), 45–58; also see Dryden's dedication to the *Aeneis* (Watson, vol. II, pp. 236–237).
[24] Elizabeth S. Sklar, "So Male a Speech: Linguistic Adequacy in Eighteenth-Century England," *American Speech* 64.4 (1989), 373.
[25] "To My Friend the Author," lines 45–47, *The Poems of John Dryden*, ed. James Kinsley, 4 vols. (Oxford: Clarendon, 1958), vol. III, p. 1436.
[26] Watson, vol. II, p. 223.

write his own epic, Dryden claims that he translates Virgil's for the honor of England, and he takes pains to establish the superiority of his version over the French and the Italian.[27] Dryden attributes his success in part to the virility of the English language: "The French have set up purity for the standard of their language; and a masculine vigour is that of ours. Like their tongue is the genius of their poets, light and trifling in comparison of the English; more proper for sonnets, madrigals, and elegies, than heroic poetry."[28] Once again, the gendered designations establish the hierarchy of linguistic values. While French is pure, it limits the creativity of its poets to "light and trifling" endeavors. The "masculine vigour" of English, on the other hand, qualifies it – and Dryden – for the highest achievement in the epic. Despite repeated complaints of the limitations of his harsh-sounding language, "clogged with monosyllables" and lacking an adequate number of vowels, Dryden claims that the English language can properly achieve the goals of heroic poetry, because "Strength and Elevation are our Standard."[29]

These examples suggest that, while little attention has been drawn to the fact, Dryden operated within a discursive context that readily attributed a cluster of gendered traits to poetry in a fairly consistent manner. The features of imagination or invention, judgment, and intellectual rigor are invariably characterized as masculine, and these constitute a standard group that I label as definitive literary qualities.[30] The heroic style, with an emphasis on strength, boldness, and excess, also employs a masculine vocabulary. In contrast, Dryden's criticism constructs a feminine balance to these poetic traits, namely sweet and smooth prosody, soft sounds, and simple ideas. Dryden privileges the masculine category as the necessary condition for poetic excellence, but he constructs his poetics on a heterosexual paradigm that binds the feminine to the masculine in a variety of ways.

THE FEMININE AND THE MASCULINE

In 1676, after more than a decade of defending the superiority of rhymed drama, Dryden admits that he has grown "weary of his long-loved mistress, Rhyme."[31] The personification, as Winn rightly suggests, signals Dryden's strong preference for the aural quality that he associates with pleasure, but the gendered comparison carries more

---

[27] Ibid., p. 242.   [28] Ibid., p. 238.   [29] Ibid., p. 247.   [30] See pages 28–31.
[31] Watson, vol. I, p. 192.

cultural freight. As a fundamental world-view, gender constitutes one of the everyday languages that Dryden uses to express his literary evaluations. Like his contemporaries, Dryden enters a discourse already saturated with gendered distinctions. The reference to rhyme as his mistress reflects Dryden's historically constituted position as a Restoration male; he describes his relationship to a literary practice in terms of a heterosexual union, and, consequently, the description inscribes the relative power associated with that perspective. In this case rhyme has become the cast-off mistress, and the poet is freed from her seduction. Dryden's gendered criticism can be understood as the dialogic threads of two discourses of value: gender and literature. As he strives to clarify literary judgment and regulate English verse, he shapes literary value through a matrix of gendered significations specific to the Restoration.

Dryden's category of the feminine generally refers to a form of prosody that emphasizes aural pleasure, and his use of the masculine indicates a significant, often heroic poetics. His critical categories dialogically intersect with the language of the hero and the genteel lady. Although his regular, unqualified application of gendered language – for instance seeing rhyme as a mistress or the English language as masculine – asserts a universal understanding of gender, his ideal categories are historically contingent upon the changing, gendered discourses of the Restoration. With its emphasis on smoothness, softness, purity, and sweetness, Dryden's concept of the feminine relies on a refined and courtly construction that is particularly prevalent among genteel women in the reign of Charles II. Similarly, Dryden's references to masculinity are overlaid with Restoration values of bravery, nationalism, and faith in empirical reason. This specific critical dialogism with gendered language suppresses the plurality of gendered constructions in Restoration discourse by continually returning to the heterosexual dynamic of the court and gentility. Unlike Rymer, whose critical attack on Desdemona borrows crude language from a lower-class femininity, and whose own critical stance rejects the politesse and dignity of gentlemanly discourse, Dryden confines his gendered referents to the elite.[32] In poetry and drama, Dryden ranges more widely, but in his criticism humble, debauched, or bawdy images rarely appear. Such consistency has the powerful effect of repressing alternative forms of sexuality and representing the values of the Restoration court as monolithic. His selectivity also

[32] For examples see selections from *A Short View of Tragedy* in *Shakespeare: The Critical Heritage*, ed. Brian Vickers, 6 vols. (London and Boston: Routledge and Kegan Paul, 1976), vol. II, pp. 25–59.

raises the value of poetry by aligning the dignity of heroic writing and the refinement of the poetic line with characters of the highest social consequence. Significantly, Dryden sets a precedent for well-mannered criticism that, with Addison's affable dignity, comes to serve as a model for eighteenth-century critical prose.

"An Account of the Ensuing Poem" prefixed to *Annus Mirabilis* (1667) offers a clear illustration of Dryden's early consciousness of the relationship between gender and literary values. Dryden's main purpose in this essay is to explain and defend the principles of wit upon which he based his heroic poem, but he structures the argument around a contrast of gendered styles. In his famous statement on the three stages of creativity, he defines "invention" as the finding of the thought, "fancy" as the molding of the thought according to judgment and propriety, and "elocution" as the "the art of clothing and adorning that thought so found and varied, in apt, significant, and sounding words."[33] This discussion of propriety first introduces Dryden's claim that the great exemplar of elocution, Virgil, has been his "master" in *Annus Mirabilis*. The emphasis on choosing the language appropriate for the subject, however, then serves as a main principle in his defense of the poem, "Verses to her Highness the Duchess," which had become the focus of hostile criticism. Dryden's sense of decorum clearly exceeds that of his contemporaries, who would judge all poetry by the standard of elevation. He addresses his detractors, who claimed that he

wanted not only height of fancy, but dignity of words to set it off. I might well answer with that of Horace, *Nunc non erat his locus* [This was not the place for such things], I knew I addressed them to a lady, and accordingly I affected the softness of expression, and the smoothness of measure, rather than the height of thought.[34]

This discrimination between poetry in general and poetry directed to a female audience demonstrates how gender operates as a fundamental epistemological division and, consequently for Dryden, as a basic critical consideration. Dryden prescribes the "softness of expression" and the "smoothness of measure" for female gratification. This judgment assumes that soft sounds please the female ear and smooth lines express the aesthetics of the feminine world. That these verses did not attain the height of thought was not a fault in his art but proof of the precision of his decorum. In his polite consideration of the feminine mind, he categorically denies the propriety of intellectual rigor.

[33] Watson, vol. I, p. 99.   [34] Ibid., p. 102.

Because of the living nature of language and its mutability throughout history, the terms Dryden uses merit closer attention.[35] Many of the words carry significations of both content and sound, or the thought and its adornment. "Soft," Dryden's most consistent sign for the feminine category of poetry, is a word of tremendous variety in meanings, many overlapping with or blending into others. In the *OED* the adjective has thirty-two main entries, each subdivided two to four times. The softness of sound (3a), defined as "low, quiet, subdued, not loud ... [a]lso, melodious, pleasing to the ear, sweet," has obvious similarities with sweetness in prosody and harmonious sound. The softness of language (10a), "ingratiating, soothing, bland, tender, sentimental," is defined in peculiarly emotional terms and reflects the word's capacity to modify the affective content of poetry. "Soft" also denotes language "free from roughness or harshness" (10b), a definition that would characterize a minimal use of punctuation to avoid sharp stops or exclamations. A soft pace (5a), which is "leisurely; easy; slow," qualifies the movement of the line adjusted to feminine standards. Dryden also uses "soft" in contrast to hard or difficult, as in *An Essay of Dramatic Poesy*, where he describes an atypical metaphor of Cleveland as so "soft and gentle that it does not shock us when we read it."[36]

Like the category of definitive literary qualities – imagination, judgment, and intellect – softness operates as a gendered signifier when read within a Restoration or eighteenth-century context. Because of its association with tenderness and impressionability, "soft" connotes that which is "weak, effeminate, unmanly" (14b).[37] Milton's paradigmatic couple from *Paradise Lost* (1667) illustrates a conception of sexual division common to that age: "For contemplation hee and valor form'd, / For Softness Shee and sweet attractive Grace."[38] Intellect and bravery belong exclusively to the male character, while a loosely defined softness and sweetness distinguish an opposing femininity. The term "the softer sex" enters proverbial discourse during the seventeenth century and often acts as a generic label for women's inferiority to men. Richard Allestree, in his phenomenally successful conduct book, *The Ladies Calling* (originally published 1673), celebrates women's "native

---

[35] James Jensen demonstrates the illusive clarity of Dryden's vocabulary in the introduction to *A Glossary of John Dryden's Critical Terms* (Minneapolis: University of Minnesota Press, 1969), p. 4.

[36] Watson, vol. 1, p. 41.

[37] All of these definitions were current during Dryden's time.

[38] *Paradise Lost*, Book VI, lines 297–298, in John Milton, *Complete Poems and Major Prose*, ed. Merritt Y. Hughes (New York: Macmillan, 1957).

softness" and "softer mold."[39] By the beginning of the eighteenth
century, references to the softness of a woman's body, mind, and spirit
were commonplace.[40] So, while Dryden's use of the "softness of
expression" clearly refers to the technical production of sound, the
language participates in several discourses at once and evokes associations
of gentle, subordinate femininity.

As the example from Allestree illustrates, Dryden's feminine descriptors
intersect with the language of the seventeenth-century conduct book, a
dialogism that is not necessarily inconsistent with the court ethos but has
ramifications for a broader sector of the reading populace. His own
Puritan background may have influenced the feminine ideal of intense
restriction that he incorporates into poetic propriety.[41] Dryden's term
"smoothness," modifying poetry that is regular and even throughout,
also refers to a woman's internal and external composure. Codes of
female decorum reinforce a direct correspondence between proper
place and visual worthiness in recognition of a woman's function both as
subordinate and object of beauty. Consequently, anger, volubility, or
emotional expression is generally prohibited as a violation of feminine
place and aesthetics. Allestree's text recommends modesty as the
fundamental principle of this internalized feminine restraint: "[Modesty]
being that which guides and regulates the whole behavior, checks and
controls all rude Exorbitancies, and is the great Civilizer of conversations
. . . [modesty] also steers every part of the outward frame. It appears in
the face in calm and meek looks." Such carriage, he continues,
epitomizes "Feminine Beauty": "An innocent Modesty, and native
simplicity of look, shall eclipse all Glaring Splendor."[42] By grounding
women's modesty in nature, Allestree's rhetoric posits an originary and
final status to feminine simplicity in opposition to wit and other
unfeminine forms of verbal dexterity. Moreover, he implies that such
"native" female beauty based in modesty is, in effect, an aesthetic of
smoothness, or the control of "all rude Exorbitancies." The discourse on
feminine conduct extends the scope of limitations to speech, calling
"discretion, silence and modesty" the fairest perfections in women: "so

[39] Richard Allestree, *The Ladies Calling. The Second Part of the Works of the Learned and Pious* (Oxford:
1687), pp. 1, 20.
[40] Antonia Fraser, *The Weaker Vessel* (New York: Vintage Books, 1984), p. 4.
[41] For a discussion of the changing role of class in the conduct literature of the late seventeenth
century, see Nancy Armstrong and Leonard Tennenhouse, eds., *The Ideology of Conduct: Essays on
Literature and the History of Sexuality* (New York: Methuen, 1987), pp. 1–24.
[42] Allestree, *The Ladies Calling*, p. 4.

pauses in discourse being well used, do make that more plainly appear, which is the best and the sweetest in it."[43] As both the "great Civilizer of conversations" and the recommended strategy in feminine speech, modesty becomes the mark of refinement in discourse, a smoothing of extremes that accrues aesthetic and social value.

Through the concept of smoothness, Dryden establishes a parallel between the cultural demands of femininity and his project for refining the English language of verse. Conversation figures in Dryden's criticism as the crucible for poetic language, in particular conversation with the court of Charles II. Discourse with greatness and good breeding, according to Dryden, has a civilizing influence unique to the Restoration: "let us ascribe to the gallantry and civility of our age the advantage which we have above [Jonson, Fletcher and Shakespeare]."[44] Dryden's explanation for the improvement of language draws on overlapping categories of class and gender. Gallantry, at this time, retains the dual connotations of courtier and lover, describing the language of address to aristocrats and to women. Dryden envisions the improvement of poetic language flowing through these two channels, from the greatness and sophistication of Charles II and the elegance and modesty of the ladies. In his Preface to *Sylvae* (1685), Dryden recommends that the wit-in-training practice, among other things, "conversation with the best company of both sexes."[45] Dryden's specific mention of "both sexes" reinforces the epistemological division between the sexes, as indicated in the gendered decorum of "An Account of the Ensuing Poem," but in this context, Dryden implies that feminine discourse benefits the poet in ways that purely masculine language cannot. The conversation of women – manifest in his conception of the feminine – is instrumental to his vision of improved English poetry.

The smoothness of feminine discourse supplements the lofty, but apparently unrefined, realm of male language. As with Dryden's example of Charles II, whose feminized French gaiety brings lightness to England's previously "constrained, melancholy way of breeding," so women bring a moderation and purification to speech.[46] Dryden's use of the term "smoothness" in his criticism corroborates the meaning. Smoothness generally indicates a style of verse that avoids hard pronunciations, uses consistent meter and maintains an equanimity in passion and thought.[47] "Smoothness," Dryden contends, is important and difficult: "'Tis no easy matter in our language to make words so

[43] Goreau, ed., *The Whole Duty of Woman*, p. 40.   [44] Watson, vol. I, p. 182.
[45] Watson, vol. II, p. 20.   [46] Watson, vol. I, p. 182.   [47] Jensen, *Dryden's Critical Terms*, p. 108.

smooth, and numbers so harmonious."[48] Ovid often stands as Dryden's example of classical smoothness, "He avoids ... all synalæphas, or cutting off one vowel when it comes before another in the following word."[49] Dryden's criticism of Ovid, however, reveals the insufficiency of metrical regularity; he complains that in "minding only smoothness, he wants both variety and majesty."[50] The principal significance of smoothness in poetry, like its counterpart in the code of femininity, lies in a restraint that yields ornamental value.

By Dryden's own acknowledgment, the "Verses to her Highness" stand as exemplary lines of the feminine style. Dryden writes the poem for the Duchess in honor of her husband's questionable victory at Lowestoft. Softness characterizes the language of the poem, which couches controversial political issues in the domestic idiom of love. Winn argues that Dryden deliberately praises the dubious military success in private terms to minimize attention to an action whose significance at that time had not fully registered.[51] By focusing on marital commitments strained by the obligations of state, Dryden subverts the national conflicts and privileges the relationship between the Duke and Duchess of York. I would add that the feminine style is fundamental to Dryden's strategy. Generalized images of romance, "the mansion of soft love," "concerns," and "chaste vows," create a calming smoothness in contrast to the graphic, violent images of war in *Annus Mirabilis*. The poem's form is very simple. Dryden sustains an iambic pentameter in the regular evenness of primarily closed couplets, including a single triplet and one alexandrine. He creates an ease and sweetness of sound through carefully modulated vowels in fair proportion with clear consonants. Rather than address the complicated political issues of the duke's victory, the feminine focus of the poem necessitates an aesthetic of soft gestures in both style and subject.

Dryden excuses the poem's simplicity by suggesting that it is meant for a female-only audience, and this explicitly gendered decorum recasts the preceding defense of *Annus Mirabilis* into gendered terms. Dryden presumably aims the heroic poem at a general and masculine audience, and its qualities of workmanship define a standard of excellence which is likewise masculine. Dryden uses the verses to the Duchess as a politic counterbalance to his showcased poem; the simple, feminine couplets, which Dryden finds "most easy," set off to advantage the bold, ambitious quatrains, notwithstanding "the trouble I had in writing [them] was

[48] Watson, vol. II, p. 40.   [49] Ibid., p. 22.   [50] Ibid.
[51] James Anderson Winn, *John Dryden and His World* (New Haven: Yale University Press, 1987), p. 159.

great." Dryden chooses the form, taken from *Gondibert*, because it is "more noble, and of greater dignity, both for sound and number, than any other verse in use amongst us."[52] Thus, the stanza's complexity and capacity for noble and dignified resonance serve as identifying features of the masculine poetic. In a poem about naval victories, Dryden sets out to improve poetic language by rejecting the modish metaphysical conceits in favor of the "proper terms of the sea."[53] Realistic language, he explains, raises poetry above "common notions" – and one might add feminine softness – by accurate depiction. Both the sense of heightening and the judgment required to achieve it form part of the matrix of masculine values in Dryden's heroic. Whereas feminine smoothness denotes an aesthetic of generalized confinement, the masculine ideal involves exceeding boundaries. He contends that the wit of heroic poetry is to improve the image in representation, to show it "as perfectly and *more delightfully* than nature."[54] The great poet renders empirical reality more pleasing through propriety of figurative language, as in the case of Virgil: "We see the objects he presents us with in their native figures, in their proper motions; but so we see them, as our own eyes could never have beheld them so beautiful in themselves."[55] The end of such elocution is "to beget admiration" or to create a sense of wonder and agreeable surprise.[56] Admiration, with its connotations of dominance and power, is a word, like "boldness," that Dryden frequently uses to signal the heroic or masculine aesthetic.[57] In contrast to soft, smooth, simple, and sweet, the masculine style of poetry defined by *Annus Mirabilis* is lofty, bold, noble, ambitious, complex, and intellectually rigorous, and it is clearly indebted to the faculties of imagination, intellect, and judgment that ultimately define literary greatness in the eighteenth century.

As with the feminine style, the masculine critical category is shaped by a language of social and political values. However, the cultural ideal of femininity, which is constructed as normative, differs from Dryden's masculine standard, which is by definition exceptional. Dryden's discourse on heroic poetry – what he calls elsewhere "the greatest work of human nature"[58] – characterizes the genre in the language of superlatives. Similarly, the masculine style is pointedly not average; aspiration and excess are key principles to its aesthetic appeal. Dryden's

---

[52] Watson, vol. 1, pp. 97, 95.   [53] Ibid., p. 96.   [54] Ibid., p. 98, emphasis mine.
[55] Ibid., p. 99.   [56] Ibid., p. 101.
[57] Cf. Jensen, *Dryden's Critical Terms*, pp. 20, 27; also "masculine," p. 77.
[58] Watson, vol. 1, p. 198.

masculine poetic dialogically intersects the discourse of the epic war-hero, a mythical paragon of patriarchal authority. In the sharp ambivalence of the post-rebellion public traditional figures of proper authority, whether kings, clergyman, fathers, or husbands, needed a more forceful interpretation of their roles.[59] The discursive solution appears to have been a concerted emphasis on honor, a male code of behavior founded in the virtues of bravery, loyalty, and honesty and epitomized by the hero. In addition to the manifold literary representations of the hero – in epic, tragedy, French romances, and translations of the classics – the panegyric of exaggerated valor and patriotism flourishes in Dryden's age.[60] For example, in the ill-fated "Instructions to a Painter" Edmund Waller glosses over the Duke of York's shortcomings and memorializes his virtue in terms of honor and duty: "The valiant duke, whose early deeds abroad / Such rage in fight and art in conduct show'd / His bright sword now a dearer int'rest draws, / His brother's glory and his country's cause."[61] Educational treatises for boys likewise emphasize the bravery of a soldier, a willingness to die in defense of your name, and a fierce loyalty to England. Milton, for instance, outlines a regimen to fit "a man to perform justly, skilfully, and magnanimously all the offices, both private and public, of peace and war."[62] The idiosyncratic heroic drama, which Dryden writes and defends, enjoys popularity during the 1660s and 1670s in part because it sensationalizes the themes of bravery and honor.[63] In his criticism, Dryden's emphasis on a masculine style of boldness, grandeur and difficulty resonates with the cultural languages of war, patriarchy, and heroism, stratifying the meaning of his literary language with the specific social and political values of the Restoration.

Thus Dryden attributes to poetry masculine characteristics that share certain qualities with Restoration notions of manhood, such as boldness, erudition, judgment, vigorous imagination, lofty vision, and strength, and he assigns feminine labels that share certain qualities with Restoration notions of femininity, such as softness, smoothness, beauty, love,

---

[59] For an account of the changing images of authority in Restoration drama see Susan Staves, *Player's Scepters: Fictions of Authority in the Restoration* (Lincoln: University of Nebraska Press, 1979).

[60] See James Sutherland, *English Literature of the Late Seventeenth Century* (Oxford: Clarendon Press, 1969), p. 4.

[61] Edmund Waller, "Instructions to a Painter," lines 11–14, in *Poems on Affairs of State: Augustan Satirical Verse, 1660–1714*, ed. George deF Lord, 7 vols. (New Haven: Yale University Press, 1963), vol. II, pp. 22.

[62] John Milton, "Of Education" (reprinted in 1673), *Complete Poems and Major Prose*, p. 632.

[63] See "Of Heroic Plays: An Essay Prefixed to *The Conquest of Granada*" (1672) in Watson, vol. I, pp. 156–168.

quietness, sweetness, and simplicity. Rather than represent eternal and unchanging notions of sex, these languages of gender are located in the Restoration court, and they constitute one set of constructions, albeit hegemonic. In "An Account" Dryden outlines these gendered categories of style, but in doing so he also imputes the relative power of patriarchal roles to his poetic categories. The gender of the heroic style, unlike the feminine, can sometimes be obscured because the masculine style operates as the poetic norm by which difference is measured. Dryden's critics, for example, want to judge his "Verses" to the duchess by the expectation that poetry, in general, should represent the pinnacle of fancy and dignity, but Dryden perceives that these are inappropriate for feminine poetry. Paradoxically, the masculine style of boundless imagination operates as the standard for poetic achievement, whereas normative femininity represents a deviation. Dryden conveys his own priority through the attention to detail and language of excellence devoted to *Annus Mirabilis*. He summarizes the feminine style in three phrases: "the softness of expression, and the smoothness of measure, rather than the height of thought." The hierarchical relationship between the sexes consequently serves as an analogy to distinguish between the ostensibly different poetics.

Dryden's evaluation of the masculine heroic is clarified by the definition and opposition to the feminine in "An Account." His conception of gendered categories, however, is not static; rather, he frequently searches for an interactive balance between the poetic virtues represented by the masculine and feminine styles. The process of distinction by which Dryden separates and prioritizes gendered referents operates simultaneously with the potential for the gendered elements to meliorate each other. In "An Account" Dryden associates a metrical style of smoothness with a female audience. Likewise, the reference to rhyme as his "long-loved mistress" figures the seduction of sound in the semblance of a woman. Dryden often casts the aural pleasures of poetry and specifically his aesthetic of confinement as a feminine force at odds with more masculine energies of creation. The greater attention to sound required by an opera, for instance, interferes with the poet's endeavor to express his thoughts. In the preface to *Albion and Albanius* (1685), Dryden constructs a gendered analogy to express this annoyance:

For Vocal Musick, though it often admits a loftiness of sound: yet always exacts an harmonious sweetness; or to distinguish yet more justly, The recitative part of the Opera requires a more masculine Beauty of expression and sound: the other, which (for want of a proper English word) I must call The Songish Part, must abound in the softness and variety of Numbers: its principal Intention, being to please the Hearing, rather than to gratify the understanding.[64]

Dryden associates the "nobler parts of verse," the recitative, with "masculine Beauty" and denigrates the aria as feminine both through his vocabulary and by position in the binary comparison. In terms of the relationship between the gendered parts of composition, the feminine is inferior because it appeals to the ear and not to the mind.[65] His description follows a Cartesian dualism, where the female represents the body and its delights, and the male signifies reason and a higher order of intellectual pleasure. Usually Dryden revels in his ability to manipulate the sounds of the English language, but here the limitations imposed by feminine music irritate him and force him to the "meanness of thought."[66] The need for "softness and variety of numbers" overrides the desire for elevated fancy and, consequently, reduces the dignity of the poet's achievement. While Dryden describes his frustration in military terms – he will never again "part with the power of the militia" – his gendered language inscribes the hegemonic authority of the heterosexual union, whereby the masculine authority of intellect ought to rule the feminine subordinate of beauty. We understand a fundamental flaw of opera to be the inversion of patriarchal order.

Opera represents an overturning of poetic priorities, but the ideal for Dryden is a cooperation between masculine qualities and the properly dependent feminine. Even in his description of the heroic in "An Account" Dryden hints at the benefit of balance. Virgil, his master in this poem, exemplifies a more feminine epic style than Juvenal. The masculine Juvenal shows "heroes drawn in their triumphal chariots, and in their full proportion," while Virgil allows "somewhat more of softness and tenderness to be shown in them."[67] The revelation of Virgil's feminine side does not diminish the master's stature, however; in Dryden's criticism Juvenal symbolizes virility *extraordinaire*, and everyone is feminized next to him. In fact, Dryden seems to approve of the feminine touch in epic style by preferring Virgil as his model. What becomes clear is that semiotic categories of gender operate not simply as a cluster of terms shared with literary values; they also provide Dryden with a paradigm for the interdependence of style and meaning.

---

[64] Watson, vol. II, p. 35.
[65] My argument concurs with Winn here; he argues that Dryden clearly prefers the verbal, intellectual arts over those appealing only to the hearing, and this partiality is often figured in gendered terms. See " 'When Beauty Fires the Blood'," esp. chapters 3–5.
[66] Watson, vol. II, p. 40. [67] Watson, vol. I, p. 101.

The marriage between masculine vigor of thought and feminine regularity of sound functions as a pervasive analogy within Dryden's criticism. Sir Walter Scott writes that Dryden "first showed that the English language was capable of uniting smoothness and strength," an idea that was accepted by the time Elizabeth Thomas wrote her elegy.[68] Her terms of praise – "Manly strength with Modern softness join" – reflect more clearly than Scott's the gendered dynamic Dryden perceives in the union. While Dryden favors the masculine recitative, he recognizes the reciprocal importance of the feminine arias. He objects, however, to their taking precedence over what he views as the more significant achievement. In a more general sense, the feminine aspects of prosody complement the masculine strength of ideas. It would be too simple to divide thought and sound into gendered categories, because, as we have seen, Dryden dictates a correspondence between each in the respectively gendered styles. Thus, heroic poetry requires the height of fancy and the elevation of sound, a sense of decorum conveyed as masculine. However, in terms of Dryden's favored principles of correction, we often find him containing the flights of masculine imagination within proper feminine bounds of melody.[69]

Keeping in mind that Dryden is not a systematic critic, I propose that he assumes a heterosexual model of balance and amelioration in his ideal for improving English verse. He joins the masculine and feminine poetics through a rationale of pleasure, stability, or duty. When he is not wholly transported by the splendor of manly imagination, he insists that poetry is amended by lyrical standards. Witness the ode that suffers in the hands of Cowley, who fails to temper intellectual power with a beautifying sound. In the Preface to *Sylvae*, Dryden describes Cowley's success in the "noble" genre with typically masculine modifiers: "As for the soul of it, which consists in the warmth and vigour of fancy, the masterly figures, and the copiousness of imagination, he has excelled all others in this kind."[70] Dryden designates the ode as unbound, heightened, and marked by excess in fancy and invention. However, he stresses the potential for improving its musicality following the example of Pindar: "somewhat of the purity of English, somewhat of more equal thoughts, somewhat of sweetness in the numbers, in one word, somewhat of a finer turn and

---

[68] W. Scott, *Life of Dryden*, p. 410.

[69] For a detailed discussion of the development of Dryden's relationship between judgment and fancy see John M. Aden, "Dryden and the Imagination: The First Phase," *PMLA* 74 (1959), 28–40, and a follow-up article by Robert D. Hume, "Dryden on Creation: 'Imagination' in the Later Criticism," *Review of English Studies*, new series, 21.83 (1970), 295–314.

[70] Watson, vol. II, p. 32.

more lyrical verse, is yet wanting."[71] Dryden aims to perfect Cowley's overly masculine ode by tuning it to feminine ideals, making it sweeter and more lyrical. Nonetheless, the masculine "soul" of poetry, which Cowley achieves, retains its privilege as the necessary condition of greatness.

Whereas lyrical perfection always plays a subordinate role in Dryden's scheme, it is important, and its association with femininity is central to the dynamism of Dryden's overall poetics. Through the historical transmission of Dryden's work, however, the influence of the feminine is obscured; Van Doren, for example, converts the feminine lyricism to a masculine flexibility. "The least effeminate of poets was not above admitting that he loved the 'sweetness' of good verse. The sweetness he means was a true sweetness, not incompatible with wit – indeed, in Dryden these are brother virtues which steadily defend and support each other."[72] In response to a perception that harmony is weak or effeminate, Van Doren anxiously purges Dryden of any femininity while assuring the reader that his passion for "sweetness" is masculine in its fraternal relationship with wit. He replaces Dryden's model of heterosexual union with homosocial bonding, thereby changing the tension between masculine strength and feminine smoothness to a comfortable, manly brotherhood. His anxiety over Dryden's masculinity suggests a misogynistic fear of feminine qualities that is uncharacteristic of Dryden and, perhaps, more aptly reflects the sharp divisions and suppressed hostility posited between the sexes in the post-World War I era. The example illustrates two important points in the use of gendered critical language: the categories of gender appear timeless and stable, but the historical contexts of gendered language dramatically affect the intention and meaning of the constructions. Secondly the cultural values attached to gendered terms can be distorted as they are invoked and regenerated by other subjects in discourse, and each new statement carries its own set of ideological languages contingent upon the subject's historical situation. Particularly when critics make gendered evaluations with unexamined assumptions of power, the meaning does not translate across time, and the reader needs to be aware of the ways in which those assumptions distort the meaning they wish to convey. While Dryden establishes a restricted poetic for female readers and writers, he recognizes the importance of the feminine qualities in poetry. Van Doren not only erases the positive associations of femininity, but he supplants Dryden's gallant embrace with suspicion and animosity toward the feminine.

[71] Ibid.   [72] Van Doren, *John Dryden*, p. ix.

COMPARATIVE CATEGORIES AND FEMININE MEN

Dryden describes his principles of poetic refinement through a gendered paradigm, and these critical terms share the language that informs the behavior of men and women in the Restoration. However, the semiotic understanding of gender in that discourse also allows Dryden to envision gender as a field of knowledge unrelated to biological entities. Consequently in his criticism we find him frequently placing male writers in feminine positions. The hierarchical relationship between the sexes serves as a useful analogue to describe the differences between two literary objects. In a typically comparative argument from "An Account," Dryden sets Ovid, who "touche[s the] tender strokes more delicately," against Virgil, "how bold, how masterly, are the strokes of Virgil!"[73] The gender-marked vocabulary allows Dryden to indicate the superiority of Virgil's elocution, an excellence based on his power to persuade and move the reader. The delicate style and tender subject of Ovid's poetry render that male poet feminine; Virgil's masterful expression earns him the masculine rubric, but these gendered labels are relative, not inherent.

The hierarchy of the sexes provides Dryden with an apparently stable metaphor, creating comparative categories into which he slides certain writers depending upon their relation to other writers. In the Preface to *Sylvae* (1685) Dryden favors "brisk" and "bold" Horace over the eminently feminine Theocritus, who is even "*softer* than Ovid."[74] In *A Discourse Concerning the Original and Progress of Satire* (1693), however, Dryden claims a personal preference for the wit of Juvenal over Horace: "[Horace's] urbanity, that is his good manners, are to be commended, but his wit is faint; and his salt, if I may dare to say is, almost insipid. Juvenal is of a more vigorous and masculine wit; he gives me as much pleasure as I can bear; he fully satisfies my expectation."[75] In the first essay Horace fills the masculine category in opposition to Theocritus, but in the later one Juvenal clearly emasculates Horace. Dryden's shift is interesting, because in both examples the quality of vigor or strength indicates the more masculine poet who consequently prevails. In this way, the discourse consistently associates strength with the masculine gender. Of course, in these examples Dryden refers to two different genres; the miscellany of 1685 primarily contained lyrics and only a few odes of Horace. Dryden prefers Juvenal over Horace in satire, which requires a more combative spirit. In the Preface to *Sylvae*, Lucretius actually earns the most masculine honors: "From this sublime and

<hr>

[73] Watson, vol. I, p. 99.   [74] Watson, vol. II, p. 30.   [75] Ibid., p. 130.

daring genius of his, it must of necessity come to pass that his thoughts must be masculine, full of argumentation, and that sufficiently warm."[76] The gender of Lucretius' writing stems from his energy and bold assertion of opinion, a dogmatism that causes Dryden some discomfort. Significantly, Lucretius, like Cowley later in the same essay, exhibits a masculine strength that is too unrestrained. In the lyric genres Dryden appreciates the balance of vigor and elegance in Horace, but the exigencies of satire differ, and there Dryden privileges Juvenal's venom over Horace's good manners. Throughout, he characterizes strength and imaginative boldness in masculine terms, while the opposition is feminized as soft, gentle, and polite.

Despite a lack of formal method, Dryden does establish a regular set of literary values as masculine. The definitive literary qualities – imagination or invention, intellect and judgment – are repeatedly associated with masculinity. Likewise Dryden considers the genres of tragedy, satire, and epic – all species of heroic poetry – manly, because the best of each demonstrates the above characteristics.[77] When Neander defends the irregular English drama against the unified French in *An Essay of Dramatic Poesy* (1667), he claims that his countrymen show genius through these definitive qualities; "there is a more masculine fancy and greater spirit in the writing than there is in any of the French."[78] Neander, who represents Dryden in the text, finds the plots of Corneille and other Frenchmen predictable and less interesting than the English plays, though they conform to the unities of the stage. He places a high premium on originality: "We have borrowed nothing from them; our plots are weaved in English looms."[79] Neander respects poetic law to the extent that it aids and does not hinder the creativity of the dramatist. To support his claim for English superiority, Neander examines the characters of the great playwrights of the previous age. In Shakespeare he finds "the largest and most comprehensive soul," granting him insight into every aspect of nature.[80] Jonson, he claims, was "the most learned and judicious writer which any theatre ever had."[81] These two supply the majority of Dryden's proof because they epitomize respectively the qualities of imagination and strength, and intellect and judgment.

While heroic genres with their emphasis on war tend to represent a masculine field of expertise, an alternative focus for tragedy, romantic

---

[76] Ibid., p. 25.
[77] For references to tragedy, satire, and epic as heroic, see Watson, vol. II, p. 87; vol. II, p. 149; Dedication to the *Aeneis, passim.*
[78] Watson, vol. I, p. 66.   [79] Ibid., p. 65.   [80] Ibid., p. 67.   [81] Ibid., p. 69.

love, is frequently cast as feminine. Earlier in the *Essay* the subject of love raises gendered questions. Eugenius considers scenes of tender emotion evidence of the superiority of the moderns. The ancients "dealt not with that soft passion, but with lust, cruelty, revenge, ambition, and those bloody actions they produced."[82] Eugenius values the representation of love, typified by Shakespeare and Fletcher, over the masculine passions of combat because its gentleness soothes the audience and raises concernment. Dryden's critical perspective reinforces a heterosexual and masculine point of view, assuming that love is a softening influence because it is associated with women. Crites rejects Eugenius' interpretation, insisting that for the Ancients love is hardy and androcentric:

Homer described his heroes men of great appetites, lovers of beef broiled upon the coals, and good fellows; contrary to the practice of the French Romance, whose heroes neither eat, nor drink, nor sleep for love. Virgil makes Aeneas a bold avower of his own virtues
        sum pius Aeneas, fama super aethera notus
which in the civility of our poets is the character of a fanfaron or Hector.[83]

With a casuistic shift of meaning, Crites turns the defect of the Ancients into an asset by appealing to a masculine code of values. Apparently, for Crites, love of meat supersedes love for women, and the virtues of indulgence and hubris outweigh self-denial and humility. Dryden's dialogue participates both in the debate over the Ancients and the Moderns and in the discourse of nationalism. The French lose on two counts; they are negatively compared to the Ancients, who offer rugged, male-centered heroes, esteemed and emulated by Englishmen, and they are contemporary authors in competition with the English for literary fame and fortune. A distinct source of Crites' contempt for the French is their modernity, which he aligns with feminine love. Crites represents such romantic love as a prohibited gender-crossing, where men become feminine through weakness and modesty. In testimony to the charm of male bonding, Dryden allows this version of love to stand: "This moderation of Crites, as it was pleasing to all the company, so it put an end to that dispute."[84] Eugenius fails to convince his friends of the fine representations of romantic love in modern plays because these tender emotions belong in an apparently feminine realm of expertise that cannot counterbalance the social and political values represented by male sociability.

---

[82] Ibid., p. 41.   [83] Ibid., p. 42.   [84] Ibid., p. 43.

Unlike the masculine categories of imagination, judgment, and intellect, areas of feminine aptitude do not constitute literary excellence. Significantly, in the *Essay* Dryden has less to say about the plays of Beaumont and Fletcher, who excel in romance, than he does of Shakespeare and Jonson: "they represented all the passions very lively, but above all love."[85] Hints of Fletcher's femininity are fully realized in Dryden's later essay, *The Grounds of Criticism in Tragedy*, prefixed to *Troilus and Cressida* (1679). More than insinuate the subject-matter of Fletcher's plays, Dryden's gendered language reinforces the dramatist's inferior abilities as a playwright. In an indirect reply to Rymer's *Tragedies of the Last Age* (1678), Dryden defends the literary virtues of English tragedy by considering Shakespeare and Fletcher as its great artisans. He structures the essay as an extended gendered comparison between the "more masculine . . . bolder and more fiery" Shakespeare and the "more soft and womanish" Fletcher.[86] For a defense of English authors, the comparative account leaves Fletcher oddly diminished. Shakespeare possesses the fount of originality, and Fletcher merely imitates. Shakespeare creates immediately recognizable characters: "Fletcher comes far short of him in this, as indeed he does almost in everything."[87] Even in the representation of love, Fletcher's apparent forte, Shakespeare exhibits superior imagination:

the excellency of [Shakespeare] was, as I have said, in the more manly passions; Fletcher's in the softer: Shakespeare writ better betwixt man and man; Fletcher, betwixt man and woman: consequently the one described friendship better; the other love. Yet Shakespeare taught Fletcher to write love: and Juliet, and Desdemona, are originals. 'Tis true, the scholar had the softer soul; but the master had the kinder. Friendship is both a virtue and a passion essentially; love is a passion only in its nature, and is not a virtue but by accident: good nature makes friendship; but effeminacy love.[88]

Dryden's preference for male friendship in Shakespeare over heterosexual romance echoes the earlier discussion of love in the *Essay*, and again the "effeminacy" of love and the "softer soul" of Fletcher give place to the representation of male sociability. Shakespeare's superiority also stems from his primacy of invention; Dryden casts Fletcher as the perpetual student of the master. The direct gendered comparison grants the male poet ascendancy in all aspects of tragedy, suggesting that excellence itself is gendered male. Interestingly, Shakespeare's masterful artwork secures his masculine status, even in creation of female characters, while

[85] Ibid., p. 69.   [86] Ibid., p. 247.   [87] Ibid., p. 251.   [88] Ibid., p. 260.

Fletcher's inferior abilities reinforce his femininity. Gender fulfills a comprehensive role in this assessment by signifying both the orientation of content and the standard of aptitude in art.

Dryden summarizes his argument in terms that mirror the dualism of the gendered aesthetic:

> Shakespeare had an universal mind, which comprehended all characters and passions; Fletcher a more confined and limited: for though he treated love in perfection, yet honour, ambition, revenge, and generally all the stronger passions, he either touched not, or not masterly. To conclude all, he was a limb of Shakespeare.[89]

Dryden's description of Shakespeare's universality shares with the masculine heroic an imagery of boundlessness and expert execution. Shakespeare's tragedies compass the world of human experience, and his portrayal is, unlike Fletcher's, masterly. The analysis of Fletcher, on the other hand, parallels the feminine aesthetic in terms of confinement and contingency. Fletcher's creativity is only as good as his limited scope, and his performance depends upon the originary genius of Shakespeare and is thus secondary. The cultural valorization of the universal over the particular, or, in Cartesian terms, the mind over the body, informs Dryden's preference for Shakespeare. Dryden's negative evaluation of Fletcher illustrates how the feminine aesthetic indicates not simply a different style but an inferior quality of art.

Within the context of this comparison, Dryden consolidates the gender of imagination and strength by giving the masculine poet precedence in both qualities. Dryden designates Shakespeare the premier English tragedian by virtue of surplus originality and vigor. Fletcher, too, provides an archetype for English tragedy; his depiction of love is "perfection," but his overall performance is weaker than Shakespeare's. While Dryden's discussion of Fletcher appears derogatory, it is only so in the comparative sense. Dryden considers Fletcher second best of his country's tragic dramatists, and though his representation of romantic love is less important than Shakespeare's "manly passions," it is to that extent worth imitating. The language of gender thus shapes Dryden's assessment of literature by providing a hierarchical paradigm of semiotic categories to which he assigns authors regardless of their sex. His consistent approval of the masculine category creates the impression of its monolithic importance, but Dryden's frequent use of comparatives suggests the need to understand the gendered assignments as relative. In

---

[89] Ibid., p. 260.

other words, simply because Dryden prefers the masculine satire of Juvenal and the manly imagination of Shakespeare, he does not, therefore, dismiss the feminized performances of Horace and Fletcher out of hand.

GALLANTRY, MODESTY AND THE FEMALE SUBJECT

Dryden's use of gendered language in the construction of gendered styles and comparative examples attaches the semiotic categories of gender to literary values regardless of the biological sex of the author. In this way critical language asserts only a loose association between gendered values and the gendered subjects participating in that discourse. Dryden often shifts the gendered status of male writers and allows them – sometimes encourages them – to adopt feminine literary traits. The gendered arrangement is not as liberating, though, for the female subject, because the actual production and reception of work by female writers is shaped by the critical preference for characteristics consistent with male identity. The gendered status of women in discourse is further encumbered by two cultural forces that do not necessarily affect that of men: the demands of gallantry and the expectations of modesty.[90] Cowley may claim that Katherine Philips' poetry is "than Man more Strong, and more than Woman Sweet," but the conventional flattery expected from male admirers renders the compliment suspect. Customs of courtesy curtail what a man can *in good taste* say about a woman. Likewise, the premium on female chastity circumscribes the range of topics and expression available to women. The modesty that distinguishes female smoothness and serves as the analogue for metrical refinement also justifies the manifold restrictions faced by women poets. Dryden's criticism and advice register a sensitivity to these cultural forces.

Although he becomes more vehement about a general standard of decency toward the end of his life, Dryden's career-long stance on the representation of modesty in literature reflects a cultural double standard for men and women. In 1685 Dryden confesses that his "luscious" rendering of Lucretius' obscene *Nature of Love* pleases him: "I am not yet so secure from that passion, but that I want my author's antidotes against it."[91] In defense he claims the integrity of a translator writing in the spirit of the original author. While Dryden enjoys the titillation, he condemns the representation of "bare-faced bawdry," and

---

[90] For a discussion of the history and use of the term "gallantry" in this study, see pp. 18–24.
[91] Watson, vol. II, p. 27.

his support, taken from Cowley, invokes the female reader as the test of
purity: "Much less can that have any place, / At which a virgin hides her
face."[92] Because social codes demand that women be excluded from
discourses that will threaten their reputations, the sexually suggestive
parts of Dryden's translation are unfit for female reading. Dryden's
awareness of the female reading subject jeopardizes his representation of
sexual knowledge and, hence, the achievement of his goal as a just
translator. In this preface, he apparently resolves the dilemma through
textual gestures that warn the female reader away from dangerous
language. Dryden explicitly directs the female readers to Theocritus,
because they "neither understand, nor will take pleasure in, such homely
expressions" of the other writers.[93] His critical discussion allows
immodesty for men under certain circumstances, but he censors it for
women.

Dryden begins to take greater responsibility for representing chastity
in the following decade, when his poetic production consists almost
entirely of translation. Dryden's new focus on chaste literature, which he
expresses in terms of morals and good taste, may actually reflect a
blurring of the gendered constituency of his audiences. He recognizes
this shared reading space, for instance, in his introductory essay to the
satires of Juvenal and Persius: "we write only for the pleasure and
entertainment of those gentlemen and ladies who, tho' they are not
scholars, are not ignorant."[94] As in polite conversation of "mixed
company," literature read by both sexes requires a standard of general
decency because of the respect due to women. While this is true,
Dryden's general emphasis on modesty may also be a response to
changes in the mores of his time. In contrast to the relative fluidity of
gendered categories in the years following the Restoration, images of
masculinity and femininity become increasingly distinct and domesticated
in the 1690s. The discourse begins to represent higher standards for the
chastity of men as well as women.[95] During the more austere reign of
William III, literary criticism undertakes a great moral purification in
the wake of Restoration licentiousness. Jeremy Collier's *A Short View of the
Immorality and Profaneness of the English Stage* (1698) is just one of the more
vituperative attacks on the indecent and irreligious drama of preceding

---

[92] Cowley's "Ode concerning wit," stanza 6, quoted in Watson, vol. II, p. 28.
[93] Watson, vol. II, p. 30.　　[94] Ibid., p. 153.
[95] Scholarship on the periodical discourses of this decade makes this point quite convincingly; see in
particular Shevelow's *Women and Print Culture,* and Shawn Lisa Maurer's "Reforming Men:
Chaste Heterosexuality in the Early English Periodical," *Restoration* 16.1 (1992), 38–55.

decades. Arbiters of social behavior voice a need for universal continence and the benefits of monogamous, heterosexual relationships. Sources as diverse as John Locke, Shaftesbury, and the periodical entitled *The Nightwalker* call for controlled male sexuality.[96] At stake in both Dryden's new recognition of audience and the insistence on male restraint is the consideration of the vulnerable female subject.

Dryden's use of the female subject as the test of modesty in his criticism reinforces the perceived need for female chastity and male gallantry. In *A Parallel Betwixt Poetry and Painting* (1695) prefaced to his translation of *De Arte Graphica*, Dryden views modesty as a standard rule of art: "The subjects both of [painting] and of [poetry], ought to have nothing of immoral, low, or filthy in them . . . [T]here are no such licences permitted in [poetry], any more than in painting, to design and colour obscene nudities." Dryden explains that Virgil, whose works he was then translating, offers a useful example in this as in most other literary skills. Throughout the *Aeneis* he maintains a respectable purity: "Neither is there any expression in that story which a Roman matron might not read without a blush."[97] With the figure of the reading female, Dryden marks chastity as the special knowledge and need of the female audience, reinscribing the moral desideratum as an aesthetic requirement. The projection of female reading subjects in literary discourse here and elsewhere functions in an ambiguous way characteristic of gallantry. On the one hand the critic respects the female reader's autonomy in the desire for special language, but, on the other hand, such precautions presuppose the fragility of female subjectivity and render it weak and in need of protection. Collier's argument for moral improvement is representative of the special role of the female: "Obscenity in any Company is a rustick uncreditable Talent; but among Women 'tis particularly rude. Such Talk would be very affrontive in Conversation and not endured by any Lady of Reputation."[98] In this way the demands

---

[96] *The Nightwalker: or, Evening Rambles in search after Lewd Women, with the Conferences Held with them, etc.* (London, 1696); John Locke, *Some Thoughts Concerning Education*, in *English Philosophers of the Seventeenth and Eighteenth Centuries: Locke, Berkeley, Hume*, Harvard Classics, ed. Charles W. Eliot, 50 vols. (New York: P.F. Collier and Son, 1910), vol. xxxvii, pp. 3–195, esp. p. 28; Shaftesbury, Anthony Ashley Cooper, *Second Characters: Or, the Language of Form*, ed. Benjamin Rand (Cambridge: Cambridge University Press, 1914), p. 161. For an insightful article on the relationship between changing views of male sexuality and aesthetic and political discourses, see John Barrell, "'The Dangerous Goddess': Masculinity, Prestige, and the Aesthetic in Early Eighteenth-Century Britain," *Cultural Critique* 12 (Spring 1989), 101–131.

[97] Watson, vol. ii, p. 187.

[98] Jeremy Collier, *A Short View of the Immorality and Profaneness of the English Stage* (1698), facsimile, preface by Arthur Freeman (New York: Garland Publishing, Inc., 1972), p. 7.

for female modesty make necessary the conventions of male gallantry. As social, discursive control over female chastity escalates, the consequences of male chivalry become more pronounced.

As a result, critics like Dryden endorse a normative morality as a general literary requirement. In his final critical work, Preface to *Fables Ancient and Modern* (1700), Dryden proposes an unconditional, if unverifiable, moral propriety: "I have written nothing which savours of immorality or profaneness; at least, I am not conscious to myself of any such intention."[99] In defense of his choice of texts, Dryden claims to select only tales "as contain in each of them some instructive moral."[100] His emphasis on didacticism rather than pleasure differs from his earlier criticism and signals a shift in the primary purpose of literature from entertainment to instruction. This emphasis on the edifying role of literature reflects the growing conviction that reading is a fundamental activity in the constitution of subjectivity, especially for women, and it therefore needs to be monitored.

Poets, critics, and moralists alike take up the responsibility for promoting appropriate subjective ideals. In his denunciation of the English stage, for instance, Collier stresses the effect drama has on its audience: "And what can be the Meaning of such Representations [of indecency], unless it be to Tincture the Audience, to extinguish Shame, and make Lewdness a Diversion? This is the natural Consequence, and therefore one would think 'twas the Intention too."[101] The extent to which Dryden shares Collier's view can be gauged by Collier's influence in this preface. Dryden belittles writers like Milbourne and Blackmore for their arguments against him, but he contends that Collier "in many things has taxed me justly; and I have pleaded guilty to all thoughts and expressions of mine which can be truly argued of obscenity, profaneness or immorality, and retract them."[102] Underlying Dryden's apology for past lewdness is the assumption that his writings have an impact on his audience. He assures his readers, "But I will no more offend against good manners: I am sensible as I ought to be of the scandal I have given by my loose writings; and make what reparation I am able, by this public acknowledgment."[103] In recognition of the power of his writing, Dryden declares that he will exclude all offensive material from the collection so that he can please and edify. He bases his editorial decisions on the apparent refinement of public behavior, or the "good manners" of his

[99] Watson, vol. II, p. 273.   [100] Ibid.   [101] Jeremy Collier, *A Short View*, p. 5.
[102] Watson, vol. II, p. 293. Note that Dryden does not accept all of Collier's charges.
[103] Ibid., pp. 285.

readers. In this way, he generalizes the needs of the vulnerable female reading subject to the entire audience.

While the claims for polite society tend to conceal the gendered dynamic impelling modest decorum, the special status of the female subject is manifest in Dryden's treatment of individual women writers. Dryden's advice to Elizabeth Thomas (1699), a poet who sent him her poems for review, reinforces an understanding of modesty as a gendered responsibility.

> [Poetry] is an unprofitable art to those who profess it; but you, who write for your diversion, may pass your hours with pleasure in it and without prejudice, always avoiding (as I know you will) the licences which Mrs. Behn allowed herself of writing loosely and giving (if I may have leave to say so) some scandal to the modesty of her sex. I confess I am the last man who ought, in justice, to arraign her, who have been myself too much a libertine in most of my poems, which I should be well contented I had time either to purge or to see them fairly burned.[104]

With characteristic gallantry, Dryden encourages Thomas to practice her art, while he politely circumscribes her efforts and aspirations within non-professional, decorous limits. The notions of leisure and modesty seem central to Dryden's conception of the female writer and provide an interesting contrast to the definitive qualities of literature. Notably, Dryden proposes the professional writer Aphra Behn as an illustration of the female author who reaches beyond the proper bounds. As a successful female dramatist, poet, and novelist, Behn symbolizes a menacing tolerance in society, which apparently rewards women for their "loose" writings.[105] Dryden issues a caution against such freedom, despite the parenthetical claim that he knows Thomas shares this understanding. After disqualifying Behn as an appropriate model, Dryden supposes that he might act in such a capacity for Thomas, but he quickly distances himself from that role by conceding a similar defect of immodesty. His confession to Thomas prefigures the public apology he will make in the Preface to *Fables*, but here the damage caused by male and female poets clearly differs. While being "too much a libertine" evidently troubles the male writer's conscience, such a display of looseness discredits a woman. Dryden operates on the assumption that

---

[104] Ibid., p. 267–268.
[105] For a summary of Behn's reputation in the 1690s and her effect on other women writers, see Jeslyn Medoff, "The Daughters of Behn and the Problems of Reputation," in Isobel Grundy and Susan Wiseman, eds., *Women, Writing, History 1640–1740* (London: B.T. Batsford Ltd., 1992), pp. 33–54.

modesty has greater material consequences for the female writing subject than for the male.

To choose an appropriate literary model for Thomas, Dryden considers the qualities of writing the female poet should emulate, and these characteristics, unsurprisingly, fall within his category of the feminine in poetry. The language of feminine gentility that informs the smoothness and regularity of feminine verse translates into Dryden's literal prescription for the female writer. As in the Preface to *Sylvae*, we find Dryden directing his female audience to Theocritus: "I would advise you not to trust too much to Virgil's Pastorals; for as excellent as they are, yet Theocritus is far above him, both in Softness of Thought and Simplicity of Expression."[106] Despite the passage of more than thirty years, Dryden recommends a version of the very same feminine decorum he identified in "An Account of the Ensuing Poem" prefixed to *Annus Mirabilis*, where he describes his poem to the Duchess of York as "the softness of expression, and the smoothness of measure, rather than the height of thought." The consistency indicates the relative stability of Dryden's conceptions of gendered categories throughout his lifetime. Frequently Dryden's own model, Virgil proves too bold an example for the female's pen, whereas Theocritus displays those qualities the female author might properly imitate. In the earlier evaluation, Dryden describes Theocritus' manifest femininity: the Greek poet excels in the pastoral with "the inimitable tenderness of his passions," appealing to the female audience with the gentle expression of emotion and an emphasis on pacific rather than martial virtues. Theocritus also avoids the display of erudition that might bar a woman's pleasure in and understanding of the text: "A simplicity shines through all he writes: he shows his art and learning by disguising both." His dialect has an "incomparable sweetness," the auditory standard required for feminine sensibility.[107] By recommending Theocritus over Virgil, Dryden steers Thomas away from the masculine and, coincidentally, most highly respected classical author in the late seventeenth century. Thus, despite granting men access to both masculine and feminine literary styles, Dryden limits the female writer to her gender, promoting a direct correspondence between the semiotic category of femininity in literary criticism and the biological female subject within discourse.

The function of gendered language in the critical evaluation of female subjects in discourse is crucial to an understanding of Dryden's famous

---

[106] Watson, vol. II, p. 268.   [107] Ibid., p. 30.

and problematic ode "To the Pious Memory of the Accomplisht Young Lady Mrs Anne Killigrew, Excellent in the two Sister-Arts of Poesie, and Painting" (1685). This ode is one of Dryden's few public statements on the art of a female poet, and its most striking characteristic is the ambiguity of his critical appraisal. The master of equivocation in his satire, Dryden has by this point in his career demonstrated an acute talent for couching uncomplimentary criticism within the language of praise, and this skill leads many critics to read the shifts in tone running throughout the Ode as instances of irony.[108] Much sophisticated analysis has been devoted to explicating the subtle, and not so subtle, ways in which Dryden attacks the young, inexperienced, dead, female poet, but few provide satisfactory reasons for why he would do so.[109] My reading of the poem is more sympathetic to those critics who read Dryden's praise of Anne Killigrew as not ironic, including Ann Messenger and James Winn.[110] However, this does not mean that I see the adulation as genuine; Messenger points out that "no poet can truly deserve the degree of praise he heaped upon her."[111] The meaning of the poem's modulated praise needs to be determined by reading the language of the poem within the discourses of its day: generic expectations for the ode and elegy, the social codes of gallantry and femininity, and the gendered values of literature.

The overlapping and contradictory principles of these three discourses complicate Dryden's project in writing a poem to dignify a volume of poetry and the family for which it is published. There is no evidence that Dryden actually knew Anne Killigrew, although he had been connected with the Killigrew family in his dramatic career.[112] Still, the occasion of celebrating the dead poet demands a certain propriety, requiring a lyrical seriousness that Dryden demonstrates in earlier commemorations of Oldham and Charles II. In the case of Anne Killigrew, though, the gendered dynamic between male poet and female subject creates the need for additional verbal delicacy in accordance with the laws of gallantry. It is worth distinguishing that Dryden does not address a

---

[108] C. Anderson Silber, "Nymphs and Satyrs: Poet, Readers and Irony in Dryden's Ode to Anne Killigrew," *Studies in Eighteenth-Century Culture* 14 (1985), 211, n. 17.

[109] Early arguments by A. D. Hope, "Anne Killigrew, or the Art of Modulating," *Southern Review* 1 (1963), 4–14, and David Vieth, "Irony in Dryden's Ode to Anne Killigrew," *Studies in Philology* 63 (1965), 91–100, initiated the semantic debate, more recently articulated by Silber and Virginia Pohli, "Formal and Informal Space in Dryden's Ode, 'To the Pious Memory of . . . Anne Killigrew'," *Restoration* 15.1 (Spring 1991), 27–40.

[110] Ann Messenger, *His and Hers: Essays in Restoration and Eighteenth-Century Literature* (Lexington: University Press of Kentucky, 1986), pp. 14–40; Winn, " 'When Beauty Fires the Blood'," pp. 89–108.

[111] Messenger, *His and Hers*, pp. 14–15.   [112] Winn, *Dryden and His World*, p. 417.

strictly female audience in the readers of Killigrew's poetry, and he is therefore not bound to follow his feminine decorum of soft expression and smooth measure without the height of thought. Nonetheless, the polite male poet is expected to treat the female subject with gentleness and modesty. The social code of gallantry assumes an unequal distribution of power, whereby the male can easily damage the female reputation, which is significantly more vulnerable to criticism because it is held to a more stringent standard of sexual control. In this respect, printed characterizations have eminently greater power over the spoken because of their broader audience and durability. A male poet in Dryden's situation must be protective of the female subject's reputation, which presumably extends to her family even after her death. Indeed, Winn identifies the protective impulse as the rationale behind Dryden's equivocal description of Killigrew's native talents.[113] However, Dryden addresses Killigrew as a woman and a poet, and this quasi-critical construction within the poem is also shaped by the gendered values of literature he held. Dryden's gendered conception of literary worth associates the qualities of literary greatness with masculinity, and the inferior, ornamental qualities of literature with the feminine. Such gendered principles are at odds with his gallantry and elegiac purpose.

Given the complex ends of the poem, Dryden's choice of the ode form is appropriate, but this decision is also the source of one of the poem's gendered conflicts. In the Preface to *Sylvae*, written that same year, Dryden explains that this genre "allows more latitude than any other," and, as the most dignified lyrical form, it is suitable for Killigrew's public elegy. As I argued earlier, Dryden's interest in perfecting the ode after the example of Pindar reveals the gendered grounds of its structure. The soul of the ode, Dryden says, lies in its "warmth and vigour of fancy, the masterly figures, and the copiousness of imagination," notions incompatible with feminine softness and simplicity. This masculine verse form, what he calls later a "noble sort of poetry," creates a tension within Dryden's critical construction of Killigrew, who also wrote odes, and this dissonance constitutes one of the poem's problematic threads.[114] In the first stanza Dryden announces a parallel between his poetic project and Killigrew's: "Hear, then, a mortal muse thy praise rehearse, / In no ignoble verse; / But such as thy own voice did practice here."[115] Given his description of the ode as "noble," and the fact that three of Killigrew's odes were included in the volume, it seems likely that Dryden

---

[113] Winn, "*When Beauty Fires the Blood*," p. 90   [114] Watson, vol. II, pp. 32–33.
[115] Kinsley, ed., *Poems*, vol. I, p. 460, lines 16–18.

draws attention to their shared practice of writing odes.[116] In the Preface to *Sylvae*, Dryden expresses the need to add musicality to the ambitious design and lofty thought of the established English ode, and he accomplishes this through the ode to Anne Killigrew. But the very virtues he strives for, particularly the expansive imagination and lyrical judgment, become ambiguous attributes in his characterization of Killigrew. For instance, he suggests that "if no clustering swarm of bees / On thy sweet mouth distilled their golden dew," it is because "heaven had not leisure to renew" those "vulgar miracles."[117] The lines propose a comparison between Killigrew's gift and Plato's eloquence – Plato was supposedly blessed by bees in infancy – but they immediately revoke the possibility by suggesting that the symbol of the golden dew has become antiquated. While he straightforwardly labels her mouth "sweet," the auditory standard for lyrical verse and a feminine attribute, he implies that she lacks rhetorical skills. Dryden grants Killigrew's abilities of sound in poetry, but he stops short of praising the astute manipulation of language, the height of thought.

A similar gendered conflict informs Dryden's praise of Killigrew's artistic proficiency in the controversial fifth stanza:

> Art she had none, yet wanted none;
> For nature did that want supply:
> So rich in treasures of her own,
> She might our boasted stores defy.[118]

Dryden's opening assertion that Killigrew lacks art ambiguously conflates the female poet with the poetry she writes. A woman's artlessness is a highly commendable trait of femininity, in keeping with Richard Allestree's preference for "native simplicity" over "glaring splendor." To the extent that Dryden addresses this quality to Killigrew the person, it stands as a compliment to her modesty. But it becomes clear as the stanza progresses that the object of Dryden's description is both her character and her poetry. A poem's lack of art, especially in the genre of the ode, is a notable failing, but one that appears inevitable, given the gendered disparity between the simplicity of the practitioner and the complexity of the form. Dryden mitigates the formal deficiency implied by gendered literary values by emphasizing Killigrew's character.

Dryden's respect for excellence in poetry, which he understood in

---

[116] Although the editor's note to Killigrew's collection puts her authorship of those odes in doubt, I follow Messenger's argument that they are almost certainly hers. See Messenger, *His and Hers*, pp. 29, 251 n. 15.

[117] Kinsley, ed., *Poems*, vol. i, lines 50–53.   [118] Ibid., lines 71–74.

gendered terms, runs counter to his responsibilities as a eulogist and a gallant, especially when the intellectual demands of poetry oppose the simplicity of the female poet. This tension produces points of strategic ambiguity in the poem that critics have been unable to satisfactorily explain. Such ambivalent lines as "Her wit was more than man, her innocence a child" seem to be navigating between the necessity of cross-gendered literary compliment and the desire to preserve and flatter the femininity of the subject. In this example, Dryden's praise follows the cultural codes for feminine propriety more closely than the standards of literary worth, which would be defined by manly wit. The opposite seems true of his characterization of Killigrew as an ambitious ruler in stanzas VI and VII. By suggesting that Killigrew's attempts in painting as well as poetry represent "such immoderate growth" that "fate alone its progress could oppose" Dryden endues the female subject with a boldness necessary to artistic greatness, but the compliment is strained because the image of masculine tyranny clashes with the otherwise modest female subject. These points of stress in the poem reveal less a sense of irony than the ambiguity characteristic of gallantry, a set of open-ended constructions resulting from the conflicting, historically situated, gendered codes.

At worst, we can say that the ode fails to negotiate between the conflicting demands of its multiple objectives, but this is true only to the extent that we focus on the stress points of the poem rather than on the successful ways in which Dryden unifies the competing discourses. The social expectations of femininity, the feminine values in poetry, and the encomium for the dead all coincide in the valorization of modesty. Not surprisingly, Dryden is most successful in the poem when he incorporates Killigrew as the symbol of moral purity, which is, incidentally, the most consistent image in the poem.[119] Dryden achieves the characterization of Killigrew's virtue to a great extent through abstraction, which he maintains through most of the poem, excepting stanza VIII. He opens and closes with Killigrew as a celestial image of refinement, offering several possibilities for her new heavenly residence. Much of the ethereal effect of the poem is due to the tenuousness of Dryden's descriptions, for he is rarely concrete or even certain.[120] Throughout the second and third stanzas, for example, Dryden proposes the details of her lineage in the conditional voice: "If by traduction came thy mind, / Our wonder is the

[119] For a review of similar arguments that contend Anne is "a suitable vehicle for larger subjects," see Earl Miner, *Dryden's Poetry* (Bloomington: Indiana University Press, 1967), esp. pp. 253–259.
[120] J. Lipking, " 'Fair Originals'," p. 62.

less to find / A soul so charming from a stock so good."[121] He minimizes the particular and material conditions of her gender by focusing on mental and spiritual traits. (Such abstraction, by the way, mutes his critical view of her art, which ought to appeal to the senses of sound and sight.) Killigrew's physical body only enters the poem briefly in the eighth stanza when Dryden describes the moment of her death, but this awkward shift to corporeality – "In earth the much-lamented virgin lies" – leads Dryden to equate Killigrew with her illustrious and pious predecessor, the poet Katherine Philips, who also died of smallpox: "Heaven, by the same disease, did both translate, / As equal were their souls, so equal were their fate."[122] The translation of the body to the heavenly soul prepares the reader for the glorious imagery of the concluding stanza, in which Killigrew leads the spirits to heaven at the apocalypse.

> And straight, with inborn vigour, on the wing,
> Like mounting larks, to the new morning sing.
> There thou, sweet saint, before the choir shalt go,
> As harbinger of heaven, the way to show,
> The way which thou so well hast learned below.[123]

This final image demonstrates Dryden's finest unification of the competing strands of his poem. Killigrew, the pure spirit and modest poet, is sublimated to the highest place after death, leading the choirs of angels to new salvation. Killigrew's sanctity, which stands in stark contrast to the modern "ordures of the stage," distinguishes her excellence in poetry, in femininity, and in the spiritual trial after death. The lines, if not frank, establish her as a symbol of consistent value in literature, society, and religion.

Dryden's ode to Anne Killigrew demonstrates the ways in which the gendered values of literature dialogically inform the languages of genre and social behavior, producing a complex matrix of values where the female poet enters public discourse. Gallantry plays a fundamental role in Dryden's depiction of Killigrew, and yet gallantry is rarely analyzed as a feature of his rhetorical stance.[124] As I suggested in chapter 1, the

---

[121] Kinsley, ed., *Poems*, vol. 1, lines 23–25.   [122] Ibid., lines 152, 163–164.
[123] Ibid., lines 191–195.
[124] While many critics suggest that Dryden's extravagant praise is part of a rhetorical stance, they rarely question the effects or the assumptions behind it. Winn is again an exception; he finds an interesting parallel "between male gallantry toward women, which assumes the hierarchy of the sexes, and professional flattery of aristocratic amateurs, which slyly subverts the social hierarchy" ("'When Beauty Fires the Blood'," p. 50), but his analysis of the ode only begins to take into account Dryden's role as a gallant, pp. 89–108.

conventions of gallantry provide a set of ritualized linguistic gestures through which the poet achieves multiple objectives by leaving the logic and intent of his meaning open. The signifiers in gallant discourse serve a meaningful purpose as gesture, quite apart from any clear or singular attachment to signifieds. The hyperbolic praise of Killigrew fulfills the obligations of the male eulogist, but it also contributes to the abstraction of the actual subject by turning the female poet into a symbol, from the "youngest virgin-daughter of the skies" to the "harbinger of heaven." Such abstraction comes at the cost of the actual representation of women; the female writing subject enters discourse here only as the ethereal image of moral perfection. The description is neither true in the sense of being an accurate depiction of Killigrew, nor false as a misrepresentation of her character; rather, the conventions of gallant discourse leave questions of truth open. Significantly, Dryden's poem incorporates Killigrew as a symbol in the ritualized language of gallantry that obscures the historical female subject. This obfuscation makes the quasi-critical judgments upon her art fundamentally unclear and, consequently, resistant to final interpretation.

In his criticism, Dryden initiates and refines a gendered critical vocabulary that later eighteenth-century critics adopt and expand. His own language, therefore, circulates throughout the period in dialogic exchange with other critics and writers, and his gendered distinctions accrue power as truth. The masculine characteristics associated with heroic literature carry the most value in Dryden's discourse, and this preference over the ornamental feminine qualities of literature tends to obscure the interdependence that he posits. The transmission of Dryden's work in the scholarship of Scott and Van Doren, for instance, simplifies the gendered balance and either constitutes the feminine as antithetical to the literary or denies it altogether. The unifying force of this representation of masculine critical value facilitates the marginalization of female authors and, indeed, the entire epistemological field that is constituted as feminine.

Consequently, it is significant that Dryden puts the gendered language of criticism to various uses, from illustrating the principle of mutual amelioration between manly imagination and feminine smoothness to providing a comparative paradigm by which male authors can occupy feminine positions. The semiotic condition of gender makes the application of feminine traits to male subjects meaningful as literary assessments, but the same flexibility is not extended to female writing and reading subjects because of the special limitations entailed by chastity and gallantry. Dryden's advice to and critical treatment of women poets is circumscribed by a fundamental assumption that cultural constructions of femininity impede the acquisition of necessary literary qualities, especially those of intellect, vigor, and judgment. Ultimately, Dryden's use of gendered language enables the denigration of the feminine subject because he incorporates patriarchal suppositions, but it would be misleading to read all of his feminine terms in this way. Rather, the literary criticism Dryden establishes incorporates a relative fluidity of gendered categories that variously emphasizes the Restoration significations of power, knowledge, and sexuality.

CHAPTER 3

Paternity and regulation in the feminine novel

> The birth and development of the novel as a genre takes place in the full light of the historical day. Bakhtin[1]

The possibility that the novel might have a recoverable history impels an irresistible search for its origins in eighteenth-century literary discourse.[2] One great paradox is that the flourishing investigation of the novel creates an instrument of academic power around a genre that was negligible before the 1740s. Within the literary hierarchy of eighteenth-century criticism, the novel occupies a low, if not anomalous, position as a new and unfixed literary form. In the contest of literary values that were debated throughout the period – Ancient vs. Modern, Classic vs. Romantic, Augustan vs. Sentimental – the aesthetic of narrative fiction does not enter as a serious factor. The elite culture accords little merit to the art of realistic narrative until the middle of the nineteenth century.[3] Prior to the achievements of Fielding and Richardson, criticism of the novel rarely identifies a clear formal purpose for the genre but is instead involved in an emphatically gendered discourse on reading, writing, and marketing of texts. As with Dryden's contemporaneous criticism, the critical prose that describes or promotes early fiction relies on gendered distinctions, but, contrary

---

[1] Mikhail M. Bakhtin, *The Dialogic Imagination: Four Essays*, ed. Michael Holquist, trans. Caryl Emerson and Michael Holquist (Austin: University of Texas Press, 1981), p. 3.

[2] Studies exclusively concerned with the origins of the novel in England begin with Ian Watt, *The Rise of the Novel: Studies in Defoe, Richardson and Fielding* (Berkeley: University of California Press, 1957). More recent works include Lennard Davis, *Factual Fictions: The Origins of the English Novel* (New York: Columbia University Press, 1983); Michael McKeon, *The Origins of the English Novel 1600–1740* (Baltimore: Johns Hopkins University Press, 1987); J. Paul Hunter, *Before Novels: The Cultural Contexts of Eighteenth-Century English Fiction* (New York: W.W. Norton & Co., 1990). Studies of women's contributions to the foundation of the novel include Jane Spencer, *The Rise of the Woman Novelist: From Aphra Behn to Jane Austen* (Oxford: Basil Blackwell, 1986), and Janet Todd, *The Sign of Angellica: Women, Writing and Fiction 1660–1800* (New York: Columbia University Press, 1989).

[3] See Gaye Tuchman and Nine E. Fortin, *Edging Women Out: Victorian Novelists, Publishers, and Social Change* (New Haven: Yale University Press, 1989); esp. chapter 1.

to expressions that celebrate the "manly" epic or tragedy, the writings on fiction focus on the feminine.

Given the authority of masculine heroic values in early critical discourse, the relative insignificance of the novel before 1740 and its pronounced femininity is hardly a surprising or innocent coincidence. However, usually only half of that equation is recognized in any given critical discussion; the relationship between the status and the gender of the genre has received little attention. One of the critical truths we have inherited is that the novel constitutes a unique form of feminine discourse, located in the private, quotidian, and subjective realms of experience.[4] This chapter aims to contextualize the "fact" of the novel's femininity by examining the earliest critical explanations of the form, found largely in the marginal spaces of the work itself – in prefaces, dedications, addresses to the reader, and epilogues. By examining the relationship between the novel's artistic inferiority and its putative femininity, the analysis complicates a second and more problematic commonplace, which is that men write the best novels in the eighteenth century. Despite the recent republication of numerous novels by women from the period, the canonical status of Defoe, Richardson, Fielding, Smollett, and Sterne remains secure both in the critical testimonies to their originary genius and in their regular place on colleges' course syllabi. The new availability of recovered texts by women from the era only draws the disparity of critical evaluation into sharper relief.

As an investigation of the epistemological languages of gender in the critical understanding of the novel, my argument is most clearly situated by the scholarship of Michael McKeon and Nancy Armstrong. Although differing in methodology and significant points of emphasis, McKeon and Armstrong tell a compatible story, one which regards the novel as a genre that mediates crucial cultural changes contingent upon the emergence of bourgeois hegemony. Both writers revise the original thesis formulated by Ian Watt and theorize the novel as a literary counterpart to the development of modern subjectivity and the expression of inner qualities of mind and virtue in opposition to external signs of aristocratic status. In *Origins of the English Novel* McKeon delineates the dialectical formation of generic categories in the mediation of epistemological and social conflicts in the late seventeenth and early eighteenth centuries. Armstrong, in *Desire and Domestic Fiction*, analyzes the construction of gender as an instrument of political ideology in

---

[4] This perception is principally indebted to Ian Watt, *Rise of the Novel*, and Nancy Armstrong, *Desire and Domestic Fiction: A Political History of the Novel* (Oxford: Oxford University Press, 1987).

domestic novels of the nineteenth century, which results in the cultural hegemony of the domestic woman. At one end of the trajectory, McKeon's account of the discourses of truth and virtue posits a set of concurrent interpretative matrices intersecting with the gendered strategies in the early criticism, but he tends to restrict the meaning of gender to social categories contingent upon class and status. At the other end, Armstrong's analysis offers a corrective view of the history of the novel that emphasizes the centrality of feminine discourses, but ultimately she overreads the historical authority of its femininity. My chapter attempts to isolate certain conventions and features of the early critical discourse on fiction that enable both the trivialization of the novel as a feminine form and the simultaneous critical elevation of certain male novelists.

Armstrong is foremost among critics in identifying the genre as a specifically feminine form of discourse which attributes to women moral and domestic authority that is capable of transforming culture. Adapting a Foucauldian conception of sexuality as a semiotic process, Armstrong argues that the development of a comprehensive nineteenth-century sign-system "depended above all else on the creation of modern gender distinctions. These came into being with the development of a strictly feminine field of knowledge, and it was within this field that novels had to situate themselves if they were to have cultural authority."[5] Femininity becomes for Armstrong the most significant feature of the genre because it allows domestic novels to renegotiate political and social relations under the guise of purely emotional changes. In this way, the popularity and omnipresence of the novel empowers the middle-class domestic female with some cultural control.

Although Armstrong's study focuses primarily on nineteenth-century texts, the striking femininity she identifies is characteristic of the early novel as well. However, the discursive strategies that enhance and ensure the gendered associations of the genre also reveal a construction of femininity that jeopardizes Armstrong's claim for female power. The type of feminine knowledge Armstrong finds in the novel is qualified by the masculinist discourse of the patriarchal society in which it is situated. For instance, in the critical discourse most representations of the domestic ideal invoke a gendered binary that distinguishes femininity as unique, and this dyadic ordering – male/female, public/private, reason/emotion – both necessitates the presence of masculine authority and subjugates the feminine priorities. Armstrong asserts that the novel reflects and promotes a feminine subjectivity, and she quickly dismisses

<hr />

[5] Armstrong, *Desire and Domestic Fiction*, p. 14.

the actual tensions between masculinity and femininity in the early discourse: "despite unsuccessful attempts such as Fielding's to place the novel in a masculine tradition of letters, novels early on assumed the distinctive features of a specialized language for women."[6] Perhaps unfortunately, the masculine context of the genre is more comprehensive than Armstrong admits and has more enduring effects on our understanding of novels, particularly those from the eighteenth century.

In its alterity the new and unregulated novel-form is symbolically feminine, and so the textual gestures that overtly feminize the genre consolidate the formal femininity, or, rather, the formlessness which is associated with the feminine. Dating at least from Aristotle's distinction between feminine matter and masculine form, Western culture has imputed a gendered dichotomy between order and that which exists uncontained and outside of it.[7] The novel's versatility and formal openness constitute a tacit femininity that underscores the more pronounced efforts to feminize the discourse, gestures that include addresses to the ladies, metaphors comparing books with female bodies, and stylistic accommodations for the female reader. The gendered constructions of the amorphous, new, literary genre provide one matrix of intelligibility through which the novel can be associated with and distinguished from existing genres, but simultaneously contained in a subordinate position.

Because many prefaces incorporate blatant attempts to seduce the reader into purchasing the text, the inferior status of the novel is compounded by the commercial grounds of its construction. The discourse of fiction uses the figure of bourgeois femininity, posited as reader and heroine, to aid the capitalistic enterprise of selling novels by suggesting an idealized identification between fictional character and the female audience that serves as the site of a fantasized femino-centric desire. However, the commercial success and feminine "taint" of the novel interfere with its recognition as art, especially within the late-eighteenth-century development of disinterested aesthetics. Throughout the period, some writers attempt to legitimate their novels through reference to the "rules" and the male tradition of letters, but after more than one hundred years of regularly published fiction, the public still perceived the novel as inferior. Anna Letitia Barbauld remarked that it was not "easy to say, why the poet, who deals in one kind of fiction,

---

[6] Ibid., p. 32.
[7] See feminist discussions of this phenomenon in Alice Jardine, *Gynesis: Configurations of Woman and Modernity* (Ithaca: Cornell University Press, 1985), esp. pp. 114–115, and Judith Butler, *Bodies that Matter: On the Discursive Limits of "Sex"* (New York: Routledge, 1993), esp. pp. 31–36.

should have so high a place allotted to him in the temple of fame; and the romance-writer so low a one as in the general estimation he is confined to."[8] The association between the novel and the construct of middle-class femininity creates a successful alliance in both commercial and cultural terms, but, as novelists strive for literary prestige, the imputed femininity of the genre detracts from its literary significance.

When the subordination of the genre becomes discursively linked with the figure of the middle-class female, cultural dismissal of either becomes dialogically reinforcing. Whether the critic chastises the novel, the reader, or the author, the logic depends upon the equation between inferiority and femininity.[9] Seen in this light, the absence of eighteenth-century female novelists from the lists of literary excellence – at least until 1975 – might not be surprising. The masculine state of the canon presents a puzzle, though, when we consider the eighteenth-century perception that the reading of fiction was an overwhelmingly feminine activity. Furthermore, according to Ian Watt and the many who are still persuaded by *The Rise of the Novel*, the greatest fiction of the time focuses on a private feminine consciousness. Certainly, a genre with such overdetermined "femininity" could be mastered by a woman. Dale Spender in her corrective study, *Mothers of the Novel*, identifies the paradoxical "truth" that only men can excel in the feminine genre:

Of the approximately 2000 novels that were written during the eighteenth century, only a very few have been preserved and passed on in the literary canon. This is in itself no cause for complaint. But when to this is added the information that about half these novels were written by women and *all* of them have since failed the test of greatness, then explanations are required. Either the laws of probability are in need of revision, or there are good grounds for hypothesizing that some other law is operating in the selection process.[10]

It is perhaps naive to hold literary quality accountable to quantity and proportion, especially when critical values reflect the unitary languages of prevailing ideologies. Indeed, "some other law" does operate in the selection process, but it is neither simplistic nor constant across time. Spender suggests that the absence of women from the eighteenth-century canon is caused by a virulent sexism that prevents "men" from seeing the literary worth of women writers.

[8] Anna Letitia Barbauld, *The British Novelists* (1810), a new edition (London, 1820), vol. 1, p. 2.
[9] Laurie Langbauer offers a deconstructive reading of the use of "women" and "romance" as the oppositional terms of the novel's definition in *Women and Romance: The Consolations of Gender in the English Novel* (Ithaca: Cornell University Press, 1990).
[10] Dale Spender, *Mothers of the Novel: 100 Good Women Writers before Jane Austen* (London: Pandora Press, 1986), p. 119.

However comforting it may be to blame the powerful for the active repression of the disadvantaged, this approach to what is more accurately a historical critical problem seems inadequate. Although she cites a valid problem in the status of women novelists, Spender fails to acknowledge the historical contingency of the critical values that inform the judgment of those women. As Michele Barrett says, "Simply to pose the question at this level is to deny what we do already know: that not only are refined details of aesthetic ranking highly culturally specific, but that there is not even any consensus across classes, let alone across cultures, as to which cultural products can legitimately be subjected to such judgements."[11] The putative femininity of a genre does not automatically entail the sovereignty of female writers within that field.

The meaning of gendered language in literary criticism cannot be reduced to a correspondence with reading and writing subjects in discourse but, rather, needs to be addressed as one epistemological field and matrix of power in the formation of critical values. Janet Todd admits that much fictional work by women from the eighteenth century falls short of established critical precepts: "By traditional literary critical standards, most are intrusively autobiographical, self-indulgent and conventional in style." She initially follows "traditional" critical standards, but she immediately questions her assessment:

Does it occur because the novels assert outmoded values which nonetheless can still appear unpleasantly seductive in modern pulp literature? ... Or is it because our critical assumptions have been fashioned through a particular body of male literature and literary criticism? Is the critical privileging of the ironic and the unified literary work as well as the assumption of a transcendental and ahistorical aesthetic against which all art can be measured historically determined?[12]

In contrast to Dale Spender, Todd explains the rejection of female writers as a condition of literary values inherited from the eighteenth century. She suggests that current critical expectations are in part shaped by a reading experience that until recently has derived from a coherent masculine tradition. Furthermore, the critical practice of privileging universal and ahistorical literary values – a development that can be traced to the emerging aesthetic in late-eighteenth-century discourse – occludes the gendered grounds of possibility for literary excellence by designating a male perspective as universal and repressing

[11] Michele Barrett, "Ideology and the Cultural Production of Gender," in Judith Newton and Deborah Rosenfelt, eds., *Feminist Criticism and Social Change* (London: Methuen, 1985), p. 78.
[12] Todd, *The Sign of Angellica*, p. 6.

alternative views as particular, poor, or trivial.[13] Because a patriarchal organization of knowledge sustains the construction of literary values in which the formation of the novel takes place, an adequate treatment of gendered subjects – writers, readers, characters – necessitates a better understanding of the role of gendered values in the early critical discourse. In particular, we might question how the gendered structure of values serves or promotes an asymmetrical privilege in the achievement of canonical status, or how male novelists apparently succeed in a feminized genre when their female contemporaries do not.

Through conventional discursive practices, fiction grows more consistently feminized throughout the eighteenth century, but at the same time the critical prose endorsing the genre attempts to control or deny that persistent femininity. In criticism, gender acts as a cultural matrix through which reading and writing subjects determine literary priorities, and, despite the imputed femininity of the novel, critics who subscribe to the definitive literary values of judgment, imagination, and intellect evaluate the genre in masculine terms. Certain practices develop in the criticism that enable literary historians of later generations to ignore or diminish the achievements of the prolific female authors. In this chapter I identify two distinct but overlapping trends. Through textual conventions that include addresses to the female reader, metonymic displacement of the text with a female body, idealized femino-centric relationships, and accommodations for linguistic modesty, publishers, editors, and authors encourage an identification between female subjects and the novel, but this gendered packaging employs the language of heterosexual romance and thus reproduces and naturalizes a paradigm of female subordination and male control. In this strategy, the discursive propriety of the match between fiction and females provides an illusion of female mastery. The pronounced gallantry of the criticism masks the circumscribed agency of the female subject, conveying the literary value of the novel in terms of private subjectivity and conduct. In a second development, critics interested in the prestige of the novel turn to the heroic genres and the masculine tradition of letters for validation, with questionable success. Here, "greatness" is secured for the novel by asserting an overriding masculinity that both protects the privilege of the male author and celebrates the achievement of the "comic Epic-Poem in Prose."

[13] Carol H. Cantrell demonstrates the value-laden gendering of these dualisms in "Analogy as Destiny: Cartesian Man and the Woman Reader," in Hilde Hein and Carolyn Korsmeyer, eds., *Aesthetics in Feminist Perspective* (Bloomington: Indiana University Press, 1993), pp. 218–228. Also see Naomi Schor, *Reading in Detail: Aesthetics and the Feminine* (New York and London: Routledge, 1989).

CONVENTIONS OF FEMININITY

The criticism under consideration dates primarily from before 1740, during a period in the discourse on fiction when definitions of the genre were loose and undetermined. Part of the disorder in the early critical discourse is a notoriously unsystematic application of generic terms;[14] my use of the terms "novel," "romance," "fiction," and "history" attempts to distinguish where possible any differences suggested by the original context, but this is frequently thwarted by the casual inter-changeability of labels in the discourse. The inconsistencies, contradictions, and multiple strategies incorporated in the early critical statements indicate a high level of what Laurie Finke refers to as the "noise" that precedes the making of a fact. Following the semiotic analyses of Bruno Latour and Steven Woolgar and feminist revisions of science by Donna Haraway and N. Katherine Hayles, Finke posits a method called the "politics of complexity" in which she aims to expose the ficticity of fact by recalling the messiness that precedes the unified narrative.[15] The "pre-novel" discourse offers a rich field for the investigation of gendered complexity that later becomes simplified or translated as literary "fact."

The perceived femininity of the eighteenth-century novel can in great measure be attributed to the constructed image of the female reader of fiction. Watt ascribes the rise in the popularity of novels during the eighteenth century to the "omnivorous reading" of the "idle fair," and it is true that the incidental references to the feminine appetite for romances appear frequently enough during the period to suggest a culture-wide perception.[16] Periodicals chastise the ubiquitous female reader, often warning her against the salacious quality of her chief reading-matter.[17] Eustace Budgell's warning in the *Spectator* registers the cultural fear of the provocative nature of fiction: "I shall also advise my fair Readers, to be in a particular manner careful how they meddle with Romances, Chocolate, Novels, and the like Inflamers; which I look upon as very dangerous."[18] Ambrose Philips advertises his periodical the *Free Thinker* as an "elevating alternative to 'the insipid Fictions of novels and

[14] See McKeon, *Origins*, pp. 26–28.
[15] Laurie Finke, *Feminist Theory, Women's Writing*, Reading Women Writing Series (Ithaca: Cornell University Press, 1992), pp. 1–28.
[16] Watt, *Rise of the Novel*, p. 44.
[17] For a discussion of the figure of the middle-class female reader as it developed in periodical literature see Kathryn Shevelow, *Women and Print Culture: The Construction of Femininity in the Early Periodical* (London: Routledge, 1989), especially chapter 2.
[18] Joseph Addison and Richard Steele, *The Spectator*, ed. Donald F. Bond, 5 vols. (Oxford: Clarendon Press, 1965), vol. III, p. 374.

Romances' in which most women indulged."[19] These writers posit a
pre-existing relationship between novels and the female sex, which
naturalizes both a feminine subjectivity susceptible to fantasy and
pleasure and a literature that caters to this reading subject.

In 1727 novelist Mary Davys reiterates the association between
women and fiction, but she implicates a wiser female reading subject:
"'Tis now for some time that those sort of writings called novels have
been a great deal out of use and fashion and that the ladies (for whose
service they were chiefly designed) have been taken up with amusements
of more use and improvement."[20] Rather than see women as the passive
recipients of sensational romance, Davys identifies a female reader who
possesses discernment and a desire for helpful literature. By the second
half of the century, though, writers commonly attribute the omnipresence
of the novel to a specifically feminine lack of taste: "So long as the British
ladies continue to encourage our hackney scribblers, by reading every
romance that appears, we need not wonder that the press should swarm
with such poor insignificant productions."[21] The discourse so thoroughly
affixes an indiscriminate and ravenous feminine readership to the novel
that this critic can blame the female readers for poor writing, even that of
men.[22] After the novel gains a certain level of cultural visibility and
prestige, a gendered understanding of the terms "novel" and "romance"
begins to shape the critical discourse, and assigns a feminine inferiority to
the romance without fully investing the novel with masculine prestige.[23]
In 1785 Clara Reeve, who challenges the gendered logic of such generic
distinctions, claims that "The learned men of our own country, have in
general affected a contempt for this kind of writing, and looked upon
Romances, as proper furniture only for a lady's Library."[24] These

---

[19] Quoted in Alison Adburgham, *Women in Print: Writing Women and Women's Magazines from the Restoration to the Accession of Victoria* (London: Allen and Unwin, 1972), p. 75.

[20] Preface to *The Works of Mrs. Davys . . . in Two Volumes* (1725), in William H. McBurney, ed., *Four Before Richardson: Selected English Novels, 1720–1727* (Lincoln: University of Nebraska Press, 1963), p. 235.

[21] *Monthly Review* (1760), vol. 23, 523.

[22] Such prejudice has passed uncritically into some contemporary evaluations of novels from the period: see Peter John Miller, "Eighteenth-Century Periodicals for Women," *History and Education Quarterly* 11.3 (1971), 279–286: "By far the most popular form of reading material for women was the novel. Indeed, its decline in quality and prestige in the late eighteenth century may well have been connected to its popularization" (280).

[23] Ros Ballaster argues for the historical association between feminine audiences and romance, but her connection between masculine audiences and the novel is implied rather than demonstrated: see "Romancing the Novel: Gender and Genre in Early Theories of Narrative," in Dale Spender, ed., *Living By the Pen: Early British Women Writers* (New York: Teachers College Press, 1992), pp. 188–200.

[24] Clara Reeve, *The Progress of Romance and the History of Charoba, Queen of Aegypt* (1785), with a bibliographical note by Esther M. McGill (New York: Facsimile Text Society, 1930), p. xi.

examples suggest that the critical discourse throughout the century assumes and naturalizes a feminine reading audience for the novel, a gesture that reciprocally shapes the understanding of the genre both as concerned with feminine subjectivity and as inferior to other masculine forms of literature. The reiteration of the image of the female reader projects a femininity about fiction that contemporary criticism of the novel inherits as a critical "truth." If men did spend their time engaged in frivolous romances, as the examples of Pepys, Temple, and even Henry Tilney suggest, the British critical discourse on fiction elides the fact.[25]

The figure of the female reader enters critical discourse in many places – as the purported dedicatee, as the audience in need of edification, as the epitome of wayward female autonomy – but its relationship to the constitution of eighteenth-century reading audiences is tenuous. As Watt argues, social and economic changes in the late seventeenth and eighteenth centuries, including the rise in female literacy and increasing leisure time, encourage the identification between female readers and fiction, but early fiction is not the exclusive discursive or material property of women. Patricia Crawford dispels the myths about women's omnivorous reading habits; even though the percentage of female literacy increased dramatically during the seventeenth century, Crawford argues that proportionally the number of male readers in society always exceeded the number of female readers.[26] Consequently women, who were barred from formal education, did not constitute a majority of the reading audience, except possibly for religious works. Ruth Perry adds that more men purchased novels in the early period, perhaps because the bookshop and coffeehouse were by social convention exclusively male preserves.[27] Neither were women the first authors of novels, despite the popular perception of "scribbling ladies." Female authorship constituted a tiny percentage of the total publication in the seventeenth century (1.2 percent from 1640 to 1700). During the 1600s women in England published only fifty-one prose works, including fictions, translations, essays, and letters.[28]

[25] Ruth Perry, *Women, Letters, and the Novel* (New York: AMS Press, 1980), p. 18.
[26] Patricia Crawford, "Women's Published Writings 1600–1700," in M. Prior, ed., *Women in English Society 1500–1800* (London: Methuen, 1985), p. 216; in 1640 10 percent of the females in England were considered literate; by the early eighteenth century the figure rises to 30 percent. For men the percentages increased from 30 percent male literacy in 1640 to 45 percent in the early eighteenth century.
[27] Perry, *Women, Letters, and the Novel*, p. 9.
[28] Crawford, "Women's Published Writings 1600–1700," 266.

The early prefaces of prose fiction likewise contradict the idea of a homogenously female audience for novels. Following the aristocratic French practice, the first authors of romantic fiction construct an elite audience of both sexes. In the preface to *Parthenissa* (1655), Roger Boyle claims that in France "he who was ignorant of the Romances of these times, was as fitt an Object for Wonder, as a phylosopher would be, who had never heard of Aristotle, or a Methmatician of Euclyd."[29] Likewise, J.D. recommends his translation of *Astrea*: "I shall onely adde the judgement of it, of the late famous Cardinall of Richelieu, that he was not to be admitted into the Academy of Wit, who had not been before well read in ASTREA."[30] In 1687 Robert Boyle (Roger's brother) designs his fiction *The Martyrdom of Theodora and of Didymus* for "young Persons of Quality of either Sex."[31] These comments identify the readers of fiction by a social status associated with class rather than with gender, and they project an impression of the novel as fundamental to the development of a learned character.

As most histories of the English novel demonstrate, the elite focus of fiction is challenged in the last quarter of the seventeenth century by competing interests from the emerging bourgeoisie. By the end of the seventeenth century, evaluations of the novel begin to incorporate a readership from a broader range of class identity. John Dunton in the *Athenian Mercury* suggests that reading romances may be unproblematic for the privileged, but it presents a danger for the lower classes: "we think 'em not at all convenient for the Vulgar, because they give 'em extravagant Idea's of practice, and before they have Judgment to byass their Fancies, generally make 'em think themselves some King or Queen."[32] In his 1715 preface to the translation of Bishop Huet's *Sur l'origine des Romans*, Stephen Lewis argues that the reading of romances has increased in popularity, appealing to men and women from a general audience: "the Romance has of late convey'd it self very far into the Esteem of this nation, and is become the Principal Diversion of the Retirement of People of all Conditions."[33] His preface suggests that the genre loses its class exclusivity, but it retains an appeal for male readers,

---

[29] Roger Boyle, preface to *Parthenissa* (London, 1655), intro. Charles Davies, Augustan Reprint Society 42 (Los Angeles: University of California Press, 1953), np.

[30] Honoré d'Urfé, *Astrea*, trans. J.D. (London, 1657), sig. a2ᵛ.

[31] Robert Boyle, preface to *Martyrdom of Theodora and of Didymus* (London, 1687), intro. Charles Davies, Augustan Reprint Society 42 (Los Angeles: University of California Press, 1953), np.

[32] Quoted in Ioan Williams, ed., *Novel and Romance: 1700–1800; A Documentary Record* (New York: Barnes and Noble, 1970), p. 29.

[33] Pierre Daniel Huet, Bishop of Avranches, *Sur l'Origine des Romans* (1670), trans. Stephen Lewis as *The History of Romances* (London, 1715), in I. Williams, ed., *Novel and Romance*, p. 45.

which he underscores with references to classical authors and an emphasis on Huet's judgment and learning. Lewis' translation serves as the introductory essay to Samuel Croxall's *A Select Collection of Novels*, whose preface likewise expresses the moral benefits of novels for "both Sexes."[34] So, as late as 1720, the discourse on fiction includes constructions of a non-gender-specific audience, which, with any expression of masculine desire for the genre, eventually becomes repressed or coded in terms of literary excellence.

Historical evidence reveals a discrepancy between the discursive construction of feminine readership and the actual constituency of the audience but, regardless of the demographic reality, the female reader becomes a commonplace figure in the prefatory pages of fiction. The commentary on fiction asserts the "femininity" of the genre through a number of conventions, the most notable being the opening address "To the Ladies." In a typical overture, the author, translator, or editor provides a justification for reading the novel. The translator of Madeleine de Scudéry's *Clelia* opens with a letter, "To the Ladies," claiming, "'Tis to the Altar of your perfections (fair Ladies) that the Incomparable Courage of the noble *Clelia* flyes for protection."[35] The translator addresses an audience marked by conspicuously feminine details – beauty, moral perfection, and intimacy. His discourse shapes an audience according to the idealized femininity represented in the fiction. George Mackenzie prefaces his *Aretina* with a similarly gallant address, "To all the Ladies of this Nation," in which he praises women as the source of all virtue necessary to protect his vulnerable new fiction.[36] Both writers ascribe to the constructed female reader the power to defend the text, implying thereby that reading their works is morally justified. Such appeals are conventional, as the examples below will suggest, and reproduce a stereotypical image of virtuous femininity.

Other writers construct a less pure female audience with the aim of educating them in proper female behavior. In *The Maiden-head Lost by Moon-light* Joseph Kepple insists in his dedication "To the Ladies" that his fiction is "the perfect Representation of the state of Innocence," by which he means the heroine's easy and frank admission of love.[37] He

---

[34] Samuel Croxall, preface to *A Select Collection of Novels* (1720), in I. Williams, ed., *Novel and Romance*, p. 72.
[35] Madeleine de Scudéry, *Clelia*, trans. (London, 1655), sig. a2ʳ.
[36] Sir George Mackenzie, preface to *Aretina; Or the Serious Romance* (London, 1660), intro. Charles Davies, Augustan Reprint Society 42 (Los Angeles: University of California Press, 1953).
[37] Joseph Kepple, *The Maiden-head Lost by Moon-light: or, the Adventure of the Meadow* (1672), reprint, in Charles C. Mish, ed., *Restoration Prose Fiction 1666–1700: An Anthology of Representative Pieces* (Lincoln: University of Nebraska Press, 1970), p. 166.

suggests that the hypocritical ladies of his society will benefit from the example of such honesty. Mary Davys dedicates *The Reform'd Coquet* "To the Ladies of Great Britain," in a playful satire on their whimsical choices in love.[38] She encourages her readers to drop the vain pastimes of masquerades, operas, and new plays and instead to read her instructive novel. Rather than invoke a moral readership for which the reading of fiction becomes a virtuous practice, Kepple and Davys address an audience whose faulty character requires edification, specifically in matters of romance. Both trends fulfill the same critical function. Whether conveyed in the hyperbolic language of virtue or the satiric representation of coquetry, these addresses to the ladies consolidate the impression of the female reader of fiction and justify the genre in terms of feminine subjectivity.

A second convention that contributes to the sense of the novel's exclusively feminine subjectivity is the metonymic displacement of the text by the figure of the heroine's body. By describing the novel itself as a female with whom the posited reader can identify, the constructed female readership serves as the site of fantasized femino-centric desire. For instance, the translator of *Clelia* asks "The Ladies" to accept [his] book because of the heroine's personal sacrifice: "But 'tis not so much the remembrance of her dangers past, as the Consideration of her paines willingly taken for your *beautifull Sex* in passing the Seas, and changing not only her *Language* but her *Country*, that invites her thus chearefully to caste her self on your Mercies . . ."[39] The personification of the text as heroine allows the translator to represent [his] own discursive labor as the autonomous and voluntary action of a gentlewoman; [he] consequently slips out of the scene of writing and proposes an ideal female coterie between reader and text. (I have bracketed the masculine pronoun because the sex of the translator is officially unknown, but there is a historical probability that it was male.) Flattering the purported reader as the source of Clelia's love and desire, the preface posits a mimetic identification between the imagined reader and this generous female, reinforcing a feminine code of behavior represented by Clelia's ideological values.

By displacing the text with the eponymous heroine, authors, translators and editors present an image of the novel as the desirable and vulnerable female body. They place the reader or patron in the role of female

[38] Mary Davys, *The Reform'd Coquet* (London, 1724), reprint, ed. Michael F. Shugrue, intro. Josephine Grieder, *Foundations of the Novel* (New York: Garland Publishing, 1973), p. iv.
[39] Scudéry, *Clelia*, sig. a2ᵛ.

guardian, and in the process coalesce text and reader in their embodiment of ideal femininity. In *The Unequal Match,* Jean de La Chapelle petitions the Dowager Countess of Tenet to shelter his fiction: "This Queen fancyed she could be nowhere so safe as under so Glorious a protection, and therefore was restless and impatient, till I had Ushered and Introduced her into your Ladyships presence." The author's language transfers the economic advantage gained from the patron from himself to the feminized and vulnerable text. This strategy valorizes the feminine bond between patron and novel-*cum*-woman and implicates the Countess' inner character as the source of the queen's desire. The convention also recasts the author's role to that of procurer, quaintly apprehensive of his protégée's appearance: "I shall have fully satisfied my vanity, if you find her Company, Madam, as agreeable as others have done, and if you can think fit to Pardon the dress she appears in, which I'm afraid will be found to have too much of the *French* in it."[40] Significantly, the literary merit of style is evaluated in the feminine arena of fashion, and measures of moral and social propriety – agreeable company – supersede other literary standards; in this way the criticism of the novel negotiates literary value through languages that supervise the female body.

The convention of substituting the heroine for the text enables other writers to make appeals on behalf of less worthy feminine characters. In *The History of the Nun* Aphra Behn closes her dedication to the Duchess of Mazarine with a recognition that her personified text might not merit the duchess' safekeeping: "if my fair unfortunate Vow-Breaker do not deserve the honour of your Graces Protection, at least, she will be found worthy of your Pity."[41] Peter Bellon displays more confidence in his patron's good nature in the anonymously published *The Reviv'd Fugitive*: "I despair not, but that you will look on this small Piece with a favorable eye, and that you will have so much bounty as to descend to this Reviv'd Fugitive, all neglected as she is."[42] Again, these metonymic strategies represent the novel as a vulnerable female but, unlike the deserving heroines whose desirability is predicated on their identification with the purported reader, the figurative bodies of these heroines are tainted and potentially offensive. The author's representation of the fiction as "fallen" woman promotes an alternative relationship based on pity, and while this construct preserves the idealized feminine virtue of the reader,

[40] [Jean de la Chapelle,] *The Unequal Match or, The Life of Mary of Anjou, Queen of Majorca* (London, 1681), np.
[41] Aphra Behn, *The History of the Nun: or, The Fair Vow-Breaker* (London, 1689), reprint, in Mish, ed., *Restoration Prose Fiction*, p. 97.
[42] [Bellon, Peter,] *The Reviv'd Fugitive: A Gallant Historical Novel* (London, 1690), p. 3.

it authorizes the titillating exposure of active female sexuality. Furthermore, the conventional displacement of the text with the image of a vulnerable female invites female readers to evaluate the novel, but not in specifically literary terms. Instead, these letters establish the novel as a genre that negotiates female bodies.

    While not all early novels project a homogeneous female audience, few exclude the female reader. Consequently, many prefaces explain the stylistic adaptations authors make for the supposed female reader, and these most frequently include an avoidance of classical learning, the enhancement of beauty, and a simple, modest form of writing. In his detailed prefatory treatise "An Apologie for Romances," Mackenzie rejects the pedantic style where the author employs inappropriate Latin and Greek phrases. In contrast, he strives for a manner that recalls Dryden's prescription for feminine poetry: "where cadence is sweet, and the epithets well adapted, without any other varnish whatsoever."[43] Like Dryden, Mackenzie derives this aesthetic from the conversation of the court, shaping a fictional discourse that is pleasing, smooth, simple, and decorous, a polite style befitting audiences that include women. The translator of Gauthier de Costes de la Calprenède's *Cassandre* emphasizes a similar aural harmony, but he advertises a far more luxurious expression, an "admirable Beauty and Lustre, deck'd in the rich Ornaments of an elegant Stile and sweetness of Language."[44] By emphasizing beauty and sweetness, the stylistic descriptions for fiction resonate with the discourse on female conduct and, like Dryden's poetic feminine, they convey the cultural significations of that pleasing, ornamental femininity. The dialogized language of these prefaces suggests the ways in which the criticism on fiction participates in the same gendered strategies as elite literary criticism, such as Dryden's.

    More conventionally, the prefaces testify to the modesty of the text for the sake of the "ladies." Henry Cogan, the translator of de Scudéry's *Ibrahim*, uses the customary female reader to verify his code of delicacy: "neither have I put any thing into my Book, which the Ladies may not read without blushing."[45] The anonymous translator of de Scudéry's *Artamène* makes similar claims: this fiction contains "so far from the least [s]ully of what might be thought vain or Fulsome, that there is not

[43] Mackenzie, *Aretina*, p. 10.
[44] Gauthier de Costes de la Calprenède, translator's preface to *Cassandre* (1644–1650), trans. (London, 1703), reprint, in I. Williams, ed., *Novel and Romance*, p. 31.
[45] Henry Cogan, preface to Madeleine de Scudéry, *Ibrahim* (1674), ed. and intro. Benjamin Boyce, Augustan Reprint Society 32 (Los Angeles: University of California Press, 1952), p. 8.

anything to provoke a blush from the most modest Virgin."[46] As with Dryden and Collier, this conventional appeal to the female reader legitimates the perceived needs of a female audience that are distinct from the male, and intimates the generosity or politeness of the author in accommodating "her." However, the identification of modesty as a particularly feminine aesthetic incurs a restriction on fictional discourse that becomes ideologically fixed to feminine subjectivity. The language of fiction consequently must conform to ideals of polite femininity.

In the early critical discourse, however, the polite ideal coexists with less restrictive feminine models. The eroticism of Behn's and Manley's texts, for instance, stands in contrast to this construction of female chastity. The discursive presence of female-authored fictions of active female sexuality should not negate the association between women and modesty; rather, the plurality of feminine images demonstrates the heterogeneity of the foundations of the genre. The interest in preserving a verbal modesty, moreover, is not inconsistent with the representation and policing of female sexuality. In 1720, W. P., the author of the *Jamaica Lady*, grudgingly submits to the virtuous requirements of his female audience: "I have taken care to write with all modesty the subject would permit, being very cautious of offending the fair sex, and should there be an expression which may seem rough or harsh, I desire it may be imputed to the sea captain [of the story] and not to the author."[47] The same author, however, expresses the desire to illustrate the depravity of "notorious women" so as to deter others of the same inclination.

These conventional statements on modesty presuppose and, hence, reinforce the presence of a female audience, but they also assert a gendered propriety in fictional language that associates pleasure in sound and beauty with feminine taste while it legislates against difficult learning and immodest language. The stylistic conventions specifically adapted for the projected female audience identify the feminine as a distinct epistemological field necessitating its own linguistic conditions. By marking the text as suitable for a feminine audience, the prefaces insinuate the author's desire to please his or her audience, and they consequently invite the imagined reader to reciprocate the generosity, creating a paradigm of reading that operates by the codes of polite gallantry rather than critical judgment.

Despite the historical evidence that suggests the genre initially engages a broader audience, the critical practices in the prefatory matter of

---

[46] [Madeleine] de Scudéry, preface to *Artamène* (1691 edn), in I. Williams, ed., *Novel and Romance*, p. 26.
[47] W. P., preface to *The Jamaica Lady* (London, 1720), in McBurney, *Four Before Richardson*, p. 87.

fiction produce an exaggerated femininity by addressing a female reader, figuring the text as female body, coalescing reader and heroine, and making stylistic accommodations for a female audience. We might, therefore, ask what interests this femininity serves. On the one hand, the construct of femininity facilitates the sale of novels by providing the site of femino-centric desire. On the other the novel form reciprocally shapes the discourse of gender by regulating proper femininity under its domain, consequently serving the interest of hegemonic order. Peter De Bolla has argued that the figure of the female reader might actually have greater implications for the control of male reading behavior: "It may now appear that it is not *women* who seem to have been caught within the prevailing male ideologies which determined their behavior, or *women* who were uniquely oppressed by male-dominated forms of representation, but that *men* were also forced into a self-image created by theory's genderization of the practice it fantasizes."[48] Following Paul Kaufman, De Bolla reads the massive technology marshaled against the female reader as a screen to hide the illicit reading of novels by men. Such uniform characterization of fiction as the province of women, he claims, preserves a pure masculine reading ethic apart from the luxurious and indulgent implications of the novel. Although De Bolla erroneously implies that such constructions oppress male subjects, and he is, in any case, too precipitous in shifting the focus of fictional discourse to its effect on male subjects, his point suggests the overriding male concern at work in the construction of femininity in critical language. Within the patriarchal context of these critical articulations, masculine authority persistently determines the configuration of gender and literary value, despite gallant gestures to the contrary. It is important to read the constructed femininity of the novel in the discourses of gendered hierarchy that inform it.

GALLANT CONTROL OF THE FEMININE GENRE

The perceived femininity of fiction continues to entice contemporary critics into granting female subjects sovereignty within that discourse: recently Dale Spender asserted that "While . . . women still wrote in every other genre, it was the novel which was recognized as 'women's form'."[49] While the novel's gendered emphasis might lead to an

---

[48] Peter De Bolla, *The Discourse of the Sublime: Readings in History, Aesthetics, and the Subject* (Oxford: Basil Blackwell, 1989), p. 271.

[49] Dale Spender, ed. *Living By the Pen: Early British Women Writers* (New York: Teachers College Press, 1992), p. 18.

evolution of female proprietorship, the masculine values of literature and the canonical ordering of novelists from the eighteenth century suggest otherwise. We need to explain how the femininity of fiction becomes suspect, or conversely, how male practice becomes the condition of fictional excellence despite the feminine character of the novel.

The femininity of the novel exists in a hierarchical relationship with a corresponding masculinity, reflecting the patriarchal organization of society. Most of the strategies that constitute fiction as feminine invoke heterosexual relations, thus making masculinity essential to femininity and vice versa. Indeed, discourse constructs and reiterates a symbolic parallel between the novel and "women's form," imputing to the genre a hegemonic desire for and anxiety surrounding women's sexuality and subjecting the novel to comparable regulation through patriarchal order. By employing the language and forms of courtship, literary criticism dialogically intersects the language of feminine conduct, consequently negotiating literary value as the legislation of female sexuality.

The criticism of early fiction is contemporaneous with Dryden's criticism of heroic literature, and the former shares with Dryden's criticism an awareness of gender as a semiotic condition. In early discussions of fiction, authors, editors, and critics fashion the identity of readers, patrons, and themselves with a consciousness of role-playing and stereotypes not necessarily restricted by categories of sex. The discourse of gender at this historical point is dominated by what Thomas Laqueur calls the one-sex system of gender differentiation, where difference is understood as a social condition of degree rather than ontological difference in kind.[50] Furthermore, the normative constructions of gender, especially for women, demonstrate a wider range of sexual expression than they would under the hegemonic influence of polite, bourgeois femininity in the mid-eighteenth century.[51] Thus, the development of modern subjectivity that Armstrong locates in the novels of the 1740s incorporates an alternative emphasis in gendered difference and normative ideology than that which operates in the discourse of Behn, Manley and early Haywood.[52] The discourse of criticism of the

---

[50] For a history of the changes in organization of gender during the period see Thomas Laqueur, *Making Sex: Bodies and Gender from the Greeks to Freud* (Cambridge: Harvard University Press, 1990), especially chapters 3 and 4; Michael McKeon, "Historicizing Patriarchy: The Emergence of Gender Difference in England, 1660–1760," *Eighteenth-Century Studies*, 28.3 (1995), 295–322; Ruth H. Bloch, "Untangling the Roots of Modern Sex Roles: A Survey of Four Centuries of Change," *Signs* 4.2 (1978), 237–252.

[51] Mary Poovey, *The Proper Lady and the Woman Writer: Ideology as Style in the Works of Mary Wollstonecraft, Mary Shelley, and Jane Austen* (Chicago: University of Chicago Press, 1984), esp. chapter 1.

[52] Ramifications of this difference are explored by Ros Ballaster in *Seductive Forms: Women's Amatory Fiction from 1684 to 1740* (Oxford: Clarendon Press, 1992).

early novel frequently forefronts the construction of female sexuality in ways that Dryden's criticism, for instance, does not. While novel-criticism often shares with Dryden a neoclassical vocabulary and rhetoric of gallantry, the archetypes of gender within each differ markedly. Whereas Dryden's gendered language intersects with the polite images of the hero and the genteel lady, authors and critics of fiction rely more heavily on the language of the languishing gallant and the ravishing mistress.

Thus, gendered language in the early discourse on fiction incorporates a construction of femininity from the Restoration that emphasizes sexual agency and its consequences. Lawrence Stone identifies, in the latter half of the seventeenth century, a growing permissiveness toward extramarital affairs and claims that it is "significant of the new attitude that the crude word 'adultery' was replaced by the rather attractive euphemism 'gallantry'."[53] Parodies of the adulteress abound in drama, poetry, and fiction: the newlywed Mrs. Pinchwife complains, "I have got the London disease they call love; I am sick of my husband, and for my gallant."[54] Rochester's Artemisia writes to her country friend of "what loves have passed" and the intrigues of the female sex, "who, born like monarchs free, / turn gypsies for a meaner liberty, / And hate restraint, though but from infamy."[55] These popular images depict a female nature of active will and sexual power, which suggests a challenging and more verbally dexterous alternative to the soft and smooth femininity of Dryden's criticism. At the same time, however, the representation of independent female desire in the context of patriarchal order always risks collapsing into an image of prostitution, and the ascendancy derived from sexual availability becomes a potential source of exploitation. This tension between feminine vulnerability and power becomes a conventional trope in the critical justifications for fiction.

The construct of active female sexuality in early fictional discourse is matched by a male counterpart, the Restoration rake. Charles II's notable promiscuity, which was such that Dryden could with impunity declare that he "Scattered his maker's image through the land," gave license to a rakish figure of masculinity.[56] Like the hero, the rake belongs

[53] Lawrence Stone, *The Family, Sex and Marriage in England 1500–1800*, abridged edition (New York: Harper and Row, 1977), p. 329.
[54] William Wycherley, *The Country Wife*, in *Restoration Plays*, intro. Brice Harris (New York: Modern Library, 1953), p. 129.
[55] Lord Rochester, John Wilmot, "Artemisia to Chloe," *Complete Poems of John Wilmot, Earl of Rochester*, ed. David M. Vieth (New Haven: Yale University Press, 1968), lines 56–58.
[56] John Dryden, "Absalom and Achitophel," *The Poems of John Dryden*, ed. James Kinsley, 4 vols. (Oxford: Clarendon Press, 1958), vol. 1, pp. 215–243, line 10.

to a tightly knit homosocial group, but rather than aspire toward the civic virtues of bravery, honor, and family, the rake's code embraces the excess of self-abasement with a competitive interest in sex, drinking, wit, and swearing. The libertine seeks women through elaborate rituals of courtship, apparently regardless of his personal welfare. Behn's Bredwell, in pursuit of the married Julia, "Swore – Wept – Vow'd – Wrote, upbraided, pray'd and rail'd; then treated lavishly – and presented high – till . . . I have presented the best part of Eight hundred a year into her Husbands hands, in Mortgage."[57] Once successful, rakes easily dismiss their conquests, who ultimately serve as conduits of sexual gratification; Dorilant in *The Country Wife* explains, "A mistress should be like a little country retreat near the town; not to dwell in constantly, but only for a night and away, to taste the town the better when a man returns."[58] The critical dialogism in the discourse of early fiction constitutes masculinity through this language of sexual license and initiative.

The figures of the mistress and her paramour are embedded in the language of gallantry that dominates the discursive structures of criticism of the early novel. As demonstrated in chapters 1 and 2, ritualized forms of gallantry temporarily reverse the power structure of the gendered hierarchy by placing the male in the position of subservient admirer and the female in control of the dispensation of favors. These roles mirror those of the courtier and king, except that at court the ends gained tend to be public and political, while the gallant aims for private, sexual, fulfillment. In Dryden's criticism, gallantry functions as a rationale for the protection of female chastity through modest discourse. In fiction, however, the ambiguity created through exaggerated forms of praise generates multiple layers of interpretation, often suggesting parallels between reading and sexual pleasure. The writers of dedications and prefaces assume the masculine prerogative of heterosexual initiative by beseeching the patronage of their female audience. These solicitations construct a feminine subjectivity that is simultaneously vulnerable and powerful in the conflated realms of love and the marketplace. Consequently, the strategies that seem to promote a feminized authority in fiction retain and reinscribe the patriarchal control of the female body. Such discursive identification registers the novel as the site of female sexuality, and, following patriarchal models, it codifies the male authority to create, sell, or police the text.

---

[57] Behn, *The Luckey Chance* (1687) in *The Works of Aphra Behn*, ed. Janet Todd, 7 vols. (Columbus: Ohio State University Press, 1996), vol. vii, pp. 223–224.
[58] Wycherley, *Country Wife*, p. 66.

Through the rhetoric of gallantry, the writer presents the entire production of a book as a favor for the projected female reader. In [his] petition "To the Ladies" the translator of de Scudéry's *Clelia* explains: "For my part (Ladies) the Grand Inducement I had to bestow those few vacant howers (I sometimes enjoy) on this worke was chiefly to pleasure you."⁵⁹ Throughout the prefatory letter, the translator cajoles [his] audience through overwrought compliments to accept the noble Clelia. [He] concludes in the same rhetorical manner by marking the translation of this romance as the gallant gesture of leisure time, and [his] feigned generosity imposes an obligation on the part of the reader to repay [his] kindness. By adopting the role of the suitor to all [his] female readers, the translator represents the act of reading the novel, and the necessary precondition of purchasing it, as a negotiation of courtship. By positing an intimacy between translator and reader analogous to sexual interaction, the letter tempts the subject with the promise of an ambiguous personal satisfaction. The translator aims to please her, after all. The address simultaneously reproduces the sexual privilege of the libertine by structurally granting the translator access to many female readers; the language of sexual conquest masks the frankly commercial motivation of [his] gallantry.

Mackenzie insinuates a similar promiscuity in his rather optimistic address "To all the Ladies of this Nation." Beginning with a cross-gendered simile comparing himself to "Moses [*sic*] trembling mother" leaving his firstborn "upon the banks of envies [*sic*] current," he constructs a complex authorial image in an awkwardly extravagant letter.⁶⁰ The novel becomes a surrogate self as he imagines his readers will "dandle it in the lapp of your protection" and allow it to "suck the breasts of your favour."⁶¹ Couched within the grandiose compliments of gallantry, such provocative images blur the distinction between maternal care and sexual fantasy. Subsequently, he grovels in homage to the ladies because, he claims, their physical beauty signifies a perfection of soul. Mackenzie's shifting persona wavers uncertainly between protecting female virtue and enacting male seduction, evoking the tension between the power and the vulnerability of the female figure constructed in the critical discourse. In a gesture of grand proportion, he declares all the women of England his patronesses: "there is none of your never enough admired Sex, but may lay claime to the patronage of all that drops from my pen."⁶² Regardless of his intentions, the over-inflated language of

---

⁵⁹ de Scudéry, *Clelia*, sig. A2ʳ.   ⁶⁰ Mackenzie, *Aretina*, p. 3.   ⁶¹ Ibid.   ⁶² Ibid., p. 4.

courtship slips into a discourse of vulgar sexuality. Compare, for instance, the dedication to the *Whore's Rhetorick*, one of the earliest pornographic fictions sold in English: "If I have not honoured you with a flat Nose, pray be pleased (fair ones) to accept the Tribute of a flat Pen."[63] Both expressions offer a prurient image of the male instrument, aligning writing with copulation. The pornographic example clarifies the phallocentrism of the act of writing and illustrates that material power – whether to avenge or to please – lies in the mastery of the pen/penis. Gallantry, or as Wollstonecraft sees it, "those pretty feminine phrases . . . men condescendingly use to soften our slavish dependence," obscures the dynamic of power by creating the illusion that females exercise control over the pen/penis, but such mastery is, in fact, a masculine prerogative.[64] Furthermore, Mackenzie solicits the commercial favor of his patronesses in terms of sexual flattery, conferring a feminine interest in fiction associated with the body rather than with the intellect. He underscores this gendered appreciation for fiction by offering a separate essay on the genre's formal features and purpose apart from his letter to the ladies.

The anonymous author of *The Obliging Mistress* further exploits the dialogism of the language of gallantry by emphasizing its political resonances. He dedicates his fiction, whose title explicitly marks the sexual discourse, with a conventional entreaty to the female patron; he hopes to employ "all the Power of your Vertue to Secure [the novel] from the rage and fury of malevolent censors."[65] His fear of government censorship differs from other writers who only dread commercial failure, but the power to which he appeals is nonetheless gender-specific: "Beauty is now the only Shroud to wrap a trembling writer in and keep him safe from Blasts, and stormy Winds." The writer's allusion to the textual practice of invoking female beauty suggests its regularity, and yet the subject of beauty clearly introduces a troubling thread in discourse. "It is like SACRED MAJESTY, to which all the World pays the tribute of awful Reverence and Devotion, and to whose absolute PREROGATIVE mankind owes its utmost Loyalty: So that it would seem no less than a crime of highest *Treason*, but to think of bringing its Power into Dispute or Question."[66] By attributing sovereignty to women and rendering

---

[63] Anon., *The Whore's Rhetorick, calculated to the meridian of London and conformed to the rules of Art* (London, 1683), sig. A3ʳ.

[64] Mary Wollstonecraft, *The Works of Mary Wollstonecraft*, ed. Janet Todd and Marilyn Butler, 7 vols. (New York: New York University Press, 1989), vol. v, p. 75.

[65] *The Obliging Mistress: Or the Fashionable Gallant* (London, 1678), np.   [66] Ibid.

himself a menial subject, the author participates in ritualistic gallant gestures. His praise is simultaneously sincere, in that he seeks the readers' approval, and false, in that the claims are patently unrealistic. The expression of his praise, though, is particularly specious because of his insistence on the royal metaphor and his emphasis on legal terminology. When the work appeared in 1678, public disapproval of Charles II's affairs, particularly with the Catholic Duchess of Portsmouth, was growing, and this carefully worded panegyric raises tensions about the courtly analogy between women and royalty. The writer's emphasis on the treasonable charge of questioning the royal prerogative suggests his dissatisfaction with the legal authority that maintains his absolute subjection to the monarch. The parallel would suggest that the subject's devotion to women or beauty is in need of as much revision as the relationship between the subject and his king, particularly when that king is himself subject to beauty. The preface illustrates a twist in the ambiguity of gallant discourse in the commentary on fiction, suggesting that the feminine power in the genre, like the king's, may be illegitimate or tyrannical.

The formulaic tropes of heterosexual romance that shape the gendered discourse on fiction present interesting obstacles and opportunities for female authors. Aphra Behn undermines hegemonic authority by adopting the male role and creating new sexual tensions with her female patron. In her dedication to "The Most Illustrious Princess The Duchess of Mazarine" Behn pleads in the voice of the devoted lover:

I was impatient for an Opportunity, to tell Your Grace, how infinitely one of Your own Sex ador'd You, and that, among all the numerous Conquests, Your Grace has made over the Hearts of Men, Your Grace has not subdu'd a more entire Slave; I assure you, Madam, there is neither Compliment nor Poetry, in this humble Declaration, but a Truth, which has cost me a great deal of Inquietude, for that Fortune has not set me in such a Station, as might justifie my Pretence to the honour and satisfaction of being ever near Your Grace, to view eternally that lovely Person, and hear that Surprizing Wit.[67]

Behn's cross-gendered appropriation of gallantry brings new dimensions to the rhetoric of courtship. Her sex gives her credibility in that her subscription as a woman is unique, unlike the common and deceitful male devotion. Behn's femininity likewise grants verity to her language; "there is neither compliment nor Poetry" in her praise, presumably

---

[67] Behn, dedication to "The History of the Nun," in Mish, ed., *Restoration Prose Fiction*, p. 96.

because there is no sexual motive to the panegyric. However, Behn's effortless assumption of male prerogative ultimately leaves the sexual innuendo open. Her enthusiasm for the duchess celebrates the spectacle of the sexual female body: "And how few Objects are there, that can render it so entire a Pleasure, as at once to hear you speak, and to look upon your Beauty."[68] Behn's revision of the sexual rhetoric, however, incorporates praise for the duchess' wit as well as her appearance. Like male authors, Behn addresses a woman in the language of extreme praise to shelter her fiction, but Behn recognizes the mental powers of her patron as well as her physical attraction, thereby drawing the feminine connection to fiction in terms of the mind and body. By calling attention to her own sex, Behn also reconstructs the dynamic between author, patron, and text as a female coterie minimizing masculine authority. Behn's feat in this instance relies on her willingness to play with gendered codes, but while she successfully co-opts the masculine instrument of discourse, she leaves the patriarchal structuring of that discourse intact.

In contrast to Behn, Mary Pix domesticates the conventions in the dedicatory epistle to her only novel, *The Inhumane Cardinal*. The years between Behn's publication of 1689 and Pix's in 1696 witness a dramatic shift in the construction of gender, in tandem with the changing economic and political ideologies following the Glorious Revolution. The figures of the domestic female and good husband gain popular favor in the periodical and fictional literature,[69] and the concomitant censure of libertinism affects critical practices. In keeping with the increasingly hegemonic codes of virtuous femininity as well as with the character of her patron, Pix emphasizes the proper female roles of wife and mother in her address to Princess Ann. Among the elements of praise she includes the princess' family lineage, "Princely Virtues," "Christian Piety," "Royal Partner" and her "Lovely Blooming Prince." Rather than mimic the would-be lover of heterosexual romance, Pix assumes the voice of an admirer of the same sex. She redirects the interest in her patron from the perspective of sexual seduction to the feminine praise of familial paragon; in the process she maintains the integrity of her own female persona.

Still, the formal conventions raise conflicts for Pix as she closes the

---

[68] Ibid. Maureen Duffy suggests that Behn may have been involved in a lesbian relationship with the bisexual duchess, Hortense Mancini: see *The Passionate Shepherdess: Aphra Behn 1640–89*, second edition (London: Methuen, 1989), p. 285.
[69] See pp. 68–70.

standard epistle. After praising the virtues of Ann's new son, Pix awkwardly shifts to the customary authorial voice:

I ought now to say something, in reference to the following Sheets; but my ravish'd Pen hath been entertain'd upon so sublime a Theme, that it disdains to descend; and my heart full of Rapture, that is, full of your *Royal Highness*, will only give me leave to endeavor the expressing, how much I am, Madam, your Royal Highness's Devoted humble Servant.[70]

Significantly, Pix skirts her critical responsibilities in favor of gallant compliment, but her awkward use of stock phrases from the sexual panegyric reveals the inadequacy of her attempt. Her "ravish'd Pen" has not been employed in sexual metaphor until this point, and her heart's "rapture" seems so discordant as to require an explanation. Unlike Behn, Pix cannot master the masculine instrument in courtly discourse, and the critical discussion of fiction is so thoroughly entrenched in its rhetoric that Pix cannot find more appropriate terms to describe her function as author. While Pix tries to change the male-oriented conventions that prevailed in prefatory materials to fiction, she finds herself caught between the gendered roles of female author and male gallant. Her inconsistency demonstrates the contradiction between the novel's discursive femininity and the dominating language of masculine privilege characteristic of gallant discourse.

In one of the earliest and most respected theoretical formulations of fiction, the Bishop of Avranches, Pierre Daniel Huet, identifies gallantry as the signal feature of the novel's literary distinction. The novel, he admits, is uniquely concerned with the female body, but it is actually homocentric for just that reason. Huet's essay, *Sur l'Origine des Romans*, translated into English in 1715, provides a history of the romance to explain France's preeminent achievement in the genre: "'Tis truly a Subject of Admiration, that we, who have yielded to others the Bays for Epic Poetry, and History, have nevertheless advanced these to so high a Perfection."[71] Although he seems quite content with this fame, his concession rather supports the gendered prejudices of British literary critics, like Dryden, who derogate the French for their ineptitude in the epic form. In this nationalistic context, the translation of Huet's French conception of fiction validates the British investment in masculine heroic genres and further consolidates the novel's femininity in England. Nevertheless, Huet suggests a native pride in the conditions of France

---

[70] Mary Pix, *The Inhumane Cardinal: or, Innocence Betray'd* (London, 1696) facsimile, intro. Constance Clark (Delmar, New York: Scholars' Facsimiles & Reprints, 1984), np.

[71] Huet, *Sur l'Origine des Romans* (1670), trans. Stephen Lewis, in I. Williams, *Novel and Romance*, p. 52.

that promote the genre: "We owe (I believe) this Advantage to the Refinement and Politeness of our Gallantry; which proceeds, in my Opinion, from the great Liberty which the Men of France allow to the Ladies."[72] The aim of the romance, for Huet, is the representation of love, and he reasons that the greater interaction between men and women provides the means to produce a more probable fiction. Hence gallantry, for Huet, establishes the grounds for verisimilitude or the formal standard of the genre.

Huet's confirmation of the role of gallantry in the foundation of the novel theorizes and legitimates the genre's fundamental interest in female sexuality and suggests the extent to which English conventions in this form are influenced by French precedent. Moreover, Huet's explanation of the nature of French gallantry discloses the male authority in the purportedly feminine genre. Even as he intimates the generosity of Frenchmen to their women, he reinforces the idea that men retain the right to control women's speech: the men "allow" the ladies to talk. Gallantry, conventionally represented in battle imagery, is coded as a gendered struggle over control of the female body:

> But in France, the Ladies go at large upon their own Parole; and being under no Custody but that of their own Heart, erect it into a Fort, more strong and secure than all the Keys, Grates, and Vigilance of the Douegnas. The Men are obliged to make a Regular and Formal Assault against this Fort, to employ so much Industry and Address to reduce it, that they have formed it into an Art scarce known to other Nations.[73]

The art of fiction, presumably, mimics this art of seduction, depicted as the male conquest, capture, or occupation of the female. Huet suggests that a good romance literally empowers the male reader in his pursuit of female prey. His construction of the genre exposes the phallocentrism of the fictional discourse, codifying the ends of fiction as male access to female sexuality.

Huet's essay offers an explanation for the complicated gendering of fictional genres in England. The language of gallantry provides a crucial framework for the critical construction of the early novel and authorizes a paradigm of masculine control over feminine subjects. Critical discourse adopts a ritualized form of compliment that reproduces the dynamic of heterosexual negotiation. The apparent femininity of the discourse, established through the exaggerated female presence in prefatory matter, is deployed through this masculine rhetoric that is

---

[72] Ibid.   [73] Ibid., p. 53.

aimed to flatter the female reader, but the pleasing ambiguity provides an illusion of female mastery that masks the conflated commercial and sexual ends of the petitions. Ultimately, the masculine authority, dialogically invoked through languages of heterosexuality, aligns control of the pen with mastery of the phallus, a conventional metonymy that symbolically governs all feminine discourse in patriarchal society.[74] Within the context of masculine authority, the genre remains the site of female sexuality, and its critical definition is thus ideologically situated. Huet's description of romance as "Fictions of Love Adventures, disposed into an Elegant Style in Prose, for the Delight and Instruction of the Reader" may be taken as a theoretical standard for fiction in its formative stages.[75] With its emphasis on love, private subjectivity, pleasure, female readers, and didacticism, this criticism of the novel dialogically intersects the regulatory languages of female sexuality.

CLASSICAL STRATEGIES

While feminine constructions of the novel primarily involve the moral or erotic discourses of the body, attempts to hypothesize its formal features tend to draw on classical theories of mimesis from Aristotle and his commentators. Although in retrospect it might seem equally appropriate for critics to find formal parallels for fiction in the feminine genres of love poetry, pastorals, or social letters, the Restoration or eighteenth-century critic is more likely to adopt masculine precedents from epic and drama, though in vague and tentative ways. Twentieth-century assessments of criticism on the novel before Henry Fielding tend to be disparaging, precisely because the formal criteria are unclear and unreliable. Fielding's revision of classical precedents in his outline of the "new province of writing" earns him an inflated reputation for influence in the critical theory of the novel.[76] Early critical strategies actually incorporate

---

[74] Sandra M. Gilbert and Susan Gubar, *The Madwoman in the Attic: The Woman Writer and the Nineteenth-Century Literary Imagination* (New Haven: Yale University Press, 1979), pp. 3–7.

[75] Huet, *Sur l'Origine des Romans*, in I. Williams, *Novel and Romance*, p. 46.

[76] Scott Elledge explains the absence of criticism on the novel in his standard collection of eighteenth-century criticism by its "primitive state": "nothing written on the theory of the novel during the eighteenth century approaches in worth or interest Fielding's essays, to be found in every copy of *Joseph Andrews* and *Tom Jones*," *Eighteenth-Century Critical Essays*, 2 vols. (Ithaca: Cornell University Press, 1961), vol. 1, p. x. I. Williams contends that early critical formulations are particularly uncertain: "until 1740 no single work had appeared which contained a coherent and integral design and which could claim to be treated seriously by its readers," *Novel and Romance*, p. 7. J. Paul Hunter is unique in his reassessment of the classical formal criteria of the genre, which, he claims, obscure or underemphasize a number of unique features that actually constitute formal distinctions: *Before Novels*, p. 30. Representative articles on Fielding's critical role

a pendulum-like dialogism that simultaneously aims to distinguish fiction from epic and tragedy while it relies on their structures for definition. Critical justifications of the novel also invoke the hegemonic purposes of pleasure and instruction, following the Horatian dictate. In the process, many writers gesture toward the "rules" as evidence of their fulfilling conventional literary expectations. This composite of critical strategies forms an alternative and competing set of literary priorities that establishes a context of masculine scholarly authority for the novel.

Huet's expression of the differences between romances and epics provides a useful example of the stylistic and thematic distinctions widely recognized between the two forms. For Huet, unlike his counterparts in England, the two types of literature carry equal cultural significance. Notably, his comparisons – translated in 1715 by Lewis – participate in a gendered critical discourse similar to Dryden's. With an allusion to Petronius, Huet claims that epics "move in a great Circumference by the Ministry of Gods and Expressions vast and audacious," while "romances preserve a much greater Simplicity, and are not so exalted, nor have the same Figures in Invention and Expression."[77] Huet identifies the language and topical parameters of the epic with a masculine sense of loftiness and grandeur that the simple and unadorned romance lacks. However, he discovers in the absence of formal features a source of fiction's imaginative potential. Epics are "more regular and correct" in conforming to established conventions, but romances, "because their Style is not so elevated, and they don't so far distend the Intellect . . . admit a greater Number of different ideas."[78] Huet suggests that the lack of mental rigor enables the relative freedom of the newer genre, but his assessment also aligns intellectual material with the classical and masculine tradition and the more entertaining but frivolous content with the tradition of romance. The distinction is consistent with the formulations of the novel that emphasize discourses that regulate the female body. Epics, on the other hand, depict the public, masculine body and its martial performance: they "make some Military Act, or Politic Conduct, their Theme, and only descant upon Love at Pleasure; whereas Romances, on the contrary, have Love for their Principal Subject, and don't concern themselves in War or Politicks, but by Accident."[79] In his

include Richmond Croom Beatty, "Criticism in Fielding's Narratives and His Estimate of Critics," *PMLA* 49 (1934), 1087–1102, and John J. Burke, "History without History: Henry Fielding's Theory of Fiction," in Donald Kay, ed., *A Provision of Human Nature: Essays on Fielding and Others in Honor of Miriam Austin Locke* (University of Alabama Press, 1977), pp. 45–63.
77 Huet, *Sur l'Origine des Romans*, in I. Williams, *Novel and Romance*, p. 47.   78 Ibid.
79 Ibid.

neat opposition between the formally established, lofty poetic of war and the unconventional, simple, and pleasing prose tale of love, Huet's binary acknowledges the gendered terms of the literary debate in which the formation of the novel takes part. On British soil, however, the comparison involves a greater disparity of worth, principally because the British literary tradition before the mid-eighteenth century attaches higher value to the formal difficulty, heroic subject, and elevated style of the epic.

Broad allusions to classical literature in the prefaces to fiction testify to the ancient tradition's prestige. In his epistle to the reader, prefixed to the translation of *Astrea*, J.D. creates a loose taxonomy by putting his romance in proximity with the Ancients: "Of all the Books that Mankind hath convers'd with, since it was first refin'd by Letters, none hath contributed so much to the civilization thereof, or gaind that esteeme and Authority with it, as those of Poetry, by which terme I meane, FICTION, in the largest extent. Under this, are comprehended the highest & noblest productions of man's wit, ROMANCES."[80] J.D. might have specified Aristotle as an authority for such claims, as Huet was to do several years later, but he establishes the classification instead by borrowing terms from ancient poetry and attenuating their meaning to incorporate the romance.[81] If J.D. stands for John Dryden, as James Winn suggests, then his ambiguity appears to be by choice rather than from ignorance.[82] J.D. appropriates the "esteeme and Authority" of the Ancients through his dialogism with classical discourse, but the vagueness of his appeal simultaneously protects that tradition. Roger Boyle's reference to the Ancients is slightly less nebulous. In his highly ambivalent preface to *Parthenissa* Boyle calls Virgil's *Aeneid* a "Romance in Numbers," using a conventional shorthand for the classical heritage J.D. describes.[83] Although Boyle is unconvinced of the fiction's worthiness, he does admit that his "way of writing Romances is less ill, than any I have yet seene Originaly in our Language."[84] The most problematic aspect is the anachronistic representation of historical characters; however, he justifies this by the precedent of Virgil and his depiction of Dido and Aeneas. By figuring Virgil as a romance writer who likewise commits factual errors, Boyle appears to denigrate the *Aeneid* rather than

---

[80] J.D., preface to d'Urfé, *Astrea*, vol. I, sig. A2^r.
[81] "According to Aristotle (who informs us, That 'tis Fiction rather than Verse which makes a Poet) a Writer of Romance may be reckon'd among the Poets" (I. Williams, *Novel and Romance*, pp. 46–47). Huet alludes to Aristotle's *Poetics*, III and VI.
[82] James A. Winn, *John Dryden and His World* (New Haven: Yale University Press, 1987), p. 147.
[83] Roger Boyle, *Parthenissa*, np.   [84] Ibid.

to commend his own fiction. Both references reveal the desire to fit the prose narrative into a respected and understood tradition, and yet they demonstrate a stubborn incompatibility between the two.

Writers discover a more profitable comparison in the delineation of form. Through the Aristotelian principle of unity of action, de Scudéry claims the epic as her model for *Ibrahim*:

> I have seen in those famous Romanzes of Antiquity, that in the Epique Poem there is a principal action whereunto all the rest, which reign over all the work, are fastned, and which makes them that they are not employed, but for the conducting of it to its perfection . . . Now those great Geniusses of antiquity, from whom I borrow my light, knowing that well-ordering is one of the principal parts of a piece, have given so excellent a one to their speaking Pictures, that it would be as much stupidity, as pride, not to imitate them.[85]

De Scudéry, or Cogan her translator, makes the conventional gesture toward a classical lineage by labeling the epic "Romanzes of Antiquity," but she elaborates the comparison by privileging the unified plot. De Scudéry's appeal reinscribes the cultural esteem for the classical tradition while it attempts to co-opt a legitimacy for the romance through the appropriation of order. Interestingly, it is in the lack of conformity to such rules that Huet finds the differences between epics and romances most advantageous to the prose fiction. De Scudéry, however, establishes her aesthetic authority by imitating hegemonic literary value, and her assimilation of the precedent reveals little of the ambivalence expressed by J.D. and Boyle. Her reference to the structure of plot anticipates the more famous British criticism by Congreve and Fielding, but again her identification with the "great Geniusses of Antiquity" demonstrates a greater ease with the comparison than either of those writers achieves. For de Scudéry there is a consistency of form and dignity in the two genres, which it would be an error of pride and stupidity not to recognize. Ironically, de Scudéry, whom Fielding uses as a negative example in his preface to *Joseph Andrews*, exemplifies the critical strategy that discursively enables Fielding's rejection of romances in favor of a classical form for the novel.

William Congreve's famous preface to *Incognita* (1692) adopts an authorizing tactic similar to de Scudéry's, but he uses the terms of dramatic criticism rather than heroic poetry. Initially, Congreve offers the now well-known distinction between romances and novels: the

---

[85] de Scudéry, *Ibrahim*, pp. 2–3.

former are "generally composed of the constant loves and invincible courages of heroes, heroines, kings and queens . . . [with] lofty language, miraculous contingencies and impossible performances," while "Novels," he claims, "are of a more familiar nature; come near us and represent to us intrigues in practice."[86] His critical gesture distances the home-grown British fiction from the invasion of French narratives and sets up categories of prose fiction based on truth claims and style. Still, he appeals to legitimate critical classifications to shore up his divisions: "And with reverence be it spoken, and the Parallel kept at due distance; there is something of equality in the Proportion which [romances and novels] bear in reference to one another, with that between Comedy and Tragedy."[87] Congreve's playful analogy suggests that the form of his novel differs as much in gravity and respect from the romance as tragedy does from comedy, but this is a comparison that he is unwilling or unable to articulate further. Instead, he shifts focus to the superiority of the stage.

Since all Traditions must indisputably give place to the Drama, and since there is no possibility of giving that life to the Writing or Repetition of a Story which it has in the Action, I resolved in another beauty to imitate Dramatick Writing, namely, in the Design, Contexture and Result of the Plot. I have not observed it before in a novel.[88]

He seems conscious of both the originality of his creative enterprise and the impropriety of it. He desires the identification with honored literary precedent, and he simultaneously resists it by reinscribing the hierarchical supremacy of drama. Although Congreve argues for the formal distinction between novels and romances, he ultimately establishes the order of the novel on the same grounds as those works he disparages. Like de Scudéry, Congreve structures his fiction according to the principle of unity:

I leave the reader at his leisure to consider, as also whether every obstacle does not, in the progress of the story, act as subservient to that purpose which at first it seems to oppose. In a comedy, this would be called the unity of action; here it may pretend to no more than an unity of contrivance.[89]

Congreve sets out to create a compelling narrative that surprises without shocking, and while he derives the organizational premise from the theatre, he yet does not make a complete identification with that superior artistic form. Action, apparently, takes place on the stage; the plot of his narrative is only contrivance. Congreve's alternating respect for an

---

[86] William Congreve, preface to *Incognita* (1692), in Paul Salzman, ed., *An Anthology of Seventeenth-Century Fiction* (Oxford: Oxford University Press, 1991), p. 474.
[87] Ibid.   [88] Ibid.   [89] Ibid., p. 475.

established aesthetic and boldness in invention and appropriation is characteristic of the difficulties early critics discovered in trying to assert a formal identity for unruly prose discourse; it is likewise symptomatic of the official statements of paternity for the strikingly feminine genre.

Such attempts at formal definition clearly indicate the author's desire to participate in sanctioned critical dialogue, and these discursive gestures are not restricted by sex. Female subjects as well as male dignify their productions by association with traditional authority. So Mary Davys introduces her narratives with a nod toward the rules of dramatic theory: "I have in every novel proposed one entire scheme or plot, and the other adventures are only incidental or collateral to it, which is the great rule prescribed by the critics, not only in tragedy and other heroic poems, but in comedy too."[90] The fact that Davys' claim relies on Aristotelian notions of unity without specific attribution indicates the pervasiveness of the ideas in her culture. The authorizing gesture has reached a level of abstraction that makes it available to those who are not classically educated, a cultural permissiveness lamented by astute critics like Addison, Swift, and Pope.

Beyond the impropriety of a female novelist appropriating the erudite masculine discourse, Davys' preface holds particular interest because its heteroglot strategies signify the conflicting directions of gendered criticism in the early novel. Her appeal to the rules, classically constituted and dispersed through the common channels of literary discourse, indicates the universality of the fiction; her claim suggests that her novels follow the pattern of ancient tragedies and epics before them. At the same time, though, she authorizes her novel through the discursive representation of her female body. She calls one novel the "brat of my brain," invested with maternal care, and she figures herself as the "relic of a clergyman and in years," desperate for monetary sustenance. Her fiction is itself involved in the regulation of female sexuality: "My whole design . . . is to endeavor to restore the purity and empire of love, and correct the vile abuses of it."[91] She constitutes her function as author in terms of normative female roles defined by the body – mother and wife – and she conveys the didactic purpose of her fiction as the reiteration and dissemination of hegemonic domestic codes. The feminine discourses with which the novel is defined involve an immanent particularity discursively fixed to the female body, and this concrete discourse of presence conflicts with the universal implications

[90] McBurney, ed., *Four Before Richardson*, pp. 235–236.   [91] Ibid., p. 236.

of classical authority. Because the critical gestures from a masculine tradition, invested in the transcendence of history and of the body, involve the repression of feminine particularity, critical prefaces like Davys' embody an ideological contradiction characteristic of a new genre of uncertain status.

Mary Delarivière Manley's preface to *The Secret History of Queen Zarah* is a more sophisticated analysis of the novel, but it, too, is representative of the gendered contest in critical discourse. Like Congreve, she distinguishes her work – "Little Histories of this Kind" – from the previously fashionable French romances, and she draws on the Aristotelian theories of drama made popular by French neoclassicists. The preface rates historical novels of probability more highly than the inflated rhetoric and artificial characters of older romances, because the former allow the reader to share the characters' emotions: "For fear and Pity in Romance as well as Tragedies are the two Instruments which move the Passion."[92] Her neoclassical reference relies on Aristotle's prescription for mimetic art rather than for unity of action, but nonetheless it locates her criticism of the novel in the discourse of established literary value, and she measures the success of realistic narratives according to the prestigious genre of tragedy. Her gesture, like other attempts to appropriate the definition of classical genres, constructs authority via literary paternity and attempts to universalize the design of her fiction.

Manley's appeal to classical authority is similarly conventional. However developed her critical discussion may be, her ostensible principles hardly apply to *The Secret History of Queen Zarah*, an elliptically written *roman-à-clef* with obvious political intentions. This discrepancy can also be explained by another, more direct appropriation at work in Manley's authorship, one that underscores the gendered dialogism of critical discourses. John L. Sutton discovered that Manley actually translated a section of a French courtesy book written by Morvan de Bellegarde, *Lettres curieuses de littérature et de morale* (1702), which in turn was a paraphrase of the sieur du Plaisir's *Sentimens sur les lettres et sur l'histoire* (1683).[93] The original French criticism of "petites histoires" refers not to the "chronique scandeleuse," a more probable forerunner to Manley's prose form, but to the "nouvelle" best represented by Mme. de Lafayette's *La Princesse de Clèves* (1678). Manley's translation of the text

[92] Mary Delarivière Manley, preface to *The Secret History of Queen Zarah* (1705) in Benjamin Boyce, ed. and intro. Augustan Reprint Society 32 (Los Angeles: University of California Press, 1952), np.
[93] John L. Sutton, "The Source of Mrs. Manley's Preface to *Queen Zarah*," *Modern Philology* (November 1984), 167–172.

from the pages of a French courtesy book designed for the ladies attests to the genre's profound connection to female subjectivity and with feminine discourses that regulate the private and subjective. The fact that the critical work doubles as advice for contemporary female subjects suggests an ideological orientation at odds with the universalizing assumptions of the masculine classical heritage. Although it asserts official forms of literary authority in order to legitimate the novel, Manley's criticism primarily addresses the subjectivity of the reader, who is at once impatient and in need of moral edification. Manley's preface thus manifests the interaction of two founding impulses in the criticism of the early novel, the masculine appeal to classical authority and the reliance on discourses of female conduct.

Manley's and du Plaisir's sensitivity to the enjoyment and edification of their audiences exemplifies a standard capitulation to the rules of literary discourse. The prevailing understanding of literary pragmatism during the eighteenth century derives from the writings of Horace, who recommends instruction as well as pleasure – dulce et utile. These goals consequently become the universal criteria of legitimation for novel-writers and provide access to the classical grounds of authority. The general appeals for profit and delight that suffuse all aspects of the literary discourse of the time reiterate a cultural desire, staking a literary territory of viability and providing the critical means to honor or dismiss a work. Some, like Blackamore, consider these desiderata self-evident: "If I understand the nature of novels aright, the design of them in general is much the same with that of poetry – to profit and delight the reader."[94] Like the broad allusions to a classical heritage, these undefined claims amount to little more than critical postures, which nonetheless signify the cultural sway of this transcendent gesture.

Other writers and critics of fiction, though, are quick to appreciate the subjective nature of these criteria, and so widen the scope of what it means to please and to educate in order to defend the romantic or licentious nature of their novels. Writers like Mackenzie and Eliza Haywood justify their work as the purveyors of important sexual knowledge. Mackenzie insists that the idealization of virtue in the romance will counteract his readers' otherwise lewd inclinations: "by these likewise lazy Ladies and luxurious Gallants, are allured to spend in their Chambers some hours, which else, the one would consecrat[e] to the Bed, and the other to the Bordell."[95] He contends further that

[94] Arthur Blackamore, *Luck at Last; or, The Happy Unfortunate*, reprint, in McBurney, ed., *Four Before Richardson*, p. 4.   [95] Mackenzie, *Aretina*, p. 7.

reading will develop the faculty of reason: "that so the curiosity might be satisfied, as well as the judgement informed."[96] Haywood, aware of the gendered complications of her position as author, defends herself against an "Aspersion which some of my own Sex have been unkind enough to throw upon me, that 'I seem to endeavour to divert more than *improve* the Minds of my Readers'."[97] She claims that her novel tends "at least to a good Moral use," but she insists that if her readers fail to see the instruction, that is owing to her success in the other novelistic requirement, to wit, "a true Description of Nature." Haywood's cavalier response to the moral dictates of the critical discourse indicates the recognized authority of the Horatian criteria as well as the flexibility of the early fictional criticism that allows for their subversion. Her prefatory advertisement of the novel promises profit and delight, but her irony suggests the erotic, rather than the moral, nature of that satisfaction.

In another context, however, Haywood expresses the normative value of fictional representations of love, especially for the sexual education of naive female readers:

[S]ometimes 'tis necessary . . . to be reminded that there have been Men so base; our Sex is of it self so weak, especially when we suffer what little share of Reason we have to be debilitated by Passion, that we stand in need of all the Helps we can procure to defend us from becoming the Victim of our own Softness.[98]

By teaching readers to distinguish the worth of a suitor, Haywood suggests, these novels perform a very vital function in the regulation of female sexuality. Her evaluation thus adapts the universal goals of judgment and learning – two categories of definitive literary value – to the feminine field of knowledge that the novel investigates.

The novel's role in policing female sexuality provides the means of credibility and literary justification for Samuel Richardson's *Pamela; Or, Virtue Rewarded* (1741). In an overstatement of the goals to divert and entertain, instruct and improve, delight and profit, Richardson insists, in the voice of the editor, that the letters that follow will "inculcate religion and morality" and "paint VICE in its proper colours."[99] Specifically, he represents the novel as a pedagogical text to "teach a man of fortune how

[96] Ibid.
[97] Eliza Haywood, dedication of *Lasselia; or the Self Abandon'd. A Novel* (1723), in I. Williams, *Novel and Romance*, p. 79.
[98] Eliza Haywood, from "The Tea-Table, or a Conversation between some Polite Persons of both sexes at a Lady's Visiting Day" (1725) in I. Williams, *Novel and Romance*, p. 82.
[99] Samuel Richardson, *Pamela; Or, Virtue Rewarded*, ed. Peter Sabor, intro. Margaret Doody (London: Penguin, 1980), p. 31.

to *use* it; the man of *passion* how to *subdue* it; and the man of *intrigue*, how, gracefully, and with honour to himself, to *reclaim* . . . [and to] give *practical* examples, worthy to be followed in the most *critical* and *affecting* cases, by the *virgin*, the *bride*, and the *wife*."[100] In other words, the novel satisfies conventional literary standards through a didactic representation of proper heterosexual activity. The critical legitimations offered by Haywood and Richardson assume and reiterate a construction of gender in which the female subject is vulnerable to male exploitation, and the representation of glorified female chastity becomes the epitome of literary quality. Claims for readers' profit and delight blend into gallant gestures to legislate feminine subjectivity, thus rendering the particular and individualized discourse of female sexuality universal. The examples of Haywood and Richardson suggest that writers interested in securing a legitimate place for fiction adopted various and sometimes contradictory authorizing strategies. Their appeals to the Horatian or Aristotelian rules appropriate the intellectual authority associated with the male tradition of letters, and their insistence on the moral instruction of the reader through the mimesis of normative heterosexual behavior reveals the negotiation of literary value as the discursive regulation of female sexuality. The consistency between the two separate but overlapping conventions is the masculine designation of the authorizing gesture.

Henry Fielding's critical writings on the novel aim to clarify some of these ambiguities. People have generally recognized in Fielding's first novel, *Joseph Andrews* (1742), a satiric exposure of and corrective to the simplistic projection of morality in *Pamela*.[101] The famous preface to that work has long been viewed as the seminal piece of eighteenth-century criticism on fiction, in part because of Fielding's claim to provide that "which I do not remember to have seen hitherto attempted in our language."[102] Rather than initiate an entirely original critical discourse, the preface actually realizes much of the potential expressed by the early and ambiguous critical gestures toward classical authority. And, just as the novel itself responds to Richardson's femino-centric and reductive concern with chastity, Fielding's prototypical critical gestures define a tradition for the novel separate from the immanent and particular discourses of feminine sexuality.

Fielding establishes his literary authority through a detached and

---

[100] Ibid.
[101] See the "General Introduction" by Martin C. Battestin in Henry Fielding, *Joseph Andrews*, ed. Battestin (Middleton: Wesleyan University Press, 1967), esp. pp. xv–xxiv.
[102] Fielding, *Joseph Andrews*, p. 3.

ironic voice that demonstrates with ease the taxonomic precision and artistic design of his "comic Epic-Poem in Prose."[103] His irony destabilizes the classical categories as he invokes them, and indicates that although he cites the recognized figures, this may not be the same hackneyed parade of the rules. Like so many authors before him, Fielding outlines a literary paternity for his novel in direct decent from the Ancients, but he humorously chooses a missing document as his forbear: "The Epic, as well as the Drama, is divided into Tragedy and Comedy. *Homer*, who was the Father of this Species of Poetry, gave us a Pattern of both these, tho' that of the latter kind is entirely lost; which *Aristotle* tells us, bore the same relation to Comedy which his *Iliad* bears to Tragedy." Fielding's ingenious argument at once appropriates the authority of Augustan heavyweights, while the lack of actual precedent allows him room for invention. He uses the epic as a model but freely adapts its definition to fit his literary design:

[A]s this poetry may be tragic or comic, I will not scruple to say it may be likewise either in verse or prose: for though it wants one particular, which the critic enumerates in the constituent parts of an epic poem, namely metre; yet, when any kind of writing contains all its other parts, such as fable, action, characters, sentiments, and diction, and is deficient in metre only, it seems I think, reasonable to refer it to the epic.[104]

Fielding's half-serious enumeration of the parts his novel will share puts him in direct contrast with Huet, who claims that the simple romance avoids the elevated language and formal conventions of the epic. The extent of his classical formalism distinguishes Fielding's critical construction of the novel and places it squarely within the masculine tradition of letters.

Indeed, he takes pains to suppress any connection with the French romance so praised by Huet:

[I]t is much fairer and more reasonable to give it a Name common with that Species [the epic] from which it differs only in a single Instance, than to confound it with those which it resembles in no other. Such are those voluminous Works, commonly called Romances, namely, *Clelia*, *Cleopatra*, *Astrea*, *Cassandra*, the *Grand Cyrus*, and innumerable others which contain, as I apprehend, very little Instruction or Entertainment.[105]

Although he suggests a fundamental formal difference between his "comic Romance" and those multi-volume fictions favored by the ladies, his argument is really based on epistemological and gendered grounds. By applying the Horatian standards, "aut prodesse aut

---

[103] Ibid., p. 4.   [104] Ibid., p. 3.   [105] Ibid., pp. 3–4.

delectare," he rejects the romance, but these are the very grounds on which romancers like Mackenzie, Haywood, and Richardson justify their fiction. One needs to ask in reference to those criteria: instruction and entertainment for whom? For authors who write and respond "to the Ladies," the answer involves the perceived needs and ideological norms of the middle-class female audience. That novel is evaluated in terms of its discursive regulation of female sexuality. Fielding clearly wants to identify a different audience. As he explains with regard to his verbal satires, which are "not necessary to be pointed out to the Classical Reader; for whose Entertainment those Parodies or Burlesque Imitations are chiefly calculated," he aims to please and edify an elite, classically educated audience, which would be historically constituted as male.

By reading Fielding's preface in a context of the competing critical strategies in the early discourse of the novel, I want to argue two contested points. First, with respect to Armstrong's dismissal of Fielding's attempts to place the genre within a classical, masculine context, he is not nearly as anomalous as she suggests.[106] Many early writers of prose fiction identify the epic and tragedy as their structural or aesthetic precedent through an appeal to the Aristotelian notions of mimesis and unified action. Men and women seek to garner from the hegemonic literary tradition a similar respect for their works, and these gestures reinscribe the value of the classics as they attempt to identify a literary space for the novel. Richardson himself appeals directly to Aristotle in his defense of tragedy in the Postscript to *Clarissa*. Consequently, the view that Fielding initiates a classical theory of the novel needs to be revised. While Fielding brings to the definition of the genre a flexible formalism achieved through an ironic relationship to classical heritage, he nonetheless manipulates a set of conventions already established in literary discourse. The conflicting critical impulses of the early discourse on the novel constitute the grounds of possibility for Fielding's sophisticated dialogism; his criticism incorporates the languages of Augustan satire, epic form and, through contrast and nullification, the feminized romance.

The identification of a classical heritage for the novel invokes an intellectual masculine authority to be distinguished from the patriarchal discourses regulating the feminine subject. The critical strategies that explicitly involve the negotiation of female sexuality – the conventions of gallantry, the edification of a female audience, the reproduction of normative sexual values – likewise constitute the grounds of masculine

---

[106] Armstrong, *Desire and Domestic Fiction*, p. 32; discussed on pp. 82–83.

authority for the production and judgment of the text. So, despite a literary justification that is essentially female-centered, the novel, unlike other literary productions, falls doubly under the jurisdiction of masculine authority. The critical construction of the novel embodies this ideological contradiction, which ultimately leaves the literary status of the genre in limbo. After 1740 the production of the novel escalates across the culture, and the critical apparatus becomes more sophisticated, with regular publications of reviews and essays.[107] As many feminist scholars have demonstrated, from 1740 onward female novelists gain a foothold in the literary marketplace, and some achieve fame. Further, Jane Spencer argues that by mid-century the cultural notions of sensibility, best exemplified in the feeling and morality of the domestic female, begin to influence critical values:

The moral utility of literature was an all-pervasive concern of eighteenth-century critics; modesty in the writer and his work was becoming an important term of praise; and simplicity and spontaneity in writing became greatly admired as the century progressed. What was happening, in fact, was that the properly "feminine" and the properly "literary" were both being redefined along the same lines.[108]

Yet, as Spencer and others note, such consistency between the literary and the feminine generally confines the female author to a circumscribed field of experience. Furthermore, the critical terms mirror these constructions of femininity through the inflected language of gallantry, the ambiguity of which leaves the skill and expertise of the female writer largely in question.[109] Masculine values of literature, on the other hand, with the emphasis on judgment, intellect, and imagination in their universal and transcendent manifestations, did not confer a similarly restraining identification for male authors.

　　With a few notable exceptions, the numerous novels published after Richardson and Fielding and before Jane Austen have generally been viewed as a bad lot, and one for which women are chiefly responsible. Watt concedes that "the majority of eighteenth-century novels were actually written by women, but this had long remained a purely quantitative assertion of dominance."[110] Terry Castle phrases the assessment as a rhetorical question: "How bad are most of the novels

---

[107] See Antonia Forster, Introduction, *Index to Book Reviews in England, 1749–1774* (Carbondale: Southern Illinois University Press, 1990), pp. 3–18.

[108] Spencer, *Rise of the Woman Novelist*, p. 77.

[109] Todd, *The Sign of Angellica*, p. 127, and Poovey, *The Proper Lady*, p. 39.

[110] Watt, *Rise of the Novel*, p. 298.

produced by English women writers in the decades before Jane Austen? Sad to say, just when one thinks one has read the very worst of them, another comes along to send one's spirits plummeting further."[111] Both suggest, though in very different ways, that gender contributes to this vexed relationship between author and the emerging genre. For Watt, "feminine sensibility" is uniquely qualified for the introspection and observation required of formal realism, which, for him, explains the success of Austen and, even, Richardson.[112] He does not, or cannot, explain why men seem so much more adept at the genre before Austen. Castle, on the other hand, identifies an aesthetically debilitating Oedipal struggle in the first generations of female novelists who wrest the power of expression from those who own the language, namely powerful men. Although it is not my intention to evaluate those novels, I want to suggest that the historical constitution of literary value in the formative stages of the genre provides some valuable insights for those who do.

The traditional landmark authors of the eighteenth-century novel – Defoe, Richardson, Fielding, Smollett, Sterne, and sometimes Burney – are overwhelmingly male, but the territory outside of these is persistently feminized. The inferiority of the novel, in the larger literary landscape, and its femininity become dialogically reinforcing, as the critical discourse defines the genre through two separate but related gendered strategies. The novel's femininity is constituted thematically by its concern with and regulation of feminine sexuality, whether erotic or puritanical; it is conveyed through a variety of textual conventions including the prefatory address to a female audience, accommodations of feminine style, conflation of reader and heroine, and metonymic displacement of the text with the female body. Rather than lead to the locus of female authority as Watt and Armstrong suggest, such inscriptions of gender actually enable the ideological confinement of femininity through the language of gallantry and the dynamic of patriarchal control. Early critical commentary codifies the role of novelist – or critic – as a masculine prerogative, and such perceptions provide the conditions of possibility for male expertise in the feminized genre. Concurrently, the critical discourse on the novel appropriates the authority and prestige of the masculine tradition of classical literature through primarily superficial claims; this uneasy relationship both reifies a sense of privilege associated with the masculine literary authority and

[111] Terry Castle, "Sublimely Bad – Review of *Secresy*," *The London Review of Books*, 23 Feb. 1995, pp. 18–19.
[112] Watt, *Rise of the Novel*, p. 298; see also chap. 5, pp. 135–174.

confirms the novel's subordinate status. Together, these early critical
tactics provide a clear masculine context for the developing genre that
adumbrates the canon-making decisions of the nineteenth and twentieth
centuries.

CHAPTER 4

Aristotle's sisters: Behn, Lennox, Fielding, and Reeve

> Criticism is a goddess easy of access and forward of advance, who
> will meet the slow and encourage the timorous.   Johnson[1]

The unprecedented increase in the practice of criticism during the
eighteenth century spawns numerous satires that, like Samuel Johnson's
famous Dick Minim papers, express anxiety over who has the right to
perform such cultural arbitration. Johnson opens this issue of the *Idler*
with a list of qualifications, ironically expressed as the standards that
culture apparently neglects:

Criticism is a study by which men grow important and formidable at a very
small expense. The power of invention has been conferred by nature upon few,
and the labour of learning those sciences which may, by mere labour, be obtained,
is too great to be willingly endured; but every man can exert such judgment as
he has upon the works of others; and he whom nature has made weak, and
idleness keeps ignorant, may yet support his vanity by the name of a critick.[2]

The satire suggests that especially bad writers can still be critics, and this
democratic access to criticism necessitates its qualitative decline. That
which distinguishes good critical work from poor can be read between
the lines: an inherent sense of invention, fostered by learning, curbed by
judgment, and sustained by strength of mind – the definitive, masculine
qualities of literature. Dick Minim represents the threat of an under-
educated literate populace gaining the leisure to pursue vanity under the
guise of wit. Johnson may deride Minim's "common course of puerile
studies," as well as the middle-class respectability he acquires when he
inherits his father's fortune, but the story of Minim underscores the
gendered conditions of possibility for the self-made critic. In terms of
social and economic history, Minim shares the same window of

---

[1] Samuel Johnson, *The Idler and The Adventurer*, ed. W. J. Bate, John M. Bullitt, L. F. Powell, *The Yale Edition of the Works of Samuel Johnson*, 16 vols. (New Haven: Yale University Press, 1963), vol. II, p. 185.
[2] Ibid., pp. 184–185.

opportunity as the female critics of the eighteenth century; yet, neither formal schooling nor economic independence, however obtained, is generally available to eighteenth-century women. Furthermore, Minim supplements his education of letters in the public forums of the pit and the coffeehouse, two arenas in which the proper lady could not gain an audience. Johnson's satire on Minim calls into question the authority of the literary critic, illustrating the need for rigorous judgment to establish order in the expanding print realm, but the example also suggests the extent to which even bad critical practice is a privilege of male experience.

Unlike Minim, the female critic faces fundamental obstacles in the gendered construction of the faculties of judgment and intellect. With the advent of the novel and the rising numbers of published women writers, the province of literature by mid-century no longer signifies an exclusively masculine preserve; however, the right to judge that discourse retains and, in fact, is further consolidated as a gendered privilege through the restrictive means of constructing authority. As Johnson's satire indicates, criticism is stratified according to the critic's demonstration of solid knowledge of the classics and "human nature," and an accurate judgment informed by the rules of taste. Within a patriarchal context, a woman's access to authority is automatically suspect, and so her exercise of judgment is similarly questioned. The mid-century discourse of polite femininity grants women expertise in a unique private epistemological realm, specifically manifest in issues of romance, emotion, morality, and education of the young. Nonetheless, this domestic orientation does not accord to women a liberal knowledge of the world and the contingent right to judge.

In fact, as feminist criticism has demonstrated, eighteenth-century discourses dictate a version of femininity at odds with the fundamental activities of learning and judgment. Through the unifying image of pure, pleasing womanhood, discourse posits the ideal woman as a source of moral authority and domestic peace. According to Ellen Messer-Davidow, the conduct literature of the late eighteenth century uniformly legislates against female judgment. The male-authored texts she investigates project a dichotomously gendered universe in which mental as well as physical traits correspond to sexual difference. Whereas men cultivate the strength of reason to fit them for the role of critic, women develop their "natural softness and sensibility," and are repeatedly encouraged to follow male judgment, especially in literature.[3] Educational programs

---

[3] Ellen Messer-Davidow, " 'For Softness She': Gender Ideology and Aesthetics in Eighteenth-Century England," in Frederick M. Keener and Susan E. Lorsch, eds., *Eighteenth-Century Women and the Arts*, Contributions to Women's Studies no. 98 (New York: Greenwood Press, 1988), p. 46. She draws

similarly correspond to gender, restricting women to studies on domestic activity, self-adornment, and subservience, as opposed to male learning in letters. At the same time, weakness and frailty become unique signs of feminine sensitivity and a source of sexual attraction.[4]

Mary Poovey argues that the cultural hegemony of this "proper lady" emerges only by the last decade of the eighteenth century, and is the result of a confluence of economic, religious, and political developments. However, this image of idealized innocence and subordination, Poovey contends, exists throughout the century and operates as the normative goal for women, if not their biological destiny.[5] The configuration of a soft and emotionally volatile female nature radically diminishes the potential for reason and judgment; it highlights a feminine aptitude for feeling and "exquisite sensibility," but it undermines the capacity for learning and complex thought. In other words, the negotiation of ideal femininity sets women apart from the contested ideal of critical authority. This chapter investigates two contradictory critical "truths" that devolve from the initial gendered conditions of criticism in the eighteenth century: first that there are no female critics from the period, and, second, that the female critics we do recover from the era represent a universal and monolithic female perspective on literature.

The gendering of critical authority contributes to the suppression of female critics during the eighteenth century, but also in the transmission of literary history. As Virginia Woolf recognized in 1928, the gendered dimensions of knowledge contribute directly to the formation of the canonical tradition:

[I]t is obvious that the values of women differ very often from the values which have been made by the other sex; naturally this is so. Yet it is the masculine values that prevail . . . This is an important book, the critic assumes, because it deals with war. This is an insignificant book because it deals with the feelings of women in a drawing-room. A scene in a battlefield is more important than a scene in a shop – everywhere and much more subtly the difference of value persists.[6]

Woolf exposes the dualistic, hierarchical system of literary standards at work in the preference for masculine topics. But in that suggestive final

---

from Dr. John Gregory, *A Father's Legacy to His Daughters* (1774), James Fordyce, *Sermons to Young Women* (1776), Vicesimus Knox, *Essays Moral and Literary* (1778), and John Bennett, *Letters to a Young Lady* (1789).

[4] See Shelley M. Bennett, "Changing Images of Women in Late Eighteenth-Century England: 'The Ladies Magazine' 1770–1810," *Arts Magazine* 55 (May 1981), 138–141.

[5] Mary Poovey, *The Proper Lady and the Woman Writer: Ideology as Style in the Works of Mary Wollstonecraft, Mary Shelley, and Jane Austen* (Chicago: University of Chicago Press, 1984), pp. 3–14.

[6] Virginia Woolf, *A Room of One's Own* (San Diego: Harcourt, Brace Jovanovich Publishers, 1929), p. 77.

clause – "everywhere and much more subtly the difference of value persists" – Woolf implies that the effects of this masculine privilege extend further. She recognizes that literary criticism, contrary to its detached tone of factuality, does not emerge into the public realm as the neutral expression of aesthetic truth. Criticism serves specific interests. Throughout the essays of *A Room of One's Own*, Woolf refers to the female writer's battle with the critical authority that is gendered male: "that persistent voice, now grumbling, now patronising, now domineering, now grieved, now shocked, now angry, now avuncular, that voice which cannot let women alone, but must be at them."[7] For Woolf, this concentration of male authority in literature leads to two unfortunate consequences. The first is that women have no tradition of their own, a motif that supplies the rationale for some of the pioneering feminist recovery of women authors in the seventies.[8] The inability to find feminine literary values, Woolf suggests, also leads female novelists to distort their writing by conforming to male standards; this assumption of gender-based critical values likewise informs feminist revision of critical practice in this century.

Writing in 1983, Lawrence Lipking speculates a history for Aristotle's sister, Arimneste, in a gesture parallel to Woolf's vision of Judith Shakespeare.[9] Just as Woolf had to imagine a chronicle of female authors in a dearth of textual evidence, so Lipking constructs a conjectural account of "critical mothers." Lipking's suggestive article points to and attempts to deconstruct the critical commonplace (that unfortunately persists) that there are no female critics before Virginia Woolf. The conclusion is easy to reach when most anthologies fail to include the work of female critics before 1930.[10] The fact that representation of early female critics is increasing in specialized texts has not yet dislodged the impression of a critical vacuum in women's early writing.[11]

---

[7] Ibid., p. 78.

[8] The title of Elaine Showalter, *A Literature of Their Own* (London: Virago, 1978) indicates a direct debt to Woolf, but collections like Ellen Moer's *Literary Women* (London: The Women's Press, 1978) answer the same objective by establishing a tradition of female authors.

[9] Lawrence Lipking, "Aristotle's Sister: A Poetics of Abandonment," *Critical Inquiry* 10 (September 1983), 61–81.

[10] L. Lipking cites Hazard Adams, *Critical Theory Since Plato* (Fort Worth: Harcourt Brace Jovanovich, 1971); in the revised edition (1992) Adams includes a six-page excerpt of Mary Wollstonecraft's writings and a seven-page piece by Germaine Necker de Staël. Similarly, David H. Richter, *The Critical Tradition: Classic Texts and Contemporary Trends* (New York: St. Martin's Press, 1989) includes four pages from de Staël as the only representation of women's writing prior to the twentieth century.

[11] For example, Robert Con Davis and Laurie Finke, eds., *Literary Criticism and Theory: The Greeks to the Present* (New York: Longman, 1989) include Aphra Behn, Anne Finch, and Eliza Haywood, among others.

In part, the inability to appreciate the critical contributions of early women writers results from a resistance to the historicity of criticism and the implications for the constructed nature of its authority. Lipking registers this lack of self-consciousness when he claims that "most poetics are not contemptuous but oblivious of women. The mainstream of theory glides over sexual issues without a ripple."[12] Contemporary critical practice inherits the legacy of "disinterestedness," the crowning glory of which is the naming of art that appeals universally and throughout time. Efforts like Woolf's, and more pointedly Lipking's, to expose the critical stance as interested threaten not only the reputation of founding critics, but the status of literature itself. To preserve a notion of literary excellence grounded in what Woolf labels "incandescence" – that state of mind unimpeded by temporal, personal concerns and, hence, universal – both Lipking and Woolf assume that gender operates as a fundamental principle of universal nature; as such the dichotomy of gendered perspectives informs two separate but equally universal traditions of literary value.

Thus, the second critical commonplace that emerges from recent feminist recovery is the assumption that female critics will represent a monolithic or essentialist "female" perspective. Actually, this reaction appears more as a hope and a fear, both of which indicate the lack of knowledge surrounding early female critics. Lipking seems to advance the thesis that Arimneste's progeny will supply a unified and coherent female voice, which, when we finally listen to it, will inform us how women really understood literature: "A patient look at history reveals some consistent patterns in literary criticism by women, as well as some significant differences from the theories of men. As other voices join with Arimneste's, she begins to make herself understood."[13] Like many earlier feminist critics, Lipking defines a "female tradition" at the level of the author or reader. He assumes that women, as women, react to literature in different ways from men; consequently, a critical tradition written by women would rectify the imbalance of the exclusively male-authored tradition.

At the same time he is aware of the limitations of his essentialist assumption. He rightly warns that the retrieval of a female-authored corpus would raise new problems: "its distinction between the sexes, not only biologically but ideologically, will inevitably serve to perpetuate sexual stereotypes."[14] We can push Lipking's concerns further. By

---

[12] L. Lipking, "Aristotle's Sister," p. 62.   [13] Ibid., p. 64.   [14] Ibid.

defining a feminist poetic as criticism written by women, we assume an understanding of gender as biologically determined, and we obscure the potential for other factors – such as class, race, historical conditions – to have an impact on the constitution of value. Erecting a female tradition of criticism presupposes an irreducible sexual binary that implicitly reinscribes the gendered hierarchy and maintains a static notion of literary value already in place. Rather than examine the process through which literary values are established as truth, this secondary tradition masks as sexual opposition the historically contingent power struggles in literary value.

Raising yet another doubt, Lipking tentatively suggests that the specter of a female critical tradition can never be realized: "the notion of a woman's poetics suggests an agreement or uniformity among women that cannot stand the test of history."[15] He reasons from the available knowledge in the history of gender, but the female-authored texts needed to confirm or deny his hypothesis are not yet available to him. Lipking's vacillation between universalizing the female critic and asserting the historical contingency of her production is characteristic of the early stage in the recovery of female critics. This chapter aims to provide specific contexts and assessments of the work of four eighteenth-century female critics in an effort to minimize the ambiguity and prejudice.

Although literary records might suggest otherwise, the act of criticism is not foreclosed to women of the eighteenth century. Rather than a universal dictate against female criticism, the discourse of proper femininity incorporates ideological contradictions that in part grant women power. As Mary Poovey points out, representations of native female domesticity invariably require instruction to cultivate these "natural" traits.[16] This cultural need authorizes some women into print; in fact, critics like Elizabeth Griffith, Clara Reeve, and Hannah More adopt the role of moralist to publish their critical judgments on literature.[17] Currently, scholars are beginning to focus on the critical activity of women in the eighteenth century in greater numbers than ever before.[18] Lipking's article challenged the very existence of Arimneste's

---

[15] Ibid.

[16] Poovey, *The Proper Lady*, p. 15.

[17] Elizabeth Griffith, *The Morality of Shakespeare's Drama Illustrated* (1775), reprint (New York: AMS Press, 1971); Hannah More, "Miscellaneous Observations on Genius, Taste, Good Sense, &c.," in *Essays on Various Subjects, Principally Designed for Young Ladies* (1777) in *Complete Works of Hannah More*, 2 vols. (New York: Harper and Brothers, 1847), vol. II, pp. 550–576 (to be discussed in chapter 5).

[18] Published works on eighteenth-century British female critics include: Ellen Argyos, "Intruding Herself into the Chair of Criticism," in Frederick Keener and Susan Losch, eds., *Eighteenth-Century Women and the Arts*, pp. 283–289; Katharine M. Rogers, "Britain's First Woman Drama Critic:

tradition, prompting a group of scholars, known as the Folger Collective, to investigate the historical reality of female-authored criticism. Their efforts resulted in an anthology which includes selections from forty-one of nearly one-hundred identified female critics.[19] This unprecedented collection of female critical voices suggests that the gendered inequality in the critical tradition "appears less Arimneste's failure to talk than our failure to listen."[20] Given that the critical discourse of the eighteenth century represents judgment as a male prerogative, the identification of these early female critics is significant in itself. The fact that these women resist cultural definitions to the extent that they present their critical opinions to an audience reinforces the need to avoid conceptions of the "proper lady" as totalizing and deterministic. Each of the critics studied here represents a gendered subject within a discourse in flux; each adopts strategies to realize her critical authority in the male-oriented discourse, testifying to the power of the individual subject to resist, alter, or reproduce hegemonic scripts.

Given my earlier caution against defining a female critical tradition along biologically determined lines, the apparent isolation of these four women in one chapter requires explanation. This chapter constitutes a specific examination of strategies used by women as collectively disadvantaged subjects within discourse, but other chapters include examples of critical work by women in dialogue with men.[21] My intention in separately treating Behn, Lennox, Fielding, and Reeve is twofold. The primary purpose, to illustrate that women did write criticism during the eighteenth century, is basic, but it nonetheless needs reiteration in order to stimulate the academic discussion necessary to their continued visibility. Women belonged to a social group that was excluded from official critical roles through legal, economic, and social conventions, but they still published prefaces, essays, reviews, and books

Elizabeth Inchbald," and Constance Clark, "Critical Remarks on the Four Taking Plays of This Season by Corinna, a Country Parson's Wife," in Mary Anne Schofield and Cecilia Macheski, eds., *Curtain Calls: British and American Women and the Theater 1660–1820* (Athens: Ohio University Press, 1991), pp. 277–308; Catherine E. Moore, "'Ladies . . . Taking the Pen in Hand': Mrs. Barbauld's Criticism of Eighteenth-Century Women Novelists," in Mary Anne Schofield and Cecilia Macheski, eds., *Fetter'd or Free? British Women Novelists, 1670–1815* (Athens: Ohio University Press, 1986).

[19] Folger Collective on Early Women Writers, eds., *Women Critics, 1660–1820: An Anthology* (Bloomington: Indiana University Press, 1995).

[20] L. Lipking, "Aristotle's Sister," pp. 63–64.

[21] In chapter 1, I mention briefly the critical opinions of Anne Finch, Jane Barker, Aphra Behn, Mary Wollstonecraft; see chapter 3 for a discussion of Behn, Mary Davys, Mary Delarivière Manley, Madeleine de Scudéry, Mary Pix, and Eliza Haywood; see chapter 5 for a treatment of Hannah More as critic.

of literary criticism during the long eighteenth century. As discursive "outlaws," their language shares a conscious sense of gendered disenfranchisement, and their methods of authorization involve the appropriation of legitimate modes of discourse. Many feminists have theorized this quality of women's writing: Laurie Finke, borrowing from Michel de Certeau, calls this "poaching"; Mary Poovey sees it as "indirection," and Kristina Straub, referring specifically to the production of female critics, defines it as the "double-vision" characteristic of the female's simultaneous appropriation of the spectator role and identification with the object.[22] Although in different ways, female critics position themselves in relation to the dominant languages of critical analysis, and their expression often includes uncomfortable dialogism rather than the gentlemanly ease of Addison.

The second objective of this chapter is to demonstrate that although these women share the discursive position of "woman" each nonetheless exhibits individual responses to her unique historical situation. Only through attention to specific cases can feminist criticism negotiate between the limitations of a homogenizing biological essentialism and the proliferating detail of historical contingency. Behn, a participant in the looser semiotics of gender in the Restoration, appropriates both the masculine voice of satire and the feminine role of modesty to undermine the social and literary customs that threaten her dramatic success. Writing in the middle of the eighteenth century, Charlotte Lennox combines neoclassical precepts with the authority of female domesticity in her unseasonable criticism of Shakespeare's representation of nature. Sarah Fielding, a contemporary of Lennox, masks her personal voice by recounting the critical dialogue of fictional men and women in an epistolary essay on *Clarissa*. In 1785, Clara Reeve also uses narrative dialogue to dramatize the gendered dynamic in the discourse on the novel in her *Progress of Romance*. The work of these four women testifies to a rich and varied heritage of female-authored criticism, suggesting a range of possibilities for even marginalized subjects to engage in hegemonic practices.

THE WOMAN DAMNS THE POET: APHRA BEHN

In a recent article, Laurie Finke argues that the critical tradition overlooks the criticism of Aphra Behn because it does not conform to the

---

[22] Laurie Finke, *Feminist Theory, Women's Writing*, Reading Women Writing Series (Ithaca: Cornell University Press, 1992), p. 10; Poovey, *The Proper Lady*, pp. 28–29; Kristina Straub, "Women, Gender and Criticism," in Davis and Finke, eds., *Literary Criticism and Theory*, pp. 855–876.

disinterestedness required by modern conceptions of literary criticism. She demonstrates how Behn's lively prefaces to her plays criticize prevailing critical orthodoxy and expose the political interestedness of Restoration theatre.[23] My analysis of Behn's dramatic criticism shares the objectives of Finke's article in that it attempts to restore her criticism to "its own history of turbulence, conflict, struggle, and ideological and political debate" by examining the discourses of its production, but this discussion addresses different contexts. Rather than read Behn's work against the disinterested critical criteria of the twentieth century and the political allegiances of the 1680s, I examine her in the gendered critical discourses of her era and demonstrate how she authorizes her judgment by mastering that semiotics. Like Dryden, Aphra Behn manipulates the flexible gender-codes circulating in Restoration discourse, revealing an understanding of sex as a social rather than an ontological condition, but her criticism, unlike her contemporary's, challenges male prerogatives and conservative notions of femininity.[24] As a public, female writer, Behn could not abide by the conventions of the soft and retiring character of Dryden's feminine prescription. Instead, Behn exhibits a fluency in both modest and libertine languages of the masculine and feminine orientation that grants her the freedom to try on different gendered roles in order to expose the gendered basis for certain critical commonplaces.

The state of dramatic criticism during the Restoration was lamented by the time Johnson wrote his life of Dryden, and it has been apologized for by scholars of the age ever since. Its major faults include superficial treatment of literature, adulatory or abusive tones, minimal systematicity, and a pervasive lack of objectivity.[25] Most critical writing occurs in the interested spaces of dedicatory epistles and prefaces to published works, where authors attempt to curry financial favor or advance a defense of their own work. Critical exchange in the Restoration is, as a result, flamboyant, violent, and frequently very funny. Complaining of the libelous nature of what passed for criticism, Dryden writes in 1693, "When they describe the writers of this age, they draw such monstrous figures of them as resemble none of us . . .

[23] Laurie Finke, "Aphra Behn and the Ideological Construction of Restoration Literary Theory," in Heidi Hutner, ed., *Rereading Aphra Behn: History, Theory, and Criticism* (Charlottesville: University Press of Virginia, 1993), pp. 17–43.

[24] I borrow the expressions "social" and "ontological" conditions of sex from Thomas Laqueur, *Making Sex: Body and Gender from the Greeks to Freud* (Cambridge: Harvard University Press, 1990).

[25] For a useful, brief review of this literature, see James and Helen Kinsley, eds., *Dryden, The Critical Heritage* (New York: Barnes and Noble, 1971), pp. 1–12.

they are all grotesque."[26] Despite claims to the contrary, Dryden was not above responding to his critics, as the portrait of Shadwell in *Mac Flecknoe* amply testifies. Yet, as that poem suggests, couched within these satirical expressions some genuine criticism emerges. In varying degrees of seriousness, most critics of the age wrestle with questions of dramatic structure and purpose by negotiating the rules and didactic imperatives imported from French neoclassicists. Aphra Behn fully participates in this dialogue, appropriating the aggressive character of language and positing critical arguments on the worth of her plays.

The bellicose nature of the critical discourse, with its partisanship and lampoons, necessitates a disruptive use of language quite unlike that of modest feminine conversation or of gallant courtship. The lack of politeness, despite Dryden's best efforts, characterizes a field of communication inappropriate for proper women, and this gender exclusivity is underscored by the elite foundations of satire on which the critical mode relies. Based in a tradition of Greek and Latin rhetoric, the densely allusive Restoration satire can be cryptic to the unlearned reader. Moreover, the satiric persona's emotional extremes, from anger to lust, represent a display of psychological states that would jeopardize a proper woman's reputation. For a variety of socially inscribed reasons, satire is a masculine discourse, and history records few effective female satirists.[27] Nonetheless, Behn adopts this form, with its open-ended inquiry and provocative display of wit, in her early critical defenses.

Behn's first critical essay, attached to *The Dutch Lover* (1673), includes a rambling satire on the role of learning in comedy. As a proponent of pleasure over instruction, Behn enters the debate between Dryden and Shadwell over the primary function of drama. Although Dryden never abandons the goal of edification in his work, he lays more emphasis on pleasing the audience, especially in his criticism of the stage. In his 1671 preface to *The Humorists*, Thomas Shadwell directly challenges Dryden's view:

Here I must take leave to Dissent from those who seem to insinuate that the ultimate end of a Poet is to delight, without correction or instruction. Methinks a Poet should never acknowledge this, for it makes him of as little use to Mankind as a Fidler or Dancing Master, who delights the fancy onely, without improving the Judgement.[28]

[26] John Dryden, *John Dryden: Of Dramatic Poesy and Other Critical Essays*, ed. George Watson, 2 vols. (London: Dent, 1962), vol. II, p. 159.

[27] See also Dustin Griffin, *Satire: A Critical Reintroduction* (Lexington: University Press of Kentucky, 1994), p. 190.

[28] Thomas Shadwell, "Preface to *The Humorists*," in J. E. Spingarn, ed., *Critical Essays of the Seventeenth Century*, 3 vols. (Bloomington: Indiana University Press, 1957), vol. II, p. 153.

Behn squarely aligns herself with Dryden, "our most unimitable Laureat," and exposes the pedantry and lack of sense in Shadwell's didactic concept of comedy.[29] Following convention, Behn positions herself through dichotomous, gendered discourses to establish the literary binaries at issue. She contends that "Plays have no great room for that which is mens great advantage over women, that is Learning,"[30] identifying the polarities of good and bad comedy with the relative education of the sexes. Behn authorizes her critical voice through repeated identification as a woman apart from the legions of overeducated "whiffling would-be wits."[31] However, as Griffin notes, the bipolar structure of the satirist's vision is only one device: "We should think of it as the satirist's point of departure rather than destination."[32] While she projects the image of an uneducated female and outsider to the main circles of critical judgment, her criticism participates in current debates, and she adopts the debased language of her brethren as she lampoons them.

Behn focuses her letter on the issue of education with an opening barb for pedants who might expect enlightenment from her comedy:

Indeed, had I hung a sign of the Immortality of the soul, of the Mystery of Godliness, or of Ecclesiastical Policie, and then had treated you with Indiscerpibility, and Essential Spissitude (words, which though I am no competent Judge of, for want of Languages, yet I fancy strongly ought to mean just nothing) . . . I were then indeed sufficiently in fault.[33]

In this attack on the impenetrability of a university style of diction, Behn sets up her initial oppositions, playing off the expectation that the reader wants to be entertained and not dumbfounded by an over-sophisticated style. Her mockery underscores the pretension of criticizing that which is meant only for pleasure. In contrast, Behn establishes her lack of learning – her "want of Languages" – as a commonsense, straightforward talent for dramatic writing.

Behn offers a tongue-in-cheek defense of comedy as reading material by comparing it to more serious books. With lucid foreshadowing of contemporary anti-intellectualism, she represents the pride of erudition as meaningless drivel:

[F]or I have heard that most of that which bears the name of Learning, and which has abused such quantities of Ink and Paper, and continually imploys so many ignorant, unhappy souls for ten, twelve, twenty years in the University (who yet poor wretches think they are doing something all the while) as Logick &

[29] Behn, *The Dutch Lover* (1673) in *The Works of Aphra Behn*, ed. Janet Todd, 7 vols. (Columbus: Ohio State University Press, 1996), vol. v, p. 162.
[30] Ibid. [31] Ibid., p. 161. [32] Griffin, *Satire*, p. 37.
[33] Behn, *Works*, ed. Todd, vol. v, p. 160.

several other things (that shall be nameless, lest I mispel them) are much more absolutely nothing than the errantest Play that e'er was writ.[34]

Her evaluation of both comedy and books of learning assumes the dual criteria of profit and delight, but she clearly valorizes the pleasure to be gleaned from reading. On the score of entertainment, dry tomes of learning rank poorly. Prevented from the benefits of a formal education, Behn stands outside the halls of academe as critic and moral superior. Because she remains grounded in the reality of her theatre world, she can afford pity for those "poor wretches" who, for all their study, remain ignorant. Her simplicity – she cannot even spell the names of such learned topics – raises her above the self-deceived scholars and asserts her clear understanding.

In keeping with the conventions of satire, Behn poses as the unsophisticated, honest spectator, whose alternative to the jaded status quo represents the vices of her opponents in gross relief.[35] For Behn, however, the satirist's assertions of simplicity resonate with the discourses of proper femininity. Dryden's recommendations for feminine verse, for instance, assume the female audience will not appreciate intellectual complexity or "the height of thought." In her role of "innocent," she capitalizes on her discursive identity as a female author to license her attack on the pedantic discourse of critics, but her letter simultaneously adopts masculine perspectives as she appropriates the language of erudition and the aggressiveness of satire.

The main body of her preface addresses the improbability that comedy truly improves anyone. "I am my self well able to affirm that none of all our English Poets, and least the Dramatique (so I think you call them) can be justly charg'd with too great reformation of mens minds or manners."[36] She discredits the lot of "wits" as profligate atheists, thereby suggesting the immoral nature of those who profess to instruct their audiences. She especially deplores the notion of imitation, or the assumption that viewers model their behavior after stage characters: "If you consider Tragedy, you'l find their best of characters unlikely patterns for a wise man to pursue . . . And as for Comedie, the finest folks you meet with there, are still unfitter for your imitation."[37] Behn's irreverent dismissal of the lofty neoclassical ideals greatly differs from Dryden's measured discussion in *Of Dramatic Poesy*, but where Dryden equivocates on learning, pleasure, and the rules, Behn exposes the

[34] Ibid.
[35] See Alvin Kernan, *The Cankered Muse* (New Haven: Yale University Press, 1959), pp. 16–17.
[36] Behn, *Works*, ed. Todd, vol. v, p. 161.   [37] Ibid.

prevailing opinion as just so much cant. Here the practicing dramatist counters the critical theory with shrewd insight into audience psychology. "I think," she says, "a Play the best divertisement that wise men have; but I do also think them nothing so, who do discourse as formallie about the rules of it, as if 'twere the grand affair of humane life."[38] Because plays are meant for entertainment, they need not be sermons nor conform to artificial precepts. Behn's disdain for "their musty rules of Unity, and God knows what besides"[39] reaffirms her outsider status and allows her to question the purported authority of the men who mouth the fashionable critical codes. She insists that drama is a less restricted field than popular criticism concedes, and this stance ultimately authorizes her vindication of female dramatists.

At the end of her epistle, Behn argues for the categorical ability of women to write for the stage, not for herself as an exception to the rule. To do so, she figuratively enters the masculine domain of the theatre pit, and she appropriates the masculine discourses in a scathing lampoon. *The Dutch Lover* failed as a stage production for several reasons, not the least of which was the pronouncement of "a long, lither, phlegmatick, white, ill-favour'd, wretched Fop." Behn writes: "This thing, I tell ye, opening that which serves it for a mouth, out issued such a noise as this to those that sate about it, that they were to expect a woful Play, God damn him, for it was a womans."[40] By reiterating the fop's charge in a context that exposes his language as vulgar and absurd, Behn counters the criticism that a woman's language, by virtue of its gender, will inevitably disappoint. She takes control of the discourse and demonstrates her power to defame. Her mimicry changes the valence of masculine discourse, turning the weapon of attack against the aggressor and revealing the "manly" oath to be ineffective next to her satire. This "sorry animal" lacks sufficient intellect to engage in debate and thus provides her with the opportunity to expand her field of attack:

I would not for a world be taken arguing with such a propertie as this; but if I thought there were a man of any tolerable parts, who could upon mature deliberation distinguish well his right hand from his left, and justly state the difference between the number of sixteen and two, yet had this prejudice upon him; I would take a little pains to make him know how much he errs.[41]

Behn clearly breaks with female decorum as she voices the anger and hostility of the unjustly demeaned dramatist. Her personal attack, though harsh, is in keeping with the "monstrous figures" in the critical

---

[38] Ibid., p. 162.   [39] Ibid., p. 163.   [40] Ibid., p. 162.   [41] Ibid.

exchange of her time. Given the decorous and highly formal codes of gallantry that characterize most communication between the sexes – and which Behn capably manipulates in the prefatory matter of her fiction – her choice of style in this preface indicates a willingness to treat men in masculine terms. Such a move would subsequently invite men to regard her equitably, which is to say not like a lady but as one of the theatrical profession. Thus, her oppositional stance ultimately gives way to a desire for insider status. She underscores this by entering the contemporary imbroglio with an attack on Ben Jonson's learning. In a probable reference to Shadwell, she accuses "the most severe of Johnsons Sect" of affectation, claiming that, apart from Dryden, "I know of none that write at such a formidable rate, but that a woman may well hope to reach their greatest hights."[42] Behn's knowledge of dramatic discourse and her personal references reveal her to be a veteran at the heart of Restoration theatre and not the unlettered outsider she initially proposes. Her satire, though, allows her to denaturalize the superiority of male learning and question its pertinence to comedy. She demonstrates all the while her skill in entertaining as she ridicules foolish men.

Behn's strategy of self-representation shifts when women become the target of her satire. In the brief address before *Sir Patient Fancy* (1678) and the famous preface to *The Luckey Chance* (1687), Behn attacks the willful blindness of moralists who condemn her plays as indecent, and this form of prejudice is conventionally charged to the ladies. In the first letter, "To the Reader," Behn's repetition of the word "Woman," in contradistinction from "Men," forefronts the female role and destabilizes the understanding of the category:

I Printed this Play with all the impatient haste one ought to do, who would be vindicated from the most unjust and silly aspersion, Woman could invent to cast on Woman; and which only my being a Woman has procured me; *That it was Baudy*, the least and most Excusable fault in the Men writers, to whose Plays they all crowd, as if they came to no other end that to hear what they condemn in this: *but from a Woman it was unnaturall.*[43]

Behn ascribes to her female audience the complaint of bawdiness, a broad category generally connoting lewdness or obscenity, especially in language. In this context, the word "bawdy" refers primarily to the use of *double entendres* in dialogue rather than the representation of sex or adultery. Behind the charge against Behn's play lies the assumption that

---

[42] Ibid.   [43] Behn, *Sir Patient Fancy* (1678), in *Works*, ed. Todd, vol. VI, p. 5.

exposure to sexual innuendo jeopardizes the purity of feminine knowledge. This gendered construction at once posits the female as naturally modest, and necessitates regulation to ensure that modesty. As a female creator of scenes of sexual banter, Behn transgresses doubly: not only does she give other members of her sex access to indecent language, but she also challenges the very construction of femininity by mastering the linguistic form of seduction. During the 1680s many claims were to be made on behalf of "the ladies" to purify the language of drama, indicating the increasing influence of the discourse of proper femininity.[44] It is unclear to what extent these "ladies" represented actual female human beings, but the trend suggests that appeals on behalf of "woman" began to signal the need for responsible standards in published and performed material. Rather than answer the charge, Behn impugns the credibility of her judges by implicating them with a hypocritical desire for the sexual knowledge they find so repellent in her. Apparently, the calls for chaste productions precede a wide-scale change in taste, and such sanitized representations, Behn implies, pertain as little to the success of comedy as the evidence of male erudition.

Behn reiterates her argument against "the old never failing Scandal – That 'tis not fit for the Ladys" nine years later in the witty and wistful preface to *The Luckey Chance*.[45] Although she maintains her stance in favor of women's ability to write plays and against the hypocrisy of feminine codes of modesty, this attack is gentler and more consistent with the notions of proper femininity. Again, she confronts the perception of her work as indecent, but here the experienced writer responds with resignation: "But Right or Wrong [the lines] must be Criminal because a Woman's."[46] Interestingly, Behn tries to obviate the charges by making her audience aware of the collaborative responsibility involved in producing a play. She invokes protection from the state by mentioning the censorship of "Dr. Davenant," and the licensing of Sir Roger L'Estrange; she claims the approval of the Master of the Revels, Charles Killigrew, and the Master players. Finally the nameless "Ladys of very great Quality, and unquestioned Fame" pronounce the play fit for chaste ears and wholly entertaining.[47] Rather than adopt the aggressive masculine voice of abuse, Behn authorizes her work through objective channels of critical authority.

[44] David Roberts, *The Ladies: Female Patronage of Restoration Drama 1660–1700* (Oxford: Clarendon Press, 1989), chapter 5.
[45] Behn, *The Luckey Chance* (1687), in *Works*, ed. Todd, vol. VII, p. 215.
[46] Ibid.   [47] Ibid., p. 217.

She reasons that anyone who still finds scandal in her play must either imagine it or suffer from immovable prejudice against the female playwright. The latter possibility provokes her defiant challenge:

[H]ad the Plays I have writ come forth under any Mans Name, and never known to have been mine; I appeal to all unbyast Judges of Sense, if they had not said that Person had made as many good Comedies, as any one Man that has writ in our Age; but a Devil on't the Woman Damns the Poet.[48]

Behn ultimately defends her play through appeal to her unique status as a female playwright. In a similar gesture, she rhetorically claims the privilege of "my Masculine Part the Poet in me," simultaneously inferring that the genius of poetry is male and that she has access to it. On the one hand she strips the language of gendered propriety in literary discourse of its gallant pretense and exposes the barriers of her sex to be artificial; on the other, she slyly manipulates the gendered codes to garner power through sympathy. Rather than pitch a battle for control of masculine forms of authority, she shifts to the role of passive female. At stake is the right to create plays: "If I must not, because of my Sex, have this Freedom, but that you will usurp all to your selves; I lay down my Quill, and you shall hear no more of me."[49] By merging all criticism of her plays into the condemnation of her sex, she represents the charge of her critics as a gross injustice. Such treatment of a woman, she suggests, is ungentlemanly: "I will be kinder to my Brothers of the Pen, than they have been to a defenceless Woman."[50] Again, we find Behn resignifying the language of her critics, but this time she adopts the voice of polite femininity to reveal the lack of gallantry among her male peers. In part, this change in strategy represents a capitulation to the normative femininity that would gain hegemonic ground after her death. But it also testifies to Behn's fluency in the multiple discourses of her era and her ability to choose the most effective means of defending her work.

Behn's consciousness of gendered constructions is vital to her critical writing; she never loses sight of her advantages and differences as a woman. This focus on her sex can be disturbing in its limited scope, and it certainly interferes with the detached objectivity most twentieth-century notions of criticism require. But her constant return to gendered conflicts suggests the extent to which her sex acted as an obstacle to standard literary authority and the respect garnered by proven playwrights. Rather than "glide over sexual issues without a ripple" – as Lipking suggests of the critical tradition – Behn's indictments expose the critical

[48] Ibid.   [49] Ibid.   [50] Ibid.

practice in the Restoration as grounded in gendered distinctions. Through her boisterous charges against the fops and ladies of fashion, she demands a reevaluation of society's critical biases. Behn's ability to exploit the social and literary controversies of her day by appropriating the different discourses of propriety and satire is a historically situated phenomenon that testifies to the turbulent state of changing codes in the Restoration. Although the critical discourse may have been personal, rancorous, political, and unsystematic, these conditions created the possibility for an enterprising and intelligent woman to express her literary judgment.

WHAT'S SO IRRITATING ABOUT CHARLOTTE LENNOX?

In *Shakespear Illustrated* Charlotte Lennox analyzes Shakespeare's use of his sources, and significantly adds "critical remarks."[51] Like Behn, Lennox adopts the language of her male contemporaries, in this case using the rhetoric of the Augustan tradition. By appropriating the "rules" and turning them against the male-oriented understanding of representation in Shakespeare, Lennox raises troubling questions about the concepts of originality and human nature. At the same time, her methods reflect the mid-century shift toward a more subjective foundation for critical judgment, drawing on her individual perception as a woman to validate her conclusions.

Lennox's text is the first full-length work of scholarly criticism by an Englishwoman and an interesting textual study for Shakespeare scholarship in the eighteenth century, but until recently it has been almost universally disparaged. Representative of the twentieth-century dismissal of her work, Brian Vickers finds the tone and tempo of her criticism especially appalling: "the catalogue of Shakespeare's 'absurdities' and 'improbabilities' grows wearisome by determined reiteration, for it is seldom that Mrs. Lennox finds anything good to say about any of Shakespeare's greatest plays, and this refusal to admit the presence of any virtues reduces her book to the level of a one-sided *idée fixe*." Significantly, however, he admits that she raises some stubborn concerns: "her literal-minded pertinacity, rather like Rymer's, does throw up some awkward questions about Shakespeare's plotting."[52] Vickers' assessment

---

[51] Charlotte Lennox, *Shakespear Illustrated: Or the Novels and Histories on which the Plays of Shakespear are Founded*, vols. I–II (London, 1753); vol. III (London, 1754).
[52] Brian Vickers, ed., *Shakespeare: The Critical Heritage*, 6 vols. (London: Routledge & Kegan Paul, 1976), vol. IV, p. 6.

takes its cues from Johnson's dedication to the work, which suggests that Lennox's discoveries regarding Shakespeare's plots can in no way diminish his literary achievement. Lennox herself, though, is less careful about Shakespeare's reputation. After reading *Shakespear Illustrated*, Samuel Richardson expressed outrage: "Methinks I love my Shakespeare, since this Attack, better than before."[53] Richardson's defensive reaction registers the potency of Lennox's criticism and suggests that it is not merely a hackneyed recitation of Shakespeare's errors, but something more disturbing.

Lennox's work has left a legacy of irritated responses. Most of her detractors confine Lennox's critical abilities to a slavish adherence to neoclassical rules following the thought of Thomas Rymer, and few refrain from coupling her with that infamous enemy of Shakespeare in ways that they would not, or could not, with a male critic. Thomas R. Loundsbury is responsible for the first twentieth-century representation of this type. After claiming that Lennox "missed her century," he adds helpfully, "had she in addition become Mrs. Rymer, the conjunction of these two stars, shooting madly from their spheres in the Shakespearean firmament, would have attracted the attention of observers for all time."[54] The "jest" is one that Karl Young "would be sorry to relinquish" and one that Vickers modifies only slightly.[55] Besides demonstrating the phenomenally sexist grounds of evaluation, this trope in the criticism of Lennox exemplifies a particular problem for the female writer entering the masculine discourse of criticism: because she is not a member of the male club, her sex becomes conspicuous and therefore a prime target for ridicule and punishment. However, most female-authored criticism is simply overlooked and consigned to obscurity. This heritage of resentment prompts the question: what is it about Lennox's text that generates such hostility?

Two recent positive appraisals attempt to identify the problematic nature of *Shakespear Illustrated*, and both significantly advance the appreciation of Lennox's work as a consistent critique of Shakespeare's representation of women. In the first of these articles, Margaret Doody reads *Shakespear Illustrated* as a companion piece to the *Female Quixote*, where Lennox vindicates the feminine tradition of the romance and the

[53] Quoted ibid.
[54] Thomas R. Loundsbury, *Shakespeare as a Dramatic Artist with an Account of his Reputation at Various Periods* (New York: Charles Scribner's Sons, 1901), p. 292.
[55] Karl Young, "Samuel Johnson on Shakespeare: One Aspect," *University of Wisconsin Studies in Language and Literature*, no. 18 (1923), 185, and Vickers (ed.), *Shakespeare*, vol. IV, p. 6.

power it accords to women.[56] In a second article, Susan Green demonstrates how Lennox's investigation of Shakespeare's female characters reveals her culture's inability to recognize female abjection.[57] Especially helpful is Green's contention that Lennox unconsciously discovers the "locus of nonmeaning" in Shakespeare's text by posing questions about the agency of women that cannot be answered by her culture.[58] However, neither article sufficiently addresses the extent to which Lennox engages the critics and the critical debates of her day. I would extend Green's argument to suggest that Lennox's questions are unanswerable because she asks that Shakespeare's representations of women be understood through dominant discourses of literary value, but the historically constituted understanding of proper womanhood and the construction of literary greatness are incommensurate. In the determination of literary value, women and women's perspective simply do not matter. When she forces the concepts of literary value to account for Shakespeare's representation of women, she is literally left with non-sense, which prompts her scorn. These frequent eruptions of indignation offend readers who have come to accept Shakespeare as the unquestioned literary paragon.

Many twentieth-century histories of British literary criticism credit the eighteenth century with the foundation of Shakespeare's international fame, and the numerous editions of his works as well as the regular performance and review of his plays certainly establish him as an enduring icon of British literature.[59] But as in the evolution of any fact, the discourses prior to cultural consensus offer a more complicated picture of Shakespeare's eighteenth-century status. The messiness reveals what culture later suppresses in the interest of preserving a monolithic sense of truth. For that reason, study of Shakespearean criticism in the eighteenth century, and especially such counter-culture texts as *Shakespear Illustrated*, provides a view of the ideological contradictions and problems that eventually become repressed in Shakespearean scholarship.

[56] Margaret Anne Doody, "Shakespeare's Novels: Charlotte Lennox Illustrated," *Studies in the Novel* 19 (Fall 1987), 296–307.
[57] Susan Green, "A Cultural Reading of Charlotte Lennox's *Shakespear Illustrated*," in J. Douglas Canfield and Deborah C. Payne, eds., *Cultural Reading of Restoration and Eighteenth-Century English Theater* (Athens: University of Georgia Press, 1995), pp. 228–257.
[58] Ibid., p. 238.
[59] Relevant books include Herbert Spencer Robinson, *English Shakespearian Criticism in the Eighteenth Century*, second edition (New York: Gordian Press, 1968) and more recently Colin Franklin, *Shakespeare Domesticated: The Eighteenth Century Editions* (Scolar Press, 1991). Vickers' series of volumes, *Shakespeare: The Critical Heritage,* is an invaluable resource for the variety of early opinions.

Criticism of Shakespeare at the time of Lennox's publication illustrates several of the principal conflicts in literary value that the eighteenth century works through, namely, the shift from an adherence to external systems of authority in the forms of classical precedent or the rules to the validation of individual perspective, subjective sensibility, and originary genius. The definitive literary values of judgment, imagination, and learning can be seen as tools of the artist or critic that manifest different potentials in each perspective, external or internal. For instance, Dryden stresses the need to balance judgment with the boldness of imagination during an age when external authority exerted more influence, but by the mid-eighteenth century "genius," a composite of judgment and imagination in which the latter holds sway, authorizes the artist to depart from established modes of success.

Shakespearean criticism serves as a sort of barometer of these changing critical codes. The punctilious French school of neoclassicism provides much of the theoretical structure for English criticism, but Shakespeare, the greatest dramatic poet of the nation, fails to conform to the French standards. Early-eighteenth-century criticism of the Bard generally focuses on the issues of the pseudo-Aristotelian unities of time, place, and action, decorum and poetic justice, and Shakespeare's knowledge of the Ancients. In an effort to compromise, British critics adopt the mode of analysis known as "praise and blame." They catalogue the list of "beauties and blemishes" in Shakespeare's plays with a tacit agreement among all (except Rymer) that the former exceed the latter. The influence of new authorities, such as Longinus and the sublime, offer an alternative set of aims and methods for criticism, with an accent on the subjective insights of the author rather than on the formal content of the work.[60] As the rules gradually fell out of fashion, imagination and the representation of human nature came to be touted as Shakespeare's unsurpassed gifts, and these were precisely the characteristics that Lennox questioned.

Because Shakespeare's education seemed less than adequate for eighteenth-century gentlemen of taste, critics tend to de-emphasize the importance of learning and instead to extol Shakespeare's knowledge of human nature. The debates over Shakespeare's qualifications as a poet indicate the extent to which "nature" was subject to negotiation in the changing codes of criticism. One defender of Shakespeare insists that the classically informed and widely accepted definition of poetry, that it is an

---

[60] Samuel H. Monk, *The Sublime: A Study of Critical Theories in XVIII-Century England*, second edition (Ann Arbor: University of Michigan Press, 1960), p. 16.

imitation of nature, excludes Shakespeare: "It is not Shakespeare who speaks the language of nature, but nature rather speaks the language of Shakespeare. He is not so much her imitator as her master, her director, her moulder. Nature is a stranger to objects which Shakespeare has rendered natural."[61] Although the statement can be read as a panegyric on Shakespeare's powers of invention and an apology for his lack of formal training, the example also illustrates the strain of competing values in mid-century criticism. The ideological value of neoclassical principles, the investment in the order of external systems, is undermined; instead, the power of the individual to direct, to master, and to mold is supreme, reflecting the rising influence of individual subjectivism.

Few critics of Shakespeare, however, go quite so far as to claim that Shakespeare changes nature. But it is nature that authorizes his departure – and those that follow him – from the classics. In "Conjectures on Original Composition" Edward Young metaphorically locates Shakespeare's genius in a different set of texts: "he was master of two books unknown to many of the profoundly read, tho' books which the last conflagration alone can destroy: the book of Nature and that of Man."[62] Originality, in this context, implies the ability to represent life in a way that previous texts did not and that was sure to transcend time. Nature becomes a source apart from and superior to the Ancients. These protective defenses of Shakespeare's knowledge are striking in that they reveal the importance of education as a determinant of literary quality, and at the same time they provide for exceptions. Notably, the quality of genius, *innate* and *rare*, separates Shakespeare from other uneducated pretenders to the revered Mount Parnassus – in particular self-made poets of the lower classes, and women. At the same time, the apotheosis of Shakespeare into "the bird of nature" signals his superiority to merely practiced poets who know the precedents and the rules.[63] Through Shakespeare, the culture debates its critical ideals with a remarkable consensus on his rank as the preeminent British poet. There are a few critics who demur, but the negative criticism of Shakespeare is to a certain extent read as an attack on British literary culture in general. Into this environment Lennox launches her sharply penned and irreverent analysis.

---

[61] William Guthrie, from *An Essay upon English Tragedy* (1747), in Vickers (ed.), *Shakespeare*, vol. III, pp. 194–195.
[62] From "Conjectures on Original Composition" (1759), in Vickers (ed.), *Shakespeare*, vol. IV, pp. 406–407.
[63] Guthrie, *English Tragedy*, in Vickers (ed.), *Shakespeare*, vol. III, p. 192.

Although Lennox's scholarship attempts to compare the sources of Shakespeare's plays for the first time, hers is not an isolated attempt to uncover origins and provide contexts for well-loved authors. In 1754 Thomas Warton published his *Observations on Spenser's Fairy Queen*, in which he demonstrated how Ariosto, Chaucer, and old romances served as models for Spenser's respected work. Johnson's praise of Warton indicates the regard with which such studies were held: "You have shown to all who shall hereafter attempt the study of our ancient authours the way to success, by directing them to the perusal of the books which those authours had read."[64] As mid-century critics become increasingly interested in the creative imagination of great authors, they begin to investigate the books which inspired them. Lennox's treatment of Shakespeare's sources challenges the popular conception of his originary genius, but it also fits into the context of critical work done by Warton and others interested in literary history and primitive texts, like Robert Lowth's research on Hebraic poetry and Hugh Blair's dissertation on the poetry of Ossian. Yet many refuse to grant Lennox's treatise a legitimate place in Shakespeare criticism. Nearly two centuries later, her analysis of the books Shakespeare read sufficiently irritates Karl Young that he reorganizes Lennox's material, greatly minimizing the romances and novels. He further argues that her scholarship is merely auxiliary to Johnson's later edition of Shakespeare: "Here, then, would be an undertaking from which Johnson's natural indolence may well have recoiled, but for which an industrious blue-stocking, with an avidity for literary routine, was peculiarly fitted."[65] With dull-witted misogyny, Young ignores the tradition of textual scholarship that Lennox shares with respectable male scholars and turns her research into a frustrated preoccupation with the trivial. His response indicates that the widespread dismissal of *Shakespear Illustrated* is largely the effect of combined sexism and Shakespeare idolatry.

Neither an imitation of Rymer, nor an adjunct to Johnson, Lennox's text deserves a fairer assessment. As Samuel Monk and others contend, literary critics distrust the absolute authority of the rules of neoclassical theory by the mid-century, but the vocabulary, nevertheless, persists alongside "beauties" of representation, "nervousness" of style, and "sublime" thought.[66] Lennox's reliance on poetic justice, probability

[64] *The Letters of Samuel Johnson*, ed. Bruce Redford, 5 vols. (Princeton: Princeton University Press, 1992–1994), p. 81.
[65] K. Young, "Samuel Johnson on Shakespeare," p. 180.
[66] See Vickers (ed.), *Shakespeare*, vol. IV, p. 4.

and the consistency of character demonstrates her participation in current critical discourse, but she joins this language of criticism with her experiential knowledge of womanhood, made intelligible through the codes of proper femininity.

The notion of poetic justice serves as Lennox's main critical principle in her condemnation of Shakespeare's *Measure for Measure* and its source, Cinthio's fifth novel of the eighth Decad. Cinthio's version provides an effective fable but is "faulty in the catastrophe" when the author rewards the lying and murderous governor with marriage to the virtuous heroine. According to Lennox, Shakespeare's addition of numerous incidents essentially weakens the plot through improbabilities and lack of unity; furthermore, Shakespeare's play is without a moral. Desiring a justified closure to the narrative, Lennox literally rewrites the conclusion. In the process she interprets the concept of poetic justice to reveal what is ideal in her system of rewards and punishments, and what constitutes vice and virtue. In Lennox's version the first male offender, who rapes a young woman, is killed for his crime; the heroine marries the evil governor whom she has already bedded, but she immediately removes herself to a cloister. "And the wretched [governor], deprived of his dignity, in disgrace with his prince, and the object of Universal Contempt and hatred, to compleat his miseries, he should feel all his former violence of passion for Epitia renewed, and falling into an Excess of Grief, for her loss . . . stab himself in despair."[67] Instead of living happily ever after – as Shakespeare and Cinthio would have it – Lennox's "hero" suffers ignobly through the deprivation of love, which ultimately drives him to suicide. Her conclusion upholds the dignity of the heroine who, she asserts, overcomes the greatest conflict of all the characters, between duty to her patriarchal ties and the preservation of her honor. Interestingly, the heroine escapes from the confines of a hated match to the female utopia of the cloister.

By recovering the perspective of the female whose honor and fate are sacrificed in the male-authored texts, Lennox reads the tale as inevitably tragic:

That Shakespear made a wrong choice of his subject, since he was resolved to torture it into a Comedy, appears by the low contrivance, absurd Intrigue, and improbable Incidents, he was obliged to introduce in order to bring about three or four Weddings, instead of one good beheading, which was the Consequence naturally expected.[68]

Lennox's language underscores the importance of point of view in the

---

[67] Lennox, *Shakespear Illustrated*, vol. I, p. 26.   [68] Ibid., p. 28.

constitution of literary values, and specifically of the category of "nature." The quick and certain punishment of the rapist is apparently what Charlotte Lennox "naturally expected," but such a rendition of nature is not entirely consistent with hegemonic discourse. Both Shakespeare and the eighteenth-century critical discourse that praised him reproduce interpretations of "nature" – or justice – skewed to favor the male perspective.[69] The pervasive double standard on sexual behavior for men and for women allows culture to turn a blind eye on male "indiscretion," and eighteenth-century literature is replete with examples of abandoned women whose seducers eventually enter successful marriages. Lennox's conviction in her dismissal of *Measure for Measure* derives from the belief in the sanctity of female purity, a value promoted by the discourse of proper femininity. The Augustan ideals she invokes, however, allow her to present as a literary flaw what might otherwise be excused as a historical difference.

Lennox starts from the commonplace, as expressed by Johnson, that Shakespeare "holds up to his readers a faithful mirrour of manners and of life," and she repeatedly tests Shakespeare's representation against her empirical understanding of the world.[70] Her perspective, unsurprisingly, is conditioned by her historical position as a middle-class woman sensitive to the vagaries of marriage and the importance of a woman's reputation. Such gendered knowledge informs her evaluation of Shakespeare's mismanagement of his source in *All's Well that Ends Well*, which provokes some of Lennox's most reproachful commentary:

He has made use of all the Incidents he found there, and added some of his own, which possibly may not be thought any Proofs either of his Invention or Judgment, since, at the same Time that they grow out of those he found formed to his Hand, yet they grow like Excrescences, and are useless and disagreeable.[71]

Rather than the "faithful mirror," Lennox discovers in Shakespeare a gross distortion of character that, when she compares it with its source, incites her scorn. Her reading appropriates the Aristotelian norm of probability, but it invokes a world-view separate from normative critical practice, a perspective that pays attention to the nuances of romantic love and the equitable treatment of female characters. Her major charge

---

[69] For a compelling interpretation of the significance of gender in rape trials, see John P. Zomchick, "'A Penetration which nothing can deceive': Gender and the Juridical Discourse in Some Eighteenth-Century Narratives," *Studies in English Literature* 29.3 (1989), 535–561.

[70] Samuel Johnson, *Johnson on Shakespeare*, 2 vols., ed. Arthur Sherbo, *Works*, 16 vols. (New Haven: Yale University Press, 1969), vol. VII, p. 62.

[71] Lennox, *Shakespear Illustrated*, vol. I, pp. 189–190.

against the play is Shakespeare's unnecessary and unconvincing lowering of the characters' dignity, which greatly damages the credibility of the outcome. At the reunion of husband and wife, Lennox prefers the properly subordinate tears and humility of Boccaccio's heroine: "In Shakespear she is cruel, artful, and insolent, and ready to make use of the king's authority to force her Husband to do her justice."[72] Boccaccio's Giletta earns the respect and love of her husband and his people through her prudent management of the Count's estate; Lennox finds Helena "less amiable" and "cunning," inadmissible qualities in the code of proper femininity. Shakespeare "shews [Helena] oppressed with Despair at the absence of the Count, incapable of either advice or consolation; giving unnecessary pain to the good Countess her mother-in-law . . . by alarming her with a pretended design of killing herself."[73] Lennox uses the Augustan rhetoric to underpin the importance of representing a compelling and admirable passion between the two principal characters. She implies that Shakespeare not only lacks creative genius in this play, but he also degrades a decent story into an offensive vision of romantic love. Her criticism points to the gap between hegemonic praise for Shakespeare's knowledge of human nature and the femino-centric concerns of marriage and female dignity.

Lennox's criticism of Shakespeare's consistency of character similarly suggests how far women are outside the purview of normative critical practice. Like Johnson, Lennox is greatly concerned with Shakespeare's sacrifice of virtue for the exigencies of theatre, but her focus typically falls on the female characters. Using the Augustan norm of the decorum of type, or the portrayal of a character consistent with her station and manner, Lennox claims that Shakespeare forfeits female sense and, more importantly, female virtue for the sake of a play's outcome. For instance, Lennox condemns the depiction of female friendship in *Othello*, an otherwise good example of Shakespeare's improvement over the source. In Cinthio's tale of the Moor, the lieutenant himself steals Disdemona's handkerchief, and the relationship between the leading female and the lieutenant's wife only provides the occasion for the lieutenant's deception. In Shakespeare,

Emilia pronounces [Othello] jealous, perceives the loss of that fatal Handkerchief, confirms some suspicions he had entertained, and though she loves her mistress to excess, chuses rather to let her suffer the bad consequences of his jealousy, than confess she had taken the handkerchief, which might have set all right

72 Ibid., p. 192.   73 Ibid., p. 191.

again; and yet this same woman, who could act so base and cruel a part against her mistress, has no greater care in dying than to be laid by her side.[74]

Emilia's behavior constitutes one nexus of "non-meaning" in Shakespeare's text, because for Lennox the contradictions cannot be explained. The dramatist's oversight is compounded by the critical appraisal of Rymer. Lennox counters Rymer's severe censure of the characters point for point, beginning with the case of Emilia: "That of Emilia though more inconsistent than any, he has taken no Notice of; and most of the Charges he brings against the others have little or no foundation."[75] The value of Lennox's criticism is precisely the way she exposes what other critics have "taken no notice of." Her dauntless critique of other male critics – she similarly engages Pope and Hamner, for instance – provides a striking illustration of the female critic's assumption of a critical authority on a level with that of men. Her gendered perspective, though, makes visible to her the roles of even minor female characters that apparently fail to stir the male critics' concern.

Lennox examines a more central character, Viola, to the same ends in her analysis of *Twelfth Night*, but the greater importance of the figure and Shakespeare's more flagrant indecorum exasperate Lennox. In Bandello's original, Nicuola is spurned by a former lover to whom she then goes dressed as a serving-boy in order to try to rekindle his love. In contrast, Viola's motivations for cross-dressing are thoroughly perplexing: "A very natural scheme this for a beautiful and virtuous young lady to throw off all at once the modesty and reservedness of her sex, mix among men, herself disguised like one, and, prest by no necessity, influenced by no passion, expose herself to all the dangerous consequences of so unworthy and shameful a situation."[76] Lennox's use of sarcasm and hyperbole indicate her frustration with Shakespeare's failure to represent the human nature she abides by, namely the mid-eighteenth-century ideology of separately gendered spheres of behavior. Lennox criticizes Viola for mixing with men and assuming a masculine appearance. Furthermore, though Bandello's heroine follows her "noble" passion at the cost of danger and potential shame, Viola possesses a distinctly unfeminine taste for adventure in planning to become the duke's page: "His person she had never seen; his affections she was informed were engaged; what then were her views and designs by submitting to be his attendant?"[77] Lennox's persistent questions and disbelief point to the constructed, as opposed to natural, quality of Shakespeare's representations.

---

[74] Ibid., pp. 128–129.   [75] Ibid., p. 129.   [76] Ibid., p. 244.   [77] Ibid., pp. 244–245.

Given his knowledge of the original, she assumes that Shakespeare changes the characters for a reason, but because the character appears unnatural to her, Shakespeare's Viola is incomprehensible.

In her unprecedented critical and scholarly work, Lennox adopts the methods of her male contemporaries to contextualize a great patriarchal figure and to broaden the critical understanding of his works through a female perspective, and in the process she reveals the gaps between the negotiation of femininity and the changing notions of literary value. The discourse of proper femininity that informs her understanding of the female characters and serves as the matrix of intelligibility for her own experience grants her authority to evaluate the private subjectivity of Shakespeare's characters; not surprisingly, Lennox's major criticism focuses on the representation of romantic love, the virtue of female characters and equitable arrangements in marriage. Lennox assumes a close identification with the female characters throughout the text, leading to the passionate defense of wronged heroines and, more interestingly, the outraged rejection of characters with whom that mirroring of self is thwarted. Straub's insight on the double-vision of female critics is applicable here. Lennox appropriates the role of observer in the masculine discourse of literary criticism, but hers is not a detached, impartial viewing. The irritation *Shakespear Illustrated* inspires derives from the irritation it expresses, and her impatience with the greatest English poet results from Lennox's insistent identification with the objects of the drama, specifically with the women. Although this double-vision prevents Lennox from achieving a pose of cool critical detachment, it leads to provocative questions that illustrate the conflicts in the discourses of gender and literary value.

THE DISPLACED VOICE OF SARAH FIELDING

Published anonymously in 1749, Sarah Fielding's *Remarks on Clarissa* shares with *Shakespear Illustrated* the mid-century contexts of the changing discourses of literary criticism and of gender.[78] Accordingly we find in Fielding's criticism a similarly gendered epistemology, whereby the feminine subject legitimately arbitrates knowledge of the private sphere, including romance, emotion, morals, and education of the young. Like Lennox, Fielding also enters the masculine critical discourse and assumes her right to judge, but her text produces considerably less

---

[78] Sarah Fielding, *Remarks on Clarissa*, intro. Peter Sabor, Augustan Reprint Society 231–232 (Los Angeles: William Andrews Clark Memorial Library, 1985).

tension then either Lennox or Behn because she carefully reproduces the gendered expectations of hegemonic discourse and masks her own judgment through fiction. Significantly, the work has only been attributed to Sarah Fielding in this century.[79] Written after her first two successful novels and one sequel, *Remarks* adopts the form of epistolary narrative by addressing the author of *Clarissa* in a personal letter. Throughout the text, Fielding narrates the conversations of several assemblies eagerly discussing the merits and problems of the novel as each installment is published. The last section of the treatise reproduces two letters exchanged between the principal "characters" of Fielding's own epistle. Thus Fielding constructs critical opinion through dialogic and textual reciprocation, displacing her voice through the fictionalized interaction of others. This, by the way, allows her to occupy both male and female perspectives on the novel and to evaluate it in the gendered terms common to novel criticism of the era, namely a didactic concern with the regulation of female behavior and the intellectual precedents of the masculine tradition of letters.

Unlike Behn and Lennox, who directly appropriate male critical methods without acknowledging the impropriety, the humble opening of Fielding's letter reveals a self-consciousness about her assumption of privilege. Rather than assert her authority, she begins by questioning the legitimacy of her text, suggesting that it "may appear very unaccountable, and whimsical."[80] Fielding's effort to establish a frame for her criticism through an address to Richardson is awkward but brief. When Peter Sabor claims that "the stiffness of this apostrophe is soon dispelled as the practiced novelist takes over from the laboring woman of letters,"[81] he unwittingly identifies an important distinction between the forms of writing and the gender of the writer. Sabor's woman of letters seems to labor, not because the matter is intellectually beyond her capacity, but because social injunctions against the display of female erudition mark the critical discourse as a masculine domain. Female judgment is out of place in the learned discourses of men. Despite the fact that Fielding is versed in Latin and Greek – her translation of Xenophon's *Memorabilia* (1762) is still standard in the twentieth century – she cannot enjoy that masculine luxury of scholastic ease.[82] On the other hand, the writing of fiction is an increasingly acceptable form of art for women, if they maintain a chaste and decorous expression. Fielding uses the socially acceptable pose of epistolary novelist as a masquerade for the subversive role of female critic.

---

[79] Ibid., p. iv.   [80] Ibid., p. 3.   [81] Ibid., p. v.
[82] Ibid., p. iii; see also biographical note to Sarah Fielding in Folger Collective, *Women Critics*, p. 80.

As opposed to Behn, who speaks forthrightly in a self-identified voice, or Lennox, who ostensibly allows her "opinion" to shape her critical expectations, Fielding essentially distances herself from the act of judgment; instead, she creates a disinterested persona who relates all the "criticisms" she has *heard* about the novel. She listens, gathers, and reports, taking great pains to establish her impartiality:

I have not willingly omitted any one Objection I have heard made to your favourite Character, from her first Appearance in the World; nor, on the contrary, have I either diminished or added to favourable Construction put on her Words or Actions. If the Grounds for the Objections are found to be deducible from the Story, I would have them remain in their full Force; but if the Answers her Admirers have given to those Objections are found to result from an impartial and attentive perusal of the Story, I would not have her deny'd the Justice they have done her.[83]

Nowhere does Fielding claim authorship; she only takes responsibility for full and accurate representation. Her strategy emphasizes the role of spectator with a tangential relationship to knowledge that authorizes the ability to judge without prejudice.

Fielding never overtly alludes to her gender in her letter to Richardson; however, she does adopt a form with strong feminine associations in the eighteenth century. The publication of private correspondence as a popular literary genre becomes common in the era, but the expertise in letter-writing, unlike most other forms, belongs to women. Madame de Sévigné and Lady Mary Wortley Montagu were recognized as exemplars in the genre, and women in general were more likely to publish their correspondence or autobiography than any other literary form except poetry.[84] As a regular practice, letters are part of the expected repertoire of female accomplishments, requiring little formal training and involving the relation of private, domestic detail. Their discursive nature is especially given to narrative, which made the form ideal for the developing genre of the novel.[85] As a published form of private expression, the letter occupies an amorphous place in literary discourse and one which women frequently find convenient for publishing their

---

[83] S. Fielding, *Remarks*, p. 3.

[84] Cynthia Lowenthal, *Lady Mary Wortley Montagu and the Eighteenth-Century Familiar Letter* (Athens: University of Georgia Press, 1994), chapter 1; Judith Phillips Stanton, "'This New-Found Path Attempting': Women Dramatists in England, 1660–1800," in Schofield and Macheski, eds., *Curtain Calls*, pp. 325–354. According to Stanton, by 1800 the numbers of women authors could be assessed in the following categories: 97 playwrights, 263 published poets, 201 published novelists, 170 religious writers, 247 letters/autobiographical writers (p. 325).

[85] See Ruth Perry, *Women, Letters and the Novel* (New York: AMS Press, 1980), esp. pp. 63–91.

ideas. Fielding uses the gendered associations of the letter-form to mitigate or mask the impropriety of her assumption of critical judgment; specifically she relates literary judgments as a form of gossip, gleaning knowledge from polite gatherings in appropriate female spaces. Criticism in her text takes place in a series of consecutive "scenes," where a regular group of characters debate the novel's length, style, and characters.

Fielding's decision to use the letter-form is, coincidentally, parallel to Richardson's own narrative technique in *Clarissa*, and so when her characters debate the merits of his epistolary form they offer an instance of "meta-criticism" on Fielding's own critical strategy. In response to Mr. Dellincourt's censure of the author's linguistic innovations – he says "you had coined new Words, and printed others as if you was writing a Spelling-book, instead of relating a Story"[86] – Fielding's spokesperson, Miss Gibson, advocates the flexibility of the genre: "Indeed, Sir, I do not pretend to be any Judge of the Accuracy of Stile, but I beg to know, if in the writing familiar Letters, many Liberties are not allowable, which in other kinds of writing might perhaps be justly condemned."[87] The exchange characterizes Fielding's dramatization of criticism as social discourse, complete with the gendered behavior required of such interactions. With a typical gesture of humility, Gibson denies her ability to judge, but she patently implies that the openness of the epistolary form obviates Dellincourt's objections. Her inquisitive and self-deprecating manner minimizes the presumption of a female correcting male judgment in a way that prefigures Richardson's later vivacious and witty heroine, Harriet Byron. Through the ostensibly recorded conversation, Fielding simultaneously defends Richardson's digressive and inventive style while she justifies her own use of the literary form. Presumably, the "many liberties" allowed accommodate her own critical dialogue. The eclecticism of the letter, or rather the symbolically feminine, inchoate possibility of the form, makes it an appropriate vehicle for so "unaccountable or whimsical" an endeavor as female-authored literary criticism.

In a more oblique endorsement of her critical strategy, Fielding defends the universal value of representing private life. Her management of the dialogue reproduces the gendered spheres of the increasingly influential middle-class ideology, which privileges a feminine understanding of common private life over the masculine interest in the history of wars and empire. Expressing the same patriarchal assumption that Virginia

[86] S. Fielding, *Remarks*, p. 12.   [87] Ibid.

Woolf observes many years later, Mr. Singleton is amused to hear that "knowing the Particulars of the Family at Harlow-place was of as much Consequence, as the knowing the Springs and Wheels on which turned the Affairs of the greatest Commonwealth that was ever heard of since the Creation of the World."[88] Fielding undermines the critical prejudice for the great and male events in history by positing, through the figure of "The Lady of the House," the moral and ethical relevance of personal minutiae:

I really think the penetrating into the Motives that actuate the Persons in a private Family, of much more general use to be known, than those concerning the Management of any Kingdom or Empire whatsoever: The latter, Princes, Governors, and Politicians only can be the better for, whilst every Parent, every Child, every Sister, and every Brother, are concerned in the former, and may take example by such who are in the same Situation with themselves.[89]

In embryonic form, the "Lady"'s argument describes the shift from the public function of literature as the instruction of princes or a statement of national character to the private purpose of literature corresponding to the needs and desires of the emerging bourgeois readership. In this way, Fielding's text anticipates the arguments for formal realism articulated by Ian Watt. The gendered epistemology of Fielding's historical position informs her assignment of roles in the critical discussion. Not surprisingly, Mr. Singleton assumes the greater importance of knowing the details of the Roman empire, whereas the lady of the house, identified solely by her domestic space, claims the universal importance of the novel's private realm. Because Fielding presents her critical views through the relation of private conversations in domestic spaces, the universal application of such private knowledge further authorizes her own criticism. More importantly, she makes a distinct claim for the importance of feminine knowledge in the novel, granting it the transcendent qualities required of art.

Fielding fully exploits the gendered spheres of knowledge in her casting of the ideal male and female critics, a device that will be used for slightly different ends by Clara Reeve. Significantly, in Fielding's critical narrative Miss Gibson wins over the reluctant male admirer, Bellario, not to herself but to Clarissa, with whom she identifies and whom she wants her friends to model. Bellario embodies the mid-century ideals of masculine sense and sensibility and operates as a conspicuous figure of desire in the text. The narrator intimates a sense of secrecy

---

[88] Ibid., p. 7.   [89] Ibid.

when she announces "the Addition of one Gentleman, whom I shall call Bellario."[90] None of the other characters merits a pseudonym taken from romances and secret histories. Fielding develops his character more than the other speakers, identifying him by critical credentials: "his known Taste and Impartiality made all those who wished Reason instead of Prejudice might judge of the Subject before them, rejoice at his Presence."[91] Bellario answers his fellow disputants "with that Candor, which is known to be one of the most distinguishing Marks of his Character."[92] Bellario and Gibson initially take opposing positions on Clarissa's capacity for love and the story's tragic ending; when Bellario ultimately capitulates to Gibson's perspective, the narrator expresses great esteem for the gentleman: "This was noble! this was candid! this was like Bellario!"[93] Finally, Bellario initiates a correspondence with Gibson for the ostensible purpose of continuing their conversation on the beauties of *Clarissa*, but as every reader of that didactic novel knows, a private correspondence between a man and woman implies, at the very least, a growing intimacy. The developing relationship between the two leading characters draws the reader's attention away from Fielding's critical endeavor; more importantly, it allows her to explore the masculine as well as the feminine critical responses to the novel.

Bellario's sixteen-page letter to Gibson, interspersed with ancient and modern references and moral reflections, dominates Fielding's text, creating an opportunity for the most sustained scholarly treatment of the novel. The criteria Bellario evaluates – the unity and proportion of the design, the justness of the action, the preservation of character and propriety of the moral – all derive from the classical tradition of criticism and French neoclassical rules. Fielding voices her learned judgments through the male figure because it is more acceptable for a gentlemen to be conversant in ancient languages and their critical traditions; the learned lady, in contrast, is a figure of contempt in fictions of the day, and a display of knowledge in Latin or Greek is considered repellent. Lady Bradshaigh wrote to Richardson: "I hate to hear Latin out of a woman's mouth. There is something in it, to me masculine."[94] Fielding's deliberate dialogism – she is literally double-voiced in this exchange of letters – reproduces the epistemological separatism of gender informing the practice of literary criticism in the eighteenth century. In keeping with the importance of originality, Bellario expresses the value of

---

[90] Ibid., p. 13.   [91] Ibid.   [92] Ibid., p. 18.   [93] Ibid., p. 31.
[94] Bridget Hill, ed., *Eighteenth-Century Women: An Anthology* (London: George Allen and Unwin, 1984), p. 56.

Richardson's unique design in *Clarissa* by comparing it with Homer's founding genius in the epic. Like the classic author, Richardson determines his own literary standards: "the painting Nature is indeed [Richardson's] Aim, but the Vehicle by which he conveys his lively Portraits to the Mind is so much his own Invention . . . Aristotle drew his Rules of Epic Poetry from Homer, and not Homer from Aristotle."[95] With equal ease Bellario quotes a "celebrated French critic," to support his emphasis on Richardson's justness and proportion.[96] Bellario further develops his critical evaluation by comparing other authors celebrated by the critical hegemony, namely Shakespeare and Milton. Significantly, Fielding does not "labor" when she creates Bellario's dissertation in educated criticism; she finds "ease" in the consistency between the masculine discourse and the male speaking subject.

In contrast to Bellario's learned exposition, Gibson's return letter describes the emotive power of the novel. Through her female character Fielding employs the rhetoric of sensibility that reflects the mid-century emphasis on internal emotional states. As scholars like John Sitter have recognized, the years following Pope's death in 1744 witness a movement away from the public, satirical forms of literature in favor of the private lyric, a retreat from the harsh world of ambition to the feminine realms of feeling.[97] Correspondingly, the critical values of the Wartons, Edward Young, and Edmund Burke, among others, reflect a new focus on personal subjectivity and heightened emotional perceptiveness. Where Bellario comments on Richardson's excellent imitation of nature, Gibson records her passionate response to the text, "his Strokes penetrate immediately to the Heart, and we feel all the Distresses he paints; we not only weep for, but with Clarissa, and accompany her, step by step, through all her Distresses."[98] Gibson's account relies on her private reading experience; it is authorized by personal testimony and not, like Bellario, by a tradition of authors and scholars.

As such, Gibson's response typifies the permissive possibilities of the changing critical discourse that Johnson derides in the figure of Dick Minim, but it also signifies the potential for women to enter critical debate based on the authority of their gendered sphere of knowledge. Fielding's narrative frequently alludes to the "intimate acquaintance" between the reader and Richardson's characters, stressing that such personal knowledge promotes instruction through imitation. Gibson's

---

[95] S. Fielding, *Remarks*, p. 35.   [96] Ibid., p. 36; the critic remains unidentified at this point.
[97] John Sitter, *Literary Loneliness in Mid-Eighteenth-Century England* (Ithaca: Cornell University Press, 1982).
[98] S. Fielding, *Remarks*, p. 51.

appreciation of Clarissa is based on an intense identification that corrects her behavior through sympathetic experience:

> Whilst we seem to live, and daily converse with her through her last Stage, our Hearts are at once rejoiced and amended, are both soften'd and elevated, till our Sensations grow too strong for any Vent, but that of Tears; nor am I ashamed to confess, that Tears without Number I have shed, whilst Mr. Belford by his Relation has kept me (as I may say) with fixed Attention in her Apartment, and made me perfectly present at her noble exalted Behaviour.[99]

Significantly, Gibson's critical processing takes place through her body; the somatic response of tears and her physical presence at Clarissa's side testify to the power of Richardson's art to affect the reader's emotional state. Such response, of course, is the empirical proof of Gibson's own sensibility and moral standards. She claims earlier that "those whose Eyes melt not at Scenes of well-wrought Distress, cannot properly be said to laugh, from a liberal and chearful Spirit."[100] Gibson ultimately tests the novel against a set of moral criteria in which Clarissa exemplifies the most worthy traits to be imitated. She closes her letter to Bellario with the hope that "every friend I love in this World [will] imitate you [Clarissa] in their Lives, and thus joyfully quit all the Cares and Troubles that disturb this mortal being."[101] Through Gibson, Fielding posits a distinctly feminine mode of critical evaluation that emphasizes the subjective identification between reader and heroine, manifest through corrective sensibility producing a didactic model of imitation. Fielding grants Gibson the last word in her dialogue, and, like Neander in Dryden's more famous critical dialogue, she seems to represent her author's perspective. However, the gendered assignment of critical methods suggests a more complicated encoding of literary values. Fielding's narrative reproduces the gendered critical modes of novel-criticism in the separation of male erudition and female emotion, but her deployment of both roles in her critical "scenes" implies the need for both perspectives to achieve critical balance and objectivity.

Ironically, Fielding maintains her critical objectivity through the fictionalized discourse of many speakers. She carefully conceals any identifying features of her own personality as she vigorously animates the minds and emotions of her characters. Fielding demonstrates a form of communal criticism through their candid exchange of ideas and consensus-building. Her final epistolary communication subverts the hierarchical ordering of critical values by representing the male and

---

[99] Ibid., p. 56.   [100] Ibid., p. 31.   [101] Ibid., p. 56.

female perspectives as complementary. The fiction of her critical authority, however, over-distances Sarah Fielding from the role of critic. Unlike the two critics already discussed, Fielding chooses to publish her criticism anonymously; this further displacement of the personal identity is characteristic of what Poovey identifies as "indirection," writing without seeking public notice.[102] She succeeds in describing the novel in both traditional, academic terms and more contemporary, subjective terms, but in doing so she reproduces the very expectations for gendered subjects that hinder the female's full entry into the realm of criticism. In an effort to be objective, she obscures the invention and judgment of her own critical voice.

THE MORAL ARTILLERY OF CLARA REEVE

The relationship between the normative ideology of the private domestic female and the numbers of published women writers is seemingly paradoxical. As the cultural investment in native female purity becomes ever more pronounced in the conduct literature of the last decades of the eighteenth century, more and more women appear in print, in fields as diverse as politics, science, and social justice. Literary criticism becomes a practicable genre, and women such as Mary Wollstonecraft, Mary Hays, and Elizabeth Inchbald publish their work in magazines and critical reviews.[103] Thus the literary discourse for Clara Reeve's *The Progress of Romance* (1785) differs considerably from that of the other critics discussed in this chapter.[104] While she may not seem a prodigy for merely attempting to publish her literary judgments, she is subject to more restrictive codes regarding the proper language in which to deliver them. In an age of "reactionaries and revolutionaries," as Janet Todd labels it, Reeve falls well within the former category.[105] However, she fully exploits the contradiction in the cultural construction of the "proper lady," entering into the public world of letters in order to promote the moral edification of youth, and particularly the female sex. Like Lennox and Fielding, Reeve supports her criticism with a fund of learning not necessarily within the scope of traditional femininity, and like all of the others she engages in the controversies and arguments of

---

[102] Poovey, *The Proper Lady*, p. 36.
[103] Janet Todd, *The Sign of Angellica: Women, Writing and Fiction, 1660–1800* (New York: Columbia University Press, 1989), chapter 12.
[104] Clara Reeve, *The Progress of Romance and The History of Charoba, Queen of Aegypt*, 2 vols. (1785), bibliographical note by Esther M. McGill (New York: Facsimile Text Society, 1930).
[105] Todd, *The Sign of Angellica*, chapter 12.

male critics, but her key authorizing strategy is the culturally specified feminine voice of morality; it provides simultaneously a position of power and propriety.

Despite dismissive accounts of *The Progress of Romance* as "of little importance," or "not strikingly original in the quality or manner of its critical judgments," Reeve's criticism plays a important role in the foundation of the novel and the negotiation of critical authority.[106] Through the course of a two-volume discussion of relationships among romance, epic, history, and novels, Reeve proposes to counter "opinions long received, and but little examined," to wit, that novels and romances, improperly confounded together, are contemptible and dangerous compared with the prestigious genres of history and epic.[107] J. Paul Hunter contends that Reeve's retrospective study achieves for the first time a definitive separation between the romance and the novel, a distinction that Reeve herself sees as historically distorted through gender and class prejudices.[108] With similar regard, Ros Ballaster argues that *The Progress of Romance* is the most important book of the period in clarifying how "the jostling over terms in this debate is precisely one of an association between the 'literary' and the masculine, and the 'popular' and the feminine."[109] Reeve holds "learned men of our country" largely responsible for the misconstruction, and she reinforces the gendered opinion by putting the arguments against the worth of novels and romances in the mouth of a male speaker. The gendered dynamic of the argument, which Reeve, like Fielding, structures in the form of a dialogue, affords compelling evidence of the intersection between social codes and critical values. By maintaining the dominant notions of biological separatism in her representation of male and female views of literature, she defines a feminine realm of authority and expertise in which she can successfully advance her critical arguments. Reeve's presumption of critical privilege certainly earns her the scorn of succeeding generations of male critics, but it is less than accurate to suppose, as Messer-Davidow does, that she "enacts the worst fears of ideologists and aestheticians alike."[110] While she sets out to clarify the

---

[106] *DNB*, eds. Leslie Stephen and Sidney Lee, 22 vols. (Oxford: Oxford University Press, 1921–1922, reprint 1967–1968), vol. XVI, p. 847; Ioan Williams, ed., *Novel and Romance, 1700–1800: A Documentary Record* (New York: Barnes & Noble, 1970), p. 298.

[107] Reeve, *Progress of Romance*, vol. I, p. 3.

[108] J. Paul Hunter, *Before Novels: The Cultural Contexts of Eighteenth-Century English Fiction* (New York: W. W. Norton, 1990), p. 26.

[109] Ros Ballaster, "Romancing the Novel: Gender and Genre in Early Theories of Narrative," in Dale Spender, ed., *Living by the Pen: Early British Women Writers* (New York: Teachers College Press, 1992), p. 191.   [110] Messer-Davidow, "'For Softness She'," p. 54.

history of the genre, her underlying principles of literary criticism reinforce the hegemonic, hierarchical vision of society.

The Progress of Romance develops as a discussion among Reeve's spokeswoman Euphrasia, her male opponent Hortensius, and a female arbitrator, Sophronia. Like Fielding's dialogue, Reeve's text represents literary criticism as social discourse, as the three interlocutors gather weekly for twelve evenings at one of the speakers' homes. Reeve, however, is much more clearly identified than Fielding, when Euphrasia claims authorship of the translation of Barclay's *Argenis*, which Reeve published as *The Phoenix* in 1772.[111] Interestingly, Hortensius expresses the desire for coverture because his male friend would certainly "indulge his splenetic humour at my expense" should he discover Hortensius closeted with women discussing romances.[112] Hortensius' fear of being exposed reflects the sense of gendered literary territory the romance and novel represent, even in the late eighteenth century. Reeve aims to separate the two genres and to distinguish the relative worth of individual examples of each based on merit. Still, throughout the text she clearly demarcates certain genres and authors as belonging to a specific sex. For instance, Hortensius claims, "Richardson is a writer all your own; your sex are more obliged to him and Addison, than to all other men-authors"; *Tristram Shandy*, however, "is not a woman's book."[113] In the case of the former, the authors' interest in virtue qualifies them for the "female cause," and in the latter, Reeve asks significantly, "what can I say of it with safety?"

In keeping with the forms of polite conversation, the language of argument is similarly gendered. Hortensius repeatedly casts the discussion in terms of combat, beginning with Euphrasia's "challenge" in daring to compare romance with epics; he demands "full satisfaction," and he suffers her "bold attack" on Homer's "extravagant sallies of imagination."[114] For her part, Euphrasia avoids any direct confrontation, preferring to shelter her opinion behind the authorities of Dr. Percy, Dr. Blackwell, Mr. Dobson, and even Lady Mary Wortley Montagu, among others. She declines "the honour of making you a convert to myself," and passes it "to abler hands."[115] Euphrasia's self-representation is necessarily balanced between the legitimate and recognized authority on the history of romances and novels and the polite lady engaged in conversation with a man. Her deference to Hortensius generally concedes to him culturally sanctioned qualities of masculinity, reflective

---

[111] Reeve, *Progress of Romance*, vol. I, p. 80.   [112] Ibid., p. 27.   [113] Ibid., p. 135; vol. II, p. 30.
[114] Reeve, *Progress of Romance* vol. I, pp, 1, 3, 20.   [115] Ibid., p. 34.

of the definitive literary categories. For instance, she admits that "I may be enabled to strike out new lights upon the subject, when my imagination is corrected by the judgment of Hortensius."[116] Her critical paradigm grants the female powers of creativity, but it reserves the higher faculty of legislative reason for the male.

Throughout, Euphrasia has recourse to her "papers and extracts," predominantly authored by men of letters, a set of "artillery and firearms" that puts Hortensius into good-humored panic. Reeve dramatizes the critic's role as the synthesizer of knowledge to minimize the presumption of female judgment, but she suggests that Euphrasia's displacement of authority irritates her male opponent. He demurs from raising objections against "what has been said by men of first-rate Genius, learning, and judgment. You have contrived so as to transfer your attack from yourself to those, whom I dare not contradict."[117] Appropriately, a woman does not enter the lists with a man. One suspects that Reeve projects in Hortensius a response from her actual readers and potential opponents. She represents the critical opinions of a woman as only that gleaned from authorities of firm standing in the intellectual community, and so she justifies her critical text while preserving the character of subordinate femininity.

While Reeve masks her understanding of history and of aesthetic criteria by appealing to male authorities, she delivers the judgment of morality entirely on her own. And in her evaluation of women novelists, she demonstrates the exclusive effects of that power. Her trajectory – from Ancient Greece through 1770 – entitles her to what may be the first serious treatment of women novelists by a female critic. Although Hortensius protests intermittently that Euphrasia is "ready enough to pay due respect to writers of your own sex, but you are rather severe upon some of ours," Euphrasia in fact subjects all the novelists, male and female alike, to the necessary criterion of pious didacticism.[118] Consequently, the novels of Sarah Fielding and Charlotte Lennox, as well as Madame Riccoboni, Frances Sheridan, and Frances Brooke receive high praise as moral entertainment and instruction.[119] Reeve treats other female writers, notably the Duchess of Newcastle, Madame de Lafayette, Aphra Behn and Mary Manley, with less enthusiasm. With the exception of the Duchess of Newcastle, who is dismissed as the "eternal scribler," the novels of these women fail because they are "very

[116] Ibid., p. 5.   [117] Ibid., p. 90.   [118] Ibid., p. 143.
[119] Reeve takes exception to Lennox's *Female Quixote*, however, because its satire is purportedly thirty years too late: *Progress of Romance*, vol. II, p. 6.

improper to be read by, or recommended to virtuous minds, and especially to youth."[120]

Reeve's treatment of de Lafayette, Behn, and Manley reveals her passionate investment in the definition of the female artist as moral exemplar, indicating the grounds of authority for her own literary achievements. She rejects de Lafayette's *The Princess of Cleves* on the basis that it promotes a dangerous image of romance: "it influences young minds in favour of a certain fatality in love matters, which encourages them to plead errors of the imagination, for faults of the heart."[121] In Behn she finds "strong marks of Genius," but "unhappily" her stories are given to "loose" turns. Reeve's combined respect and disappointment yield an expression of unexpected feeling for Behn: "Let us do justice to her merits, and cast the veil of compassion over her faults."[122] Manley does not fare so well; her scandal chronicles, Reeve hopefully predicts, "are sinking gradually into oblivion. I am sorry to say they were once in fashion, which obliges me to mention them, otherwise I had rather be spared the pain of disgracing an Author of my own sex."[123] Reeve's intention to remain silent on Manley's works – she refuses to even offer a title – indicates a lacuna in the critical language available. Except for *The Princess of Cleves*, Reeve never specifies the faults of this "class" of writers. Her language of propriety does not permit the identification of those offenses because that would implicate her own knowledge. She might respond as she does to *Tristram Shandy*, "What can I say of it with safety?" Instead she casts the improper female writers into the void: silenced, veiled, in oblivion.

Reeve allows women writers to enter the pantheon of great artists only when they perform a service to their sex and the world by promoting virtue. Eliza Haywood's role as the fallen and converted female artist illustrates the case in point. Reeve spares her the fate of Behn and Manley, because "she had the singular good fortune to recover a lost reputation, and the yet greater honour to atone for her errors. – She devoted the remainder of her life and labours to the service of virtue."[124] As a critic dedicated to the ideal of female moral purity, Reeve can commit the story of Haywood's fame to posterity because it corresponds to her critical and moral vocabulary. She describes Haywood's improprieties as sins against virtue, collapsing the literary under the greater moral imperative. Reeve herself plays the role of moral censor, saving Haywood from the calumny that Hortensius would impute to her

---

[120] Reeve, *Progress of Romance*, vol. I, pp. 74, 117.   [121] Ibid., p. 115.   [122] Ibid., p. 118.
[123] Ibid., p. 119.   [124] Ibid., p. 121.

and indicating that her reputation as a literary artist depends upon her standing as a proper lady.

Unlike Fielding's Gibson, who delights in the intense emotional effect of novel-reading, Reeve frequently worries that unmonitored novel-reading will seriously damage the minds of unsophisticated readers. Euphrasia answers the charge that novels are enervating and dangerous by stressing the importance in selection. Hortensius contends that the danger is greater for the female sex because they read more novels, but all reading, Euphrasia claims, is potentially harmful for the young without proper guidance and moral contexts. The responsibility for this proper selection falls within the feminine sphere: "It is certainly the duty of every Mother, to consider seriously, the consequences of suffering children to read all the books that fall in their way indiscriminately."[125] She provides a list of suitable books that includes several conduct books, moral guides and sermons, all of Richardson's works and the *Spectator*, *Tatler*, and *Rambler*. Reeve's pedagogical paradigm differs strikingly from the one in which she was reared, having supposedly read the parliamentary debates and Greek and Roman history at her father's knee.[126] Her femino-centric pedagogy and limited reading list initially appear to deny the intellectual conditions that enable her own entry into the field of letters, and, hence, reinforce the dominant ideological division between masculine intellect and feminine morality that hinders females in the critical role. However, her insistence on the mother's choice in educating her children necessitates a form of critical judgment for women that contests notions of feminine dependence on male reason. By detailing the potential good and danger inherent in the reading of novels, and by assigning to women the duty of discriminating proper texts, Reeve makes a serious argument in favor of female critical authority. According to late-eighteenth-century constructions of native female purity, women are uniquely qualified for the cause of morality, and hence for the role of reading censor as she conceives it.

Reeve's pride in her feminine sense of morality is understandably piqued when her critical honesty is impugned in an exchange of letters published in the *Gentleman's Magazine* (1786). In a letter signed merely A.S, Anna Seward, a recognized poet and correspondent of the literati, condemns Reeve's *Progress of Romance* because of her expressed

---

[125] Ibid., vol. II, p. 101.
[126] *DNB*, vol. XVI, p. 847; also see Miriam Leranbaum, "'Mistresses of Orthodoxy': Education in the Lives and Writings of Late Eighteenth-Century English Women Writers," *Proceedings of the American Philosophical Society*, 121.4 (August 1977), 281–301.

preference for *Pamela* over *Clarissa* and *Sir Charles Grandison*. Seward takes personal offense at the judgment because she had formerly entertained high notions of Reeve's mind based upon "repeated perusals of the *English Baron*," Reeve's most famous novel. Seward ungenerously concludes:

The *English Baron*, its author well knows, is better written than *Pamela*, that dim dawn of an illustrious genius; and the heart of Clara Reeves, less candid and sincere than her imagination is happy, with the co-operation of that eternal misleader self-conceit, suggested this too common practice of disingenuous spirits, to attempt the degradation of a superior writer, by extolling a work of his, which they know they can themselves excel, above those higher efforts of his genius, which they feel unattainable.[127]

Seward explains the apparently ludicrous preference for *Pamela* as a calculated deception by Reeve to grant her own novel more favorable consideration. She doubly assails Reeve's moral standing by implicating her as a liar and vainglorious author.

Seward's public accusation forces Reeve to reenter the public sphere in the particularly difficult position of self-defense. Reeve's response indicates the extent to which her public role depends upon a reputation of modesty and moral righteousness.

Had the writer of that letter only imputed to me an error in judgement, I might have sat down in silence under the charge . . . But this unmerciful critic charges me with disingenuousness, and a design to mislead the judgement of others; a fault of a much higher nature, which I shall not take to myself while I have power to prove myself innocent of it.[128]

It is far worse for a female critic to be condemned on grounds of a bad heart than of a weak mind. Less concerned about errors in judgment, Reeve fails to address Seward's literary point altogether. Instead she deflects the charge of insulting Richardson by claiming intimate friendship with and approval of that novelist's sole-surviving daughter. Presumably, if Richardson's daughter can support his treatment in *The Progress of Romance*, then it cannot be degrading, and therefore Reeve cannot be guilty of the sort of disingenuousness with which she is charged.

The negotiation of critical authority in this exchange reveals a gap between the moral and aesthetic grounds of judgment akin to the incommensurate debates of literary value and femininity in *Shakespear*

---

[127] Anna Seward, "Correspondence between Anna Seward and Clara Reeve from the Gentleman's Magazine (1786)," in Folger Collective, eds., *Women Critics*, pp. 166–167.
[128] Folger Collective, eds., *Women Critics*, p. 168.

Illustrated. In her retaliatory letter, Seward calls upon cultural consensus to justify her charges against Reeve:

> Had Miss Reeve apologized to the world for her strange dissent from the universal voice on that subject – had she only said that *Pamela* was more to her taste than *Clarissa*, or *Sir Charles Grandison*, that taste had perhaps been pitied in silence; but the cool arrogance of an absolute decision, that Pamela is the *chef d'œuvre* of Richardson, must prove a daring contradiction of the general opinion, which deserved the pointed reprehension it has met.[129]

Seward takes issue with Reeve's assertion of critical authority; she distinguishes between the harmless statement of opinion and the more dangerous representation of critical truth. The latter, when it dissents from recognized opinion, *requires* public denunciation. Seward assumes the voice of critical hegemony to authorize her rejection of Reeve's competence as a critic. Reeve, on the other hand, is more invested in the moral authority of her position than the ability to determine aesthetic ranking. The two pursue different ends in their critical practice, and each fails to accommodate the vision of the other. Reeve evaluates novels on their pedagogical value for young female readers, and Seward – at least here – doctrinally follows a critical consensus that overlooks the specific needs of women and children in its attempt at universality. Reeve does not specify her objections to *Clarissa*, but, given her preference for happy endings, she probably finds the tragedy difficult to recommend. In her first letter, Seward offers Johnson's opinion of *Clarissa* to justify her perspective, an authority she did not always bow to but which held sufficient critical clout. In the second, she appeals to the construct of a "universal voice" as the final tribunal.

Each woman's critical grounding involves different gendered assumptions that further divides them. Seward's outrage at Reeve's flouting critical convention may be tinged with the surprise or shock at a woman's presumption. Alternatively, Reeve's assumption of the moral didacticism – which in part enables the arrogance of absolute decision – is compounded by her position as a woman. Furthermore Reeve does not shrink from drawing gendered inferences from the language and tone of A.S.'s letter. She closes her reply with the explanation "that I have addressed my reply as to a man; for I cannot conceive it possible that so much malevolence, with so little delicacy, could proceed from the pen of one of my own sex."[130] Reeve reads Seward's letter as illiberal and indecorous, employing a shameful form of language inconsistent with

---

[129] Ibid., pp. 170–1.   [130] Ibid., p. 170.

reigning notions of femininity. According to Reeve's principles, the hostility of Seward's attack, like Behn's loose narratives and Manley's scandalous reports, is distinctly unfeminine, and within an ontological understanding of gender, such signs negate the possibility of representing the female. Again, confronted with the writing of a woman that does not figure into her concept of woman, she reasserts her understanding of gender and erases the female author.

In *The Progress of Romance*, Reeve uses the role of moral censor to authorize her entry into the realm of critical judgment while retaining the privileges accorded to women in the late-eighteenth-century discourse of the proper lady, but her strategy involves considerable aesthetic restrictions. Limited to didactic concerns for children and young ladies and to the representation of pure womanhood, Reeve's critical purview is constrained to a domestic purpose and vocabulary. Her inability to speak about *Tristram Shandy* or Manley because of their indecency exemplifies the ways in which gendered discourses impinge upon the construction of literary values, as well as limit the scope of the female critic. The dialogic effect of gendered and critical discourses produces a filter of femininity through which only women who conform to the properly feminine code emerge. All others are blotted out, veiled, or – in the case of Seward – refused her female identity. The interaction with Seward points to the incommensurability between the ontologically gendered female and the critical desire for objective universality. Reeve's investment in the moral and didactic function of literature is the necessary condition for her critical judgment, but through it she addresses an increasingly minor set of aesthetic criteria in the late eighteenth century, as disinterestedness and the transcendent values in art supersede the Augustan ideals of profit and delight. Reeve's criticism, nonetheless, has great historical interest with respect to both the field of novel-studies and the transition of literary values that takes place throughout the century. Like Behn, Lennox, and Fielding, her criticism represents what the discourse eventually simplifies and represses, and with it the feminine perspective that challenges and complicates masculine critical objectivity.

WHERE ARE THEY NOW?

As part of the newly empowered literate classes, eighteenth-century women could gain access to that easy and forward goddess, Criticism, approaching her through methods both of clever indirection and bold appropriation. Given the critical publications of Behn, Lennox, Fielding, and Reeve, the purported silence of Aristotle's sisters raises questions. What happened to these critical efforts? What were the contemporary reactions? How were they treated in subsequent generations? Reeve's critical selectivity demonstrates the process of silencing that Behn was subject to less than a hundred years after her death. Evidently, by Virginia Woolf's time, the early female critics had been erased from the annals of literary history altogether. Despite the overwhelming consistency in the repression of female critical voices, it would be a mistake to see this as an inevitable course of events or a predetermined, identical experience for every woman. Myra Jehlen reminds us that agents and statements exert unequal influence in discourse "because of the spaces in which they are articulated and because of the political and social networks that are being organized around them."[131] Eighteenth-century literary discourse preserves judgment as a masculine privilege, a condition that favors the reiteration of critical statements made by men but not by women. For instance, Dryden's prefaces were imitated, modified, and discussed in public networks like coffeehouses and periodicals, as well as reproduced in prestigious, bound volumes. Dryden's collected works were published in a variety of permutations in five different editions, many reprinted more than once, before the end of the eighteenth century.[132] For various reasons, criticism by female authors did not benefit from these forms of repetition or the status of cultural "truth" thereby attained.

Behn's works enjoyed considerable esteem throughout the 1690s; no less than five versions or editions of her collected "Histories and Novels" were published between 1696 and 1700, and eight of her fifteen published plays were reprinted between her death in 1689 and 1700.[133] Significantly, however, none of the plays prefaced by her vituperative critical comments went through a second printing before the twentieth century. Behn was given new presence in the 1915 collection of her works by Montague Summers, reissued in 1967. A scholarly edition of Behn's works in seven volumes was completed by Janet Todd in 1996. (For full citations see my bibliography.) Charlotte Lennox had the fortune – or misfortune, as it seems – to criticize the most popular literary subject of the eighteenth century, and hence to participate in the proliferating discourses of Bardology. Despite Lennox's opposition to the culture's

---

[131] Judith Walkowitz, Myra Jehlen, and Bell Chevigny, "Patrolling the Borders: Feminist Historiography and the New Historicism," *Radical History Review* 43 (Winter 1989), 43.

[132] Kinsley and Kinsley, eds., *Dryden: The Critical Heritage*, p. 7.

[133] For a detailed list of Aphra Behn's publications see Mary Ann O'Donnell, *Aphra Behn: An Annotated Bibliography of Primary and Secondary Sources* (New York: Garland, 1986).

growing attachment to Shakespeare, her work was initially received with modest praise. Samuel Johnson showed his esteem for it by writing the dedication to volumes I and II and by referring to Lennox's research in his edition of Shakespeare. Reviewers in the *Gentleman's Magazine* and the *Monthly Review* were impressed with Lennox's rigor and knowledge, achievements that contemporary critics do not grant her.[134] While many people have criticized *Shakespear Illustrated*, it has not been reprinted since its original publication.[135] In terms of commentary within discourse, Fielding's *Remarks on Clarissa* is the least successful of the four examples considered here; this anonymous tract was published only once, and it inspired no acclaim, either in her time or in the twentieth century. Fielding enjoyed widespread popularity for her novel *David Simple* (1744) and for her collection of children's stories *The Governess* (1749). Both were reprinted in several editions, and the latter appeared in several languages. *Remarks* benefited from no such popularity, and even Richardson had little to say of the work. Sabor observes, however, that Richardson did make liberal use of Fielding's ideas in his subsequent editions of the novel without attribution.[136] Just as Young credits Lennox's scholarship to Johnson's overarching design, William Merritt Sale, Jr. suggests that the "little piece by a lady . . . might have been fostered by Richardson as part of a publicity program."[137] The assumption of male critical initiative and female dependence is an apparently powerful force in the erasure of female critical authority. Unlike *Shakespear Illustrated*, *Remarks on Clarissa* is available in two facsimile reproductions, as is Reeve's *Progress of Romance*.[138] However, neither is annotated or corrected. As mentioned before, *The Progress of Romance* has received mostly negative commentary in the history of novel criticism, but it is beginning to be recognized for its achievement.

All four critics are represented in the Folger Collective's new anthology, *Women Critics, 1660–1820*, but these selections are understandably brief. *Women Critics* begins to establish a context for the critical enterprises by eighteenth-century women, but much remains to be done in order to understand the significance of these contributions. The very

---

[134] *Monthly Review* (August 1753), vol. 9, 145; (April 1754), vol. 10, 309; *Gentleman's Magazine* (1753), vol. 23, 256; (1754), vol. 24, 233.

[135] All three volumes of *Shakespear Illustrated* are available on microfilm: The Eighteenth Century, Research Publications, Reel no. 3907, location 14 (vols. 1–2) and Reel no. 3575, location 5 (vol. 3).

[136] S. Fielding, *Remarks*, p. iv.

[137] William Merritt Sale, *Samuel Richardson: A Bibliographical Record of His Literary Career with Historical Notes* (New Haven: Yale University Press, 1936), p. 131.

[138] In addition to the Augustan Reprint Society edition of *Remarks*, and the Facsimile Text Society version of *Progress*, Garland reproduced both in 1970.

innovation of this collection suggests the repressive power of the literary tradition. Inattention to the critical perspectives of women functions as a process of simplification in the transmission of critical truths through time. The examples of these four women suggest that a reason for their repression lies in their tenacious hold on the particular, the private, the female, in literature. As the critical discourse of the late eighteenth century begins to formalize and embrace an aesthetic of transcendent, universal values and perspectives, the insistence on the needs and views of women and youth can be dismissed as marginal, a censure that continues to be launched against feminist criticism today. Of course, what such gestures of erasure fail to recognize is the extent to which the universal is constituted as a masculine perspective, defined by and grounded in its opposition to the feminine particular.[139]

According to Lipking, the absence of female critics from the tradition of literary criticism results in an impoverished, lopsided interpretation of literature: "But no one speaks for Aristotle's sister. The classic line of literary theory has hardly acknowledged the existence of two sexes, let alone the possibility that women might read and interpret literature in some way of their own."[140] In part, this is true; each of the female critics discussed in this chapter revises hegemonic critical views by asserting criteria from a female perspective. Their writings represent the products of female subjects within a discourse constituted as masculine, and, as such, they expose the limitations of a masculinist criticism. Most instructive is the way in which Lennox and Reeve, for instance, point to the gap between the negotiation of dominant critical authority and the contested category of femininity. Yet, these female critics demand to be read on their own terms, in their own historical and discursive spaces. Literary criticism throughout the century incorporates a gendered hierarchy that remains in place; however, the specific configuration of the genders and the literary expressions of "masculinity" and "femininity" change significantly between Behn and Reeve. Their individual self-authorizing strategies demonstrate the variety of techniques taken to realize a public voice. Behn alternately takes on satire or modesty as character roles; Lennox bends Augustan rules to the feminine discourse of domesticity; Fielding masks herself behind the dialogue of masculine learning and female sensibility, and Reeve maintains the conservative gendered status quo by speaking through the voice of morality.

---

[139] See Naomi Schor, *Reading in Detail: Aesthetics and the Feminine* (New York and London: Routledge, 1989), esp. part 1.
[140] L. Lipking, "Aristotle's Sister," p. 62.

While each woman negotiates the gendered expectations of the form in which she writes, none apologizes for what appears to be a transgression of critical prerogative. None apparently finds the role of critic too incongruous for the female subject. Given the long silence of Aristotle's sisters, we might justly be surprised by these early critical writings by women, but our wonder would be more profitably directed toward the forces that originally obscured the texts, which caused little consternation at their debut.

CHAPTER 5

Returning to the beautiful

> The Fair sex has just as much understanding as the male, but it is
> a beautiful understanding, whereas ours should be a deep
> understanding, an expression that signifies the sublime.   Kant[1]

From Addison's papers on the *Pleasures of the Imagination* (1712) through
Kant's *Critique of Judgment* (1790), the literary discourse of the eighteenth
century demonstrates a determined interest in how and why objects of
art produce their effects on individual subjects. Traditional accounts of
the aesthetic, including the long-standing scholarship of Samuel H.
Monk, tend to view the eighteenth century as the birthplace of
aesthetics, but these standard histories often understand eighteenth-century
discourse as a partial and confused attempt to reach Romantic
subjectivism.[2] Only recently have the ideological implications of the
historicity of aesthetics been explored. As Martha Woodmansee
demonstrates, the disinterestedness of art and the critic, a hallmark of
modern aesthetics, evolves in response to the interests of the unpatronized
literati facing a rise in popular literacy and the emerging bourgeois
marketplace.[3] In England, the political dimensions of this struggle are
evident in the discussion of the sublime and the beautiful, which signals
a challenge to the patrician model of classical authority by the modern,
subjective orientation of criticism. A matrix of discourses involved in
the formation of the modern subject underpins this shift in literary

---

[1] Immanuel Kant, *Observations on the Feeling of the Beautiful and the Sublime,* trans. John T. Goldthwait
(Berkeley: University California Press, 1960), p. 78.

[2] For example, see George Dickie, *Aesthetics: An Introduction* (New York: Pegasus, 1971), pp. 9–32;
Samuel H. Monk, *The Sublime: A Study of Critical Theories in XVIII-Century England,* second edition
(Ann Arbor: University of Michigan Press, 1960): "it is with Wordsworth that the experience that
lay behind the eighteenth-century sublime reached its apotheosis. All that had been written in
theory or in enthusiasm during our period seems to be a darkening of wisdom with counsel in
contrast to Wordsworth's concrete expression of his imaginative interpretation of the enduring
spiritual values of the external world," p. 231.

[3] Martha Woodmansee, *The Author, Art, and the Market: Rereading the History of Aesthetics* (New York:
Columbia University Press, 1994).

authority, at the core of which is the coalescing system of modern gendered difference.

Recent studies have focused on the development of the aesthetic under the aegis of colonial expansion and capitalist economics in eighteenth-century England in an effort to posit a complicity between aesthetic theory and political hegemony. David Simpson, in his comments tellingly entitled "Updating the Sublime," suggests that the sublime has not always been with us, "but it has," he claims, "certainly been more with us, white, male, western, members of so-called 'developed' countries."[4] Because of its obvious concern with power, the sublime has been recognized at least since the 1980s as a discourse enmeshed in the political ideologies of its historical construction and owned by representatives of the reigning hegemony. According to W. J. T. Mitchell, Edmund Burke's notion of the sublime corresponds to the rights of patriarchs – kings, fathers, husbands – while the beautiful is imputed to the dominated object: Burke "regards [the gendered analogy] not just as a matter of sensory or aesthetic decorum but as a figure for the natural foundations of all political and cosmic order, the universal structure of domination, master and slavery."[5] These critics recognize gender as part of the paradigmatic power structure of the aesthetic, but they fail to register the ramifications of such a fundamental parallel. In particular, the role of beauty and its dialogic context in femininity are minimized or overlooked.[6]

Of greater concern in the demystification of the aesthetic is the formation of the modern subject. Peter De Bolla and Terry Eagleton, though in very different ways, read the eighteenth-century aesthetic as a problematic negotiation of power under a political regime in transition from totalitarianism to a bourgeois republic. De Bolla's analysis proceeds structurally, in that he identifies a doubled discourse on and of the sublime in the mid-eighteenth century that initially describes the moral and political category of the sublime as "excess" and immediately produces a corresponding legislative discourse to control that surplus.[7] The compelling feature of the sublime lies in the radical subjectivity of

---

[4] David Simpson, "Commentary: Updating the Sublime," *Studies in Romanticism* 26.2 (Summer 1987), 255.

[5] W. J. T. Mitchell, *Iconology: Image, Text, Ideology* (Chicago: University of Chicago Press, 1986), p. 130.

[6] Frances Ferguson observes that most recent treatments of the sublime all but ignore the beautiful in the haste to get to the " 'real' subject"; "The Sublime of Edmund Burke, or the Bathos of Experience," *Glyph* 8 (Baltimore: The Johns Hopkins University Press, 1981), 69.

[7] Peter De Bolla, *The Discourse of the Sublime: Readings in History, Aesthetics, and the Subject* (Oxford: Basil Blackwell, 1989).

the individual perceiver, whose unreliable response is socially and politically undesirable and hence needs to be policed. De Bolla locates this discourse of control in rhetoric and literary theory. For Eagleton the aesthetic is a discourse of rationalized somatic response that can be both liberating and oppressive.[8] He identifies the complicity between aesthetic and political theory in the common appeal to universalized human feeling or sentiment, derived from the discourse of moral philosophy. The aesthetic is *the* legitimating bourgeois discourse, but it has a contradictory effect. On the one hand, the discourse of the sublime authorizes the freedom of the autonomous and self-determined subject, and on the other the rationale of moral human nature and affective social bonding renders the individual's consent to political authority pleasing.

The historicizing of the political and ethical imbrication in the aesthetic clearly exposes the structure of patriarchal ideology at its foundation, and both De Bolla and Eagleton acknowledge the participation of the aesthetic in gendered discourse because of the explicit ways in which the sublime and beautiful are coded as masculine and feminine. However, neither treats the ideological force of gendered paradigms with adequate attention to the implications for gendered subjects. De Bolla cites the sexual analogue for the sublime as the "transport" or sexual orgasm resulting from coitus, but he suggests that the gendered subjectivity produced in the discourse operates primarily within a homoerotic economy, where male subjects are at risk of seduction by the powerful, public, rhetoric of other men.[9] He addresses the feminine subject only as the much maligned reader of novels, a narrow and flawed evaluation of the production of the feminine subject in aesthetics.[10] He ignores her representation both as a more diverse reader and as the essential counterpart to the masculine subject of the sublime. These are two concerns I will address below.

From the outset, Eagleton minimizes the role of gender in his polemical defense of socialist criticism, and the effects of this decision are manifest in his assessment of the most blatant appropriations of gender in the aesthetic.[11] For instance, he addresses the gendered binary of Burke's *Philosophical Enquiry into the Origin of our Ideas of the Sublime and Beautiful* as the figuration of two organizations of power: "The distinction between the beautiful and the sublime, then, is that between woman and

[8] Terry Eagleton, *The Ideology of the Aesthetic* (Oxford: Basil Blackwell, 1990).
[9] De Bolla, *Discourse of the Sublime*, pp. 56–58.   [10] Ibid., pp. 252–278.
[11] Eagleton, *Ideology of the Aesthetic*, pp. 5–7.

man; but it is also the difference between what Louis Althusser had called the ideological and the repressive state apparatuses."[12] He implies that in Burke the aesthetic that is used to delude the individual into voluntary subjection is feminine, whereas the authentic power is masculine, a paradigm baldly construed in Eagleton's unproblematized metaphor: "The law is male, but hegemony is a woman."[13] He draws on Mary Wollstonecraft's critique of Burke to illustrate the sexism involved, but his concern is primarily with how Burke aestheticizes morality and power in order to justify his conservative vision of society. In their respective treatments of the aesthetic, then, neither De Bolla nor Eagleton theorizes the role of gender sufficiently. This neglect minimizes the significance of the beautiful in ideological accounts, a critical tendency that reinscribes the terms of the aesthetic's gendered analogy by subordinating and repressing the feminine.

Mary Poovey's analysis in her chapter on the economic and political roots of the British aesthetic begins to recover the feminine category.[14] She advances the understanding of gendered aesthetics in two important ways. First, she analyzes the impact of the gendered dynamic between judge and object, and second she suggests the problems created for the female subject as both aestheticized object and commodity of the marriage market. Poovey illustrates how two models of desire derived from moral philosophy – one acquisitive and based in bodily need, and one disinterested and based in contemplation – overlap in economic and aesthetic theories. Edmund Burke, for instance, explains the basis of aesthetic judgment through the opposing models of lust and love. In lust, desire answers the body's biological urgency by merely acquiring a mate, but in love a man discriminates among variety: "Men are carried to the sex in general, as it is the sex, and by the common law of nature; but they are attached to particulars by personal beauty."[15] For Poovey, Burke's appropriation of the sexed subject naturalizes the roles of male judge and female object of beauty.

Moreover, she argues that because Burke formulates the capacity for aesthetic preference in terms of female beauty, he renders the conventions of heterosexual differentiation – "man's relation to an aestheticized reading of sex and an eroticized reading of difference" – the basis for

---

[12] Ibid., p. 55.   [13] Ibid., p. 58.

[14] "Aesthetics and Political Economy in the Eighteenth Century: The Place of Gender in the Social Constitution of Knowledge," in George Levine, ed., *Aesthetics and Ideology* (New Brunswick: Rutgers University Press, 1994).

[15] Edmund Burke, *A Philosophical Enquiry into the Origin of our Ideas of the Sublime and Beautiful*, ed. J. T. Boulton (London: Routledge, 1958), p. 42.

social distinctions and discrimination. Poovey's analysis denaturalizes Burke's gendered binaries by exposing the economic models of desire that authorize the assumptions about human behavior that underlie his aesthetic system. "Thus sexual difference, which exists in nature, becomes the fundamental organizing dichotomy of a semantic system that produces distinctions – and therefore discriminations – in excess of the natural, originary difference."[16] The eighteenth-century semantic system has a crucial bearing on the bartering of female subjects in the bourgeois marriage market, since in that arena men are no longer contemplative observers but acquisitive dealers. Poovey sees Wollstonecraft as a pivotal critic of these gendered practices. According to Wollstonecraft, the degradation of the female in her society stems from her "natural" subordination to men, but this is complicated and entrenched by her position as an object of exchange whose value is discriminated by the male in aesthetic terms. Furthermore, this act of discrimination repeatedly fetishizes women in an economy designed to satisfy and resuscitate male desire: "the aesthetic stance articulated as an alternative to the acquisitive relation to objects – disinterested contemplation – positions women as objects to be appreciated imaginatively; in so doing, it leaves no room for expressing the sexual desires that aesthetics also inscribes *in* the woman so that she can fulfill the task of inciting male desire."[17] Poovey's insight suggests that in addition to the debasement of humanity in economic trade, the aesthetic objectification of women also sanctions a wholesale erasure of female expression, leaving a vacant female body on to which the male viewer fantasizes his own desire. Poovey reads the role of gender, and woman in particular, as the site of contradictions in late eighteenth-century aesthetics that point to its denied relationship to political economy. Unlike Eagleton and De Bolla, she foregrounds the way in which the aesthetic appropriates masculine discourses of power to sustain and naturalize the asymmetrical gendered positions in a system of discrimination and exchange.

These ideological critiques challenge the traditional acceptance of aesthetics as the disinterested discourse of artistic appreciation by re-placing it within the historical discourses of its production and examining, respectively, the structural, political, and gendered implications of its emergence. De Bolla and Eagleton represent the aesthetic as a complex and contradictory thesis of modern subjectivity. Poovey demonstrates the impact of overlapping discourses on the construction

---

[16] Mary Poovey, "Aesthetics and Political Economy," pp. 89–90.   [17] Ibid., p. 97.

of gendered subjectivity. All theorize the mid-century shift in focus to the subject as a multi-dimensional cultural project contemporaneous with the bourgeois rise to power. None, however, examines the aesthetic as a discourse informing literary judgment.[18]

While its roots in other intellectual discourses cannot and need not be denied, the mid-century discussion of aesthetics also negotiates the structure of literary authority with a new interest in the power of individual subjectivity and a corresponding anxiety over controlling the reading subject. More importantly for the argument of this book, the shift in focus to a subjective literary response – analyzed in the aesthetic of the sublime and the beautiful – occurs simultaneously with the emergent model of modern gendered difference, which posits an ontological rather than a social understanding of sex. The contemporaneity of these two changes has yet to be examined, the study of which is especially significant, given the dialogic construction of the categories of aesthetics and gender. Under an empirical impulse, critics tend to locate the source of aesthetic judgment in individual perception, which is *theorized* as universal and predictable. The tension between the construct of the autonomous subject, whose sense perceptions in *practice* are variable, and the desire for a set of stable criteria for aesthetic truth, yields a pronounced didacticism within the critical discourse. Because the sexes are seen to be ontologically separate beings rather than different versions of the same creature, and because a sex-specific universality is insistently reiterated, the critical discourse constructs the reading subject through categories of sexual difference. This chapter focuses on the discourse of the sublime and the beautiful in the context of the historical change in literary and gendered values and pays particular attention to the projection and regulation of the gendered reader.

Consequently, the field of aesthetics under question is narrow, in contrast to the traditional philosophical understanding of the term. Rather than address enduring questions of beauty and taste inherited from Plato – a practice Arthur C. Danto criticizes as the "continuity model of history"[19] – I will isolate the terms of contention in the literary and gendered debates of the middle years of the eighteenth century. Adapting from Eagleton, I use the term "aesthetics" to signify a

---

[18] De Bolla is less interested in what the sublime is than how it functions to provide a place for the subject to emerge. Similarly for Eagleton: the aesthetic is a putatively functionless concept that actually serves numerous purposes in political hegemony. Poovey analyses the aesthetic function, particularly as a system of discrimination between the sexes, but her suggestive chapter focuses on social qualities rather than on literary or artistic ones.

[19] See his foreword to Woodmansee, *Author, Art, and the Market*, xii–xv.

discourse that negotiates artistic value through the rational understanding of sense perceptions, and this discourse is implicated in moral and political as well as literary phenomena. My use of "beauty," therefore, should be distinguished from the more general notion implied by the word "aesthetics," although eighteenth-century theorists frequently do not make such discrimination. According to Walter J. Hipple, "beauty" in eighteenth-century parlance can be understood "in the comprehensive sense of serious positive aesthetic value (in which case sublimity is a species of it) or in the narrow sense of a particular aesthetic mode which contrasts with sublimity."[20] It is with the latter definition that I am concerned. My use of "sublime" and "beautiful" refers to the categories that emerge from the distinct split in the construction of aesthetics that occurs in the eighteenth century, where the sublime comes to represent the experience and qualities of grandeur, height, speed, expanse, and power, while the beautiful signifies the apprehension and qualities of smoothness, delicacy, smallness, harmony. Following De Bolla, I am interested in structure, but unlike him I focus on beauty as the dialectic double of sublimity, where the beautiful provides the conditions of possibility for the sublime. With one qualification that I will elaborate below, my understanding of the literary qualities of the sublime and the beautiful follows Monk's suggestion that *"Beauty* came to include, generally speaking, those qualities and gentle emotions that neo-classical art sought to embody; *sublimity* might contain anything else that seemed susceptible of giving aesthetic pleasure provided that it was grand enough and might conceivably 'transport'."[21] Because these literary concepts are mapped on to gendered categories, the discursive control over reading subjects closely corresponds to the hegemonic constructions of gender.

MID-CENTURY TRANSITIONS IN VALUE

The literary criticism of Wordsworth and Coleridge strikes readers as utterly different from the neoclassical criticism of Dryden and Pope, reflecting the pronounced shift from rule-oriented evaluation to a reliance on subjective human response. Literary discourse of the mid-century manifests this transition as conflict or ambiguity. Richard

[20] Walter J. Hipple Jr., "Philosophical Language and the Theory of Beauty in the Eighteenth Century," in Howard Anderson and John S. Shea, eds., *Studies in Criticism and Aesthetics 1660–1800: Essays in Honor of Samuel Holt Monk* (Minneapolis: University of Minnesota Press, 1967), p. 228.
[21] Monk, *The Sublime*, p. 55.

Hurd's language characterizes the dialogism between the older model of external authority and the increasing influence of subjectivism: "The art of poetry," he predicts in 1766, "will be universally the art of pleasing, and all its rules but so many means which experience finds most conducive to that end."[22] By subordinating the utility of poetry to its production of pleasure, Hurd signals the departure of didactic paradigms within poetry, a gesture representative of a discourse that ultimately divorces art from the use-value associated with crafts.[23] He appeals, nonetheless, to those "who like a principle the better for seeing it in Greek," and thus acknowledges the persistence of Ancient authorities as the standard of critical truths. His own expression – the "art" of poetry, with "all its rules" – carries the residual vocabulary of poetic laws, but the verification of these dicta lies not in the classics but in collective experience. In order to preserve a unified notion of poetry based on pleasure, Hurd theorizes the subjective response as universal. His recourse to general experience characterizes the mid-century articulation of custom as a sanction for internalized literary truths that elude empirical verification.

The universalizing gesture, however common, is not unproblematic, as David Hume's "Of the Standard of Taste" (1757) attests. Hume maintains that standards exist, although identifying any example of beauty or deformity is fraught with contention: "Though the principles of taste be universal, and nearly, if not entirely, the same in all men, yet few are qualified to give judgment on any work of art, or establish their own sentiment as the standard of beauty."[24] Taste is the product of sentiment – the mental apprehension of sense stimuli – educated by reason; because organs of perception are rarely perfect and because prejudice and lack of good sense frequently deform reason, few individuals are qualified to ascertain the "true standard of taste and beauty."[25] At stake in these discussions is the right to judge. The autonomy of subjective response represents an unruly and unpredictable source of knowledge, and hence a precarious base for "true" judgment. The construct of universality acts as a control on literary imagination, while it serves to reinforce hegemonic values.

---

[22] "A Dissertation on the Idea of Universal Poetry," in Scott Elledge, ed., *Eighteenth-Century Critical Essays*, 2 vols. (Ithaca: Cornell University Press, 1961), vol. II, p. 860.

[23] For a feminist analysis of the separation, see Josephine Donovan, "Everyday Use and Moments of Being: Toward a Nondominative Aesthetic," in Hilde Hein and Carolyn Korsmeyer, eds., *Aesthetics in Feminist Perspective* (Bloomington: Indiana University Press, 1993), pp. 53–67.

[24] In Elledge, ed., *Eighteenth-Century Critical Essays*, vol. II, p. 822.

[25] Ibid., p. 823.

Conflict in literary authority accompanies a pronounced change in poetic style, and this discourse borrows the language of gender with its implications of power. Under the influence of Dryden's criticism, the earlier eighteenth century favors the concepts of balance, decorum, and mimesis in its valorization of classical models and Pope's perfect couplets. At mid-century, poetic ideals move away from Augustan balance toward a bolder experimentation in form and diction and the representation of more extreme pathos. Many scholars have addressed this revolution in "taste," noting various places in the discourse for the "emergence" of the sublime.[26] With the retreat of order, symmetry, and balance and the rise of excess, power, and grandeur, this version of literary history invites a gendered parallel, where feminine beauty of the earlier eighteenth century is vanquished by the immanent masculine sublime. One might reach this conclusion from Monk's description of the beautiful as Augustan style and the sublime as anything else that transports the reader. Retaining the association between balanced, ornamental beauty and femininity and between the excessive emotional force of the sublime and masculinity, it is necessary to emphasize that within each historical era gendered language encodes and enforces a binary structure of literary values. To cast the Augustan style as feminine is to erase the dominant masculine emphases of tragedy, epic, and satire. Furthermore, to envisage the sublime as the *autonomous* aesthetic consistent with discursive constructions of masculinity is to oversimplify the gendered dynamic that sustains that aesthetic mode. The dialogism between the historically contingent organization of sexual difference and the changing models of literary value continues throughout the entire period but, as the models shift, the interactions and their implications change likewise. Before I address the aesthetic in treatises by Burke, Lord Kames and Hannah More, I will outline the transition in literary values and the historically concurrent shift in gendered codes to provide a context in which to interpret the strikingly gendered language of aesthetics.

Rather than read the sublime as the aesthetic discovery of the mid-eighteenth century, or the beautiful as the inheritance from

26 While Monk's scholarship on eighteenth-century aesthetic thought is still standard, other studies include: Walter J. Hipple, *The Beautiful, the Sublime and the Picturesque in Eighteenth-Century British Aesthetic Theory* (Carbondale: Southern Illinois University Press, 1957); Marjorie Hope Nicolson, *Mountain Gloom and Mountain Glory: The Development of the Aesthetics of the Infinite* (Ithaca: Cornell University Press, 1959); Thomas Weiskel, *The Romantic Sublime: Studies in the Structure and Psychology of Transcendence* (Baltimore: The Johns Hopkins University Press, 1976). John Sitter's *Literary Loneliness in Mid-Eighteenth-Century England* (Ithaca: Cornell University Press, 1982) is also pertinent.

Plotinus, a gendered analysis suggests that the more immediate origins of these literary ideals can be found in the Augustan discourse they apparently displace. The descriptions of the sublime as transcendent power and the beautiful as harmony strongly recall Dryden's gendered categories of criticism, where the masculine heroic is signified by bold flights of imagination and the heightening of emotion through apt, significant language, and the feminine poetic encompasses softness, smoothness, modesty, and balance.[27] For the purposes of the argument it may be useful to summarize Dryden's gendered categories that I analyzed in chapter 2. In the "Account of the Ensuing Poem" prefixed to *Annus Mirabilis*, Dryden characterizes the heroic style as masculine, and he makes war its evident subject: "I have found myself so warm in celebrating the praises of military men . . . that it is no wonder if they inspired me with thoughts above my ordinary level . . . All other greatness in subjects is only counterfeit, it will not endure the test of danger; the greatness of arms is only real."[28] The grandeur of the subject demands an "elocution" "in apt, significant and sounding words," much like the "masterly" strokes of Virgil. Such descriptions "well wrought" are "the adequate delight of heroic poesy, for they beget admiration, which is its proper object."[29] Dryden's experience in writing heroic poetry has many of the hallmarks of the sublime; it "warms" him; it elevates thought "above my ordinary level"; it forces him to contemplate real danger. His formal prescriptions likewise resonate with the rhetorical concept described in Longinus' *On the Sublime*, requiring apt and meaningful eloquence and, more importantly, begetting admiration. He distinguishes this heroic poesy from his "feminine" poem, in which he "affected the softness of expression and the smoothness of measure." Because he addresses this verse to a lady, Dryden does not attempt "the height of fancy" or the "dignity of words."[30] Dryden's criticism incorporates a model of gendered hierarchy between the heroic masculine as admirable, lofty, and heated and the pleasing feminine as

---

[27] Without attending to the gendered language of style, Frans De Bruyn and James Grantham Turner have recently suggested the continuity in literary ideals from the heroic through the sublime in terms of political danger and sexual energy: De Bruyn, " 'Hooking the Leviathan': The Eclipse of the Heroic and the Emergence of the Sublime in Eighteenth-Century British Literature," *The Eighteenth Century: A Journal of Theory and Interpretation* 28.3 (1987), 195–215; Turner, " 'Illustrious Depravity' and the Erotic Sublime," ed. Paul J. Korshin, *The Age of Johnson* 2 (New York: AMS, 1989), pp. 1–38, and "The Libertine Sublime: Love and Death in Restoration England," *Studies in Eighteenth-Century Culture* 19 (1989), 99–115.

[28] John Dryden, *John Dryden: Of Dramatic Poesy and Other Critical Essays*, ed. George Watson, second edtion, 2 vols. (London: Dent and New York: Dutton, 1968), vol. 1, p. 97.

[29] Ibid., pp. 98, 99, 101.   [30] Ibid., p. 102.

smooth regularity that would literally translate into the gendered terms of the sublime and the beautiful.

Although Monk finds no evidence to conclude that Dryden advanced a coherent theory of the sublime, Dryden's criticism appears to incorporate Longinian precepts, especially in his use of the term "boldness" and in his attraction, if not acquiescence, to erring genius.[31] The reciprocal influence of Dryden's criticism can be registered by the increased reliance on his critical terms in successive translations of *On The Sublime*. The treatise attributed to Longinus was first translated into English in 1652 by John Hall; he interpreted "hupsous" as the "height of eloquence," stressing the formal function of the Longinian concept. Boileau's 1674 French translation which, according to William Smith, was "not always faithful to the Text, yet ha[d] an elegance and a spirit,"[32] probably influenced the men of letters in England more than Hall's because of its forceful representation of the sublime as an idea of emotional strength and content.[33] In 1698 an anonymous translation was published, and in 1712 Leonard Welsted translated Boileau's text into English. In 1739 William Smith reviewed all three, finding Welsted's a "misrepresented and mangled" version of Boileau, and dismissing Hall's and the 1698 anonymous translation as less than adequate. Supplanting the former translations, Smith's *Dionysius Longinus on the Sublime* was the standard version during the mid-century shift to subjective aesthetics, published in five editions through 1800 and becoming a regularly used text in male education by 1766.[34] Significantly, Smith's text demonstrates the greatest dialogism with Dryden's masculine heroic. Because of its numerous reprintings and its privileged function in education, Smith's translation provides a clear example of how gendered language is dispersed through official channels of literary culture. It also suggests one cause of the heavy resonance between the heroic and the sublime, marked by a common set of masculine descriptors.

Dryden first mentions Longinus in his "Apology for Heroic Poetry and Poetic Licence" (1677), apparently after having read Boileau's translation.[35] In his argument for the propriety of strong rhetorical figures in the heroic style, Dryden exonerates the erring genius of Milton and Cowley by appeal to Longinus' principles and examples. Throughout,

---

[31] Monk, *The Sublime*, p. 44.
[32] William Smith, trans., *Dionysius Longinus on the Sublime: Translated from the Greek, with Notes and Observations, and Some Account of the Life, Writings and Character of the Author,* second edition (London, 1742), preface, np.
[33] Monk, *The Sublime*, p. 36.
[34] De Bolla, *Discourse of the Sublime,* p. 35, n. 10; Monk, *The Sublime*, p. 24.
[35] Watson, ed., *John Dryden: Of Dramatic Poesy,* vol. I, p. 195, headnote.

Dryden makes frequent recourse to "boldness," his favored term of the masculine style. He shows characteristic circumspection in setting limits "betwixt the boldness and rashness of a poet."[36] However, "The boldest strokes of poetry," he claims, "when they are managed artfully, are those which most delight the reader."[37] The term represents the height of imagination, expressive of extreme energy and properly applied to heroic poetry.

In chapter 8 of *On the Sublime*, Longinus delineates the five sources of sublimity and, he claims, *contra* Caecilius, that emotion is not a *necessary* part of the style. He draws on an example from Homer's *Odyssey* to demonstrate; a modern translation of which reads as follows:

such as (in addition to tens of thousands of others) those exceedingly bold lines of the poet about the Aloadae:

They both were eager to set Ossa on Olympus, on Ossa Pelion, shaker of woods, so that heaven might be passable to them.

And there is the still greater line after these:

And now they would have ended it.[38]

Since Dryden would have been a mere 21 years of age when Hall published his translation, his influence on that version of *On the Sublime* is, apparently, nil: the word "boldness" does not appear at all in Hall's translation of chapter 8. He describes the first source of sublimity as a "regular vastnesse of thought." He translates the passage on Homer: "for example (not to instance a thousand others) what a daring speech of the Poet is this concerning the Aloide."[39] The anonymous version of 1698 adopts the word "bold" as a modifier of the sublime. The source of sublimity is "a largeness and height of Spirit, and Thought"; the example from Homer is "that bold description of, as daring an attempt of the Giants against Heaven. . . and that which follows, which pushes it higher."[40] In Welsted "boldness" is used as a synonym for sublimity. The primary source of the sublime is "a certain Force and Superiority of Genius."[41] Welsted interprets the praise of Homer thus: "where he speaks with so much boldness of the Aloides . . . What follows is yet more

---

[36] Ibid., p. 199.   [37] Ibid., p. 200.

[38] James A. Arieti and John M. Crossett, trans., *Longinus: On the Sublime*, Texts and Studies in Religion (New York: Edwin Mellen Press, 1985), pp. 50–51. All modern quotations will be taken from this translation.

[39] John Hall, trans., *Peri Hupsous, or Dionysius Longinus of the Height of Eloquence. Rendred Out of the Originall* (London, 1652), p. xii.

[40] Anonymous, trans., *An Essay on the Sublime: Translated from the Greek* (Oxford, 1698), pp. 15, 16.

[41] Leonard Welsted, trans., *The Works of Dionysius Longinus, On the Sublime: Or a Treatise Concerning the Sovereign Perfection of Writing, Translated from the Greek* (London, 1712), p. 20.

strong."[42] In contrast, Smith's translation of chapter 8 repeatedly uses
"boldness" to confer a sense of the imaginative and rhetorical strength of
the sublime. For instance, he translates the first source of sublimity as
"Boldness and Grandeur of thoughts."[43] His dependence on the word in
the example from the *Odyssey* is telling: "as among a thousand Instances,
we may see, from what the Poet has said, with so much Boldness, of the
Aloides ... But with the Boldness of what he afterwards adds, is yet
greater."[44] The literary use of "boldness" resonates with martial and
libertine discourses, signifying a cluster of masculine privileges including
invention, vigor, difficulty, and courage. Smith's reliance on "boldness"
as a source of and synonym for the sublime style imposes the ideological
values of Dryden's masculine heroic on the emergent aesthetic mode.

The influence of Dryden's tropes of height, heat, speed, and masculine
understanding can also be traced in the translations of Longinus' chapter
33, "Whether Excellence with Faults is Better than Faultless Mediocrity."
Dryden alludes to the section directly in his "Apology for Heroic
Poetry," citing Longinus' preference for Homer's genius over the
perfectly regular poetry of Apollonius and Theocritus. Although George
Watson claims that the duration of Longinus' influence on Dryden
ended with the publication of Rymer's *Tragedies of the Last Age* (1678),
Dryden's description of Theocritus in comparison with Lucretius in the
Preface to *Sylvae* (1685) borrows its principles from Longinus.[45] As I
mentioned in chapter 2, Dryden defends the irregular poetry of
Lucretius by stressing his achievement in creativity:

From this sublime and daring genius of his, it must of necessity come to pass that
his thoughts must be masculine, full of argumentation, and that sufficiently
warm. From the same fiery temper proceeds the loftiness of his expressions, and
the perpetual torrent of his verse, where the barrenness of his subject does not
too much constrain the quickness of his fancy.[46]

Dryden's description of genius compounds the warmth of emotion with
a pointedly masculine fecundity of intellect that, as a matter of course,
results in reckless verse. His insistence on the necessity of the relation
between the sublime and the masculine heat of argument naturalizes the
gendered comparison in a way that the discourse of the sublime readily

[42] Ibid., p. 22.
[43] Smith, trans., *Dionysus Longinus on the Sublime*, p. 16. The modern translation reads, "a solid thrust of conception" (Arieti and Crossett, trans., *Longinus*, p. 46).
[44] Smith, trans., *Dionysus Longinus on the Sublime*, p. 17.
[45] Watson, ed., *John Dryden: Of Dramatic Poesy*, follows Monk and T. R. Henn's *Longinus and English Criticism* (1934); see vol. I, p. 197, note 3.
[46] Watson, ed., *John Dryden: Of Dramatic Poesy*, vol. II, p. 25.

assimilates. Smith, for instance, characterizes Longinus himself in sublime terms that reiterate the gendered parallel: "He has a high and masculine turn of Thought, unknown to any other Writer, which inforced him to give all possible Strength and Energy to his Words."[47] In the Preface to *Sylvae*, Dryden uses feminine modifiers to describe the less impressive poetry of Theocritus. The "inimitable tenderness," the "simplicity" and the delicate touch of Theocritus recommend this poet to women, who ought to emulate his "softness of thought and simplicity of expression."[48] Just as Longinus gives faint praise to the poets who strive for correctness, Dryden's language reveals his admiration for the rare and forcible artist, and the gendered qualifiers underscore the hierarchical dichotomy.

Longinus makes his case for the magnificence of the sublime writer over the careful and exacting author through a series of rhetorical questions and comparisons. The modern translation of a characteristic phrase reads: "And, too (heaven knows), should the more numerous excellences in speeches and writings justifiably carry off first prizes or the greater ones?"[49] Hall's translation of this passage, as elsewhere, suffers from a lack of defined vocabulary: "Yet, nevertheless I think the greatest vertues, although not equally regnant in the whole piece, ought to carry the suffrage for precedency, were it for no other cause then their height and greatnesse."[50] Like the other translators before Smith, Hall's diction conveys the formal meaning of the Longinian text but, without rhetorical structure and evocative imagery, it lacks incisiveness and conviction. The 1698 version offers also a bland description of erring genius: "And I will uphold that Sublime, tho' it does not always keep an even pace, still deserves the first rank in Composures."[51] Welsted's version flounders in verbiage: "In one word, I cannot but think that the Sublime, tho' it does not equally support it self thro' the whole, provided this is only owing to its Grandeur and Elevation, carries the Day from all the rest."[52] With the exception of Welsted's "Grandeur" and "Elevation," lost in a string of qualifications, none of the earlier translations employs Dryden's implicitly gendered vocabulary, adhering, instead, to the technical understanding of the sublime as unequal but nonetheless first in rank. Smith's translation of this description of erring genius, on the other hand, borrows Dryden's heroic imagery: "the great and noble

---

[47] Smith, trans., *Dionysus Longinus on the Sublime*, p. xxv.
[48] Watson, ed., *John Dryden: Of Dramatic Poesy*, vol. II, pp. 30, 268.
[49] Arieti and Crossett, trans., *Longinus*, p. 160.   [50] Hall, trans., *Peri Hupsous*, p. lxi.
[51] Anon., trans., *Essay on the Sublime*, p. 70.   [52] Welsted, trans., *Works of Dionysus Longinus*, p. 99.

Flights, tho' they cannot every where boast an Equality of Perfection, yet ought to carry off the Prize, by the sole Merit of their own intrinsic Grandeur."53 Unlike the earlier translators, Smith adopts language that recalls Dryden's gendered binaries in his translation of the comparative passage that follows. According to Smith, Eratosthenes offers a "complete and delicate Performance," but cannot be rated higher than Archilochus, "who flies off into many and brave Irregularities, a godlike Spirit bearing him forwards in the noblest Career."54 Here the sublimity of Archilochus receives a heroic shading by casting his literary invention as brave and noble. Conversely, Smith interprets the work of Bacchylides and Io "smoothly, delicately, and correctly," indicative of the inferior, ornamental style that Dryden reserves for the feminine. The gendered distinctions in Smith's translation forge a feminine association with correctness, consistent with the Augustan regularity that becomes suspect by mid-century. The literary genius that rises above rules is in turn impressed with masculinity.

Even though the sublime represents the height of aesthetic achievement in mid-century, its dialogism with heroism is not unproblematic. In fact, the social and political implications of heroic iconoclasm raise conflicts with the bourgeois male ideal that had begun to form. From the mid- to the late eighteenth century, heroic genres experience a general decline in prestige as their warlike, antisocial values become antithetical to the sentimental virtues of a burgeoning middle-class readership. The cultural transition is made manifest by the weakened authority of classical literature. In Alexander Pope's youth, the epic was perceived to be an important cultural text for the indoctrination of proper manhood.55 By 1798 the Edgeworths' treatise on *Practical Education* maintains that an education in the classics no longer serves to prepare men or women for their respective roles in society.56 According to Frans De Bruyn, the mid-century discourse does not completely suppress the heroic, whose long-standing appeal continues to exert influence; rather, the literary discourse displaces some of the more dangerous masculine values of the heroic into the category of the sublime. However, De Bruyn concludes that the hero becomes neutralized as a threat to the state and is transformed "into an aesthetic object whose scope of influence on the

53 Smith, trans., *Dionysus Longinus on the Sublime*, p. 79.   54 Ibid., p. 80.
55 Carolyn D. Williams, *Pope, Homer and Manliness: Some Aspects of Eighteenth-Century Classical Learning* (London: Routledge, 1993), esp. pp. 38–63.
56 Miriam Leranbaum, " 'Mistresses of Orthodoxy': Education in the Lives and Writings of Late Eighteenth-Century English Women Writers," *Proceedings of the American Philosophical Society* 121.4 (August 1977), 298.

observer has been carefully circumscribed."[57] Because circumscription within the sublime is not a stable constraint – as the analyses of De Bolla and Eagleton suggest – consideration of the hero bears further examination.

Reevaluation of the hero takes place along the same cultural axes as the formulation of the aesthetic, based on sentimental human nature in service of conservative political objectives. For example, in *The Adventurer* (1753) Joseph Warton argues in favor of Ulysses over Achilles as the pedagogical model for male youth in a way that recalls Sarah Fielding's defense of domestic fiction in 1749. The *Iliad*, Warton contends,

by displaying the dire effects of discord among rulers may rectify the conduct of princes and may be called "The Manual of Monarchs," whereas the patience, the prudence, the wisdom, the temperance, and fortitude of Ulysses afford a pattern the utility of which is not confined within the compass of courts and palaces, but descends and diffuses its influence over common life and daily practice. If the fairest examples ought to be placed before us in an age prone to imitation, if patriotism be preferable to implacability, if an eager desire to return to one's country and family be more manly and noble than an eager desire to be revenged of an enemy, then should our eyes rather be fixed on Ulysses than Achilles.[58]

Warton's rejection of Achilles evidences the change in class-oriented values attendant upon the increasing wealth, power, and, of course, literacy of the bourgeoisie. Like Fielding, Warton defends the representation of behavior that reinforces the experience of the civilized, middle-class reader, but, for Warton, this imitation is political nonetheless. Warton insists that the "predominant passion" of Ulysses, and consequently the work's moral precept, is a love of one's country, and this socio-political virtue marks the *Odyssey*, for Warton, as emphatically masculine. Significantly, this corrective version of masculinity represented by Ulysses challenges the previously celebrated figure of the war hero, Achilles; the latter provides a dangerous example of "courage" and "firmness," whereas the former displays the more amenable qualities of "constancy" and "humanity."[59] Warton suggests a significant change in accepted standards of male conduct: what amounts to the domestic, civic virtues of Ulysses are considered more "manly" than the martial prowess of Achilles. Nonetheless, the sublime hero is aesthetically more important: "Let the *Iliad* be ever ranked at the head of human compositions for its spirit and sublimity, but let not the milder and perhaps, more insinuating

[57] De Bruyn, " 'Hooking the Leviathan'," p. 197.
[58] In Elledge, ed., *Eighteenth-Century Critical Essays*, vol. II, pp. 704–705.
[59] Ibid., p. 705; cf. Sitter, *Literary Loneliness*, pp. 104–134.

and attractive beauties of the *Odyssey* be despised and overlooked."[60] In a comparison that anticipates the gendered separation of the sublime and the beautiful in Burke, Warton extols the energy and violence of the *Iliad* as the universal aesthetic preference, while he hopes to secure the ornamental and softer *Odyssey* from contempt. His artistic ranking conflicts with the ideological objectives of bourgeois representation, a friction that indicates a fundamental contradiction in the aestheticization of political values.

Hume's essay on "taste" suggests a more resolute rejection of the brute hero, based on moral repugnance. Unlike taste, morality appears to be beyond the vicissitudes of fashion and the vagaries of national or individual character and, hence, to be indisputable. The apparent stability of morals authorizes their legislative role in the formation of taste. Hume allows that the *representation* of morality may change from age to age, but the universal standard needs to be enforced through repudiation of its deformity in art, a belief that ultimately empowers his objection to aggressive or brutal heroes. He respects the literary reputation of Homer and the Greek tragedians, but his moral principles prevent him from appreciating their illustration of violent characters:

We are not interested in the fortunes and sentiments of such rough heroes; we are displeased to find the limits of vice and virtue so much confounded; and whatever indulgence we may give to the writer on account of his prejudices, we cannot prevail on ourselves to enter into his sentiments, or bear an affection to characters which we plainly discover to be blamable.[61]

For Hume, a collective dissociation from the rough hero testifies to the standard of moral principle he claims for humanity. If morality is universal, then the representation of vicious characters in the classics should be condemned, even if they were formerly esteemed as cultural and literary icons. Hume's criticism, like Warton's, indicates the rejection of violence in favor of civility as the standard of masculine worth; it does not, however, allow for the aestheticization of the hero in a politically circumscribed realm of the sublime. On the contrary, his assumption that the sensitivity of taste is controlled by moral sentiment obviates the need for more overt displacement of questionable representations. He suggests that heroes have inherently lost their persuasive power over the enlightened man of taste.

The mid-century assessment of heroic discourse sheds light on the changing values of masculinity. The discursive representation of proper

---

[60] In Elledge, ed., *Eighteenth-Century Critical Essays*, vol. II, p. 705.   [61] Ibid., p. 827.

manhood – like its feminine counterpart – undergoes significant transformation as one part of the nexus of cultural discourses constituting bourgeois authority. Unlike the feminine character, though, the masculine is revised on two fronts, the public and the private. As indicated in the rejection of the hero, the mid-century male ideal compounds moral sentimentality with civic pride. Masculine honor, in contrast to the Restoration credo of loyalty to the king and a willingness to die for your country, is encapsulated in what Joseph Warton calls "the duties of universal benevolence, of charity, and of hospitality."[62] Physical power and its potential for destruction are subdued to the gracious responsibilities of the patriarch, a voluntary check to precipitate violence symbolized by Sir Charles Grandison's sheathed sword. The widespread embrace of a belief in "good nature" at the mid-century inspires a short-lived dichotomy in masculine public character. In fiction, the stories of Grandison and the Man of Feeling exemplify the frankness and generosity of the "good man." These characters model the benignity of heart and proper affective sensibility in their financial beneficence and emotional sympathy. The opposing side of mankind, according to Henry Fielding, practices the "art of thriving" in an increasingly duplicitous commercial society. Fielding writes a Theophrastic account of "bad" men, marked by their ill-nature and cunning, to protect the "good man" by making him aware of threats to both his virtue and his pocketbook.[63] Both "good" and "bad" constructs illustrate the mid-century's negotiation of the emerging power of the middle-class male, regulating his economic behavior in society through a discourse of internalized moral sentiment. As the aristocratic code of honor signified by external forms of status loses persuasive power, the bourgeois values of inner worth gain cultural authority.[64]

The force of bourgeois ideology also affects the construction of the private character of men, specifically in the reinvestment of male sexuality. In the wake of Restoration representations of male licentiousness, early-eighteenth-century writers – including Steele, Shaftesbury, and Defoe – issue warnings against sexual promiscuity as an effeminizing and

---

[62] Ibid., p. 708.
[63] Henry Fielding, "An Essay on the Knowledge of the Characters of Men," in *The Complete Works of Henry Fielding*, ed. William Ernest Henley, 16 vols. (New York: Croscup and Sterling, Co., 1902), vol. XIV, p. 282.
[64] This is one of the major themes of Michael McKeon's ideological history of the novel: see *Origins of the English Novel 1600–1740* (Baltimore: The Johns Hopkins University Press, 1987), chapter 4; see also his "Historicizing Patriarchy: The Emergence of Gender Difference in England, 1660–1760," *Eighteenth-Century Studies* 28.3 (1995), 295–322.

luxurious tendency. By mid-century, Enlightenment discourses sanction sexual appetite as an essential aspect of *male* nature, productive of happiness.[65] This construction of masculinity allows for active male desire, as long as it is directed at a proper object (i.e., a woman) and performed behind closed doors. Adultery when prompted by "nature" poses little problem for a man. In an expression that clarifies the class contingencies of the attitude, Samuel Johnson claims that a husband "does not do his wife a very material injury . . . if, for instance, from mere wantonness of appetite, he steals privately to her chambermaid."[66] Subject to the policing discourses of moral sentiment, the construction of male sexual energy has important implications for the aesthetic transitions in the era, as John Barrell has noted. "Masculinity," he claims, "now becomes a matter of virility rather than of abstinence, of the ability to enjoy the pleasures of sexuality rather than to resist them," and this validation of pleasure authorizes the polite enjoyment of erotic art when it is confined within the private sphere.[67] In his *Enquiry*, Burke argues for sexual fulfillment as an essential male pleasure: "the generation of mankind is a great purpose, and it is requisite that men should be animated to the pursuit of it by some great incentive. It is therefore attended with a very high pleasure."[68] More than justify male sexuality, these aesthetic constructions model artistic pleasure on a naturalized understanding of male sexual energy. Furthermore, as Poovey has suggested, Burke enlists the rationale of male sexual need based on nature to authorize the aesthetic of beauty in the individual discrimination of a marriage partner.[69]

Although mid-century constructions of male sexuality encourage a liberal heterosexual practice, the corresponding construction of bourgeois female sexuality becomes more restricted. According to Thomas Laqueur, after medical science in the mid-century verifies that female orgasm is unnecessary for conception, it becomes possible to render female sexuality passive and contingent upon the male.[70] The ideal of proper

[65] Roy Porter, "Mixed Feelings: The Enlightenment and Sexuality in Eighteenth-Century Britain," in Paul-Gabriel Bouce, ed., *Sexuality in Eighteenth-Century Britain* (Manchester: Manchester University Press, 1982), p. 8.

[66] James Boswell, *The Life of Samuel Johnson*, introduction by Claude Rawson (New York: Alfred A. Knopf, 1906, 1992), p. 350.

[67] John Barrell, "'The Dangerous Goddess': Masculinity, Prestige, and the Aesthetic in Early Eighteenth-Century Britain," *Cultural Critique* 12 (Spring, 1989), p. 111.

[68] Burke, *Philosophical Enquiry*, p. 41.

[69] Poovey, "Aesthetics and Political Economy," pp. 89–90.

[70] *Making Sex: Bodies and Gender from the Greeks to Freud* (Cambridge: Harvard University Press, 1990), p. 3, and chapter 3.

womanhood that would become hegemonic by the end of the eighteenth century reinforces the ontological separation of the sexes that this model of human sexuality projects. Hence, the domestic ideology that corresponds with feminine purity and moral authority divorces sexual desire from the female will but, implicitly, authorizes masculine sexual agency within the private sphere. Recognition of the masculine right to sexual access within the domestic domain qualifies the notion of separate spheres, and puts into question the status of female authority within the home. The economic contingency of middle-class women, codified into law by Hardwicke's Clandestine Marriage Act (1754) and Blackstone's *Commentaries*, further defines the subordination of woman within the domestic arena.[71] So while masculine power is constrained through a civilizing process in public behavior, the private man is granted autonomy through sexual and economic authority over the shrinking sovereignty of the female subject.[72]

Much of the conduct literature of the middle and late eighteenth century sentimentalizes women's role in an overt program of reconciling her to this contingent status. The Reverend James Fordyce, for instance, champions women as

the mothers and formers of a rational and immortal offspring; to be a kind of softer companions, who, by nameless delightful sympathies and endearments, might improve our pleasures and soothe our pains; to lighten the load of domestic cares, and by that means leave us more at leisure for rougher labours, or severer studies; and finally, to spread a certain grace and embellishment over human life.[73]

As in Burke's treatise, the female functions simultaneously in a procreative and an aesthetic capacity. By improving male pleasure and soothing his pain, the domestic woman acts as a reward for civilized man's "rougher labors"; pleasure and pain, not incidentally, are the founding sentiments of Burke's categories of the beautiful and the sublime. Fordyce values this idealized domesticity as a form of artistic enhancement of private life, suggesting that a woman's aesthetic role within the household becomes a surrogate occupation, as the shift in economic and social structures diminishes the opportunities for her public responsibilities.

---

[71] See William Cobbett, *The Parliamentary History of England, from the Earliest Period to the Year 1803* (London, 1813), vol. xv, pp. 2–3; and William Blackstone, *Commentaries on the Laws of England* (London, 1765) reprint (London: Dawsons, 1966), vol. i, p. 430.

[72] See Susan Moller Okin, "Women and the Making of the Sentimental Family," *Philosophy and Public Affairs* 11.1 (1982), 65–88.

[73] James Fordyce, *Sermons to Young Women: In Two Volumes*, new edition (Boston, Mass., 1767), vol. i, p. 144.

The aesthetic function of private femininity translates into critical evaluations of the female author, effectively circumscribing her agency in the literary realm as well. Much criticism of women operates along the same principles as the sentimentalized portrait of Fordyce's conduct manual. Cibber, for instance, whose *Lives of the Poets* was published in the same year as Warton's criticism of the *Iliad*, digresses into an encomium of female purity in the middle of his biography on Katherine Philips. His consideration of the female poet initiates an aestheticization of the entire female sex:

[W]hoever has ... scrutinized the heart, will find that more real virtue, more genuine and unaffected goodness exist amongst the female sex, than the other, and were their minds cultivated with equal care, and did they move in the bustle of life, they would not fall short of the men in the acute excellences; but the softness of their natures exempts them from action, and the blushes of beauty are not to be effaced by the rough storms of adversity.[74]

In keeping with the bourgeois construction of femininity, Cibber invests the female character with a greater share of the internal virtues common to human nature. That native goodness, however, requires passivity, and thus the "softness of their natures" exempts women from action. At the same time as masculine sexuality becomes the model and rationale for aesthetic excellence, Cibber implies that female passivity and virtue disqualify women from literary success, "the acute excellences" of men. Furthermore, the female's function as aesthetic object displaces her function as artist, as the "blushes of beauty" need to be spared from the "rough storms of adversity." Underlying Cibber's criticism is an economy of male desire akin to that expressed by Fordyce; those "blushes of beauty" enhance her value for the male viewer. Thus, the literary discourse appropriates the social codes of gender to restrict access to aesthetic power and to preserve the private, sexual rewards that female beauty represents for the male.

The change in gendered structures of power is apparent in the bourgeois understanding of marriage at mid-century. In the early eighteenth century a union of mutuality between the sexes is a current but fading model for marital bliss. The *Ladies Dictionary* offers this definition under the heading of marriage: "To be a help and comfort to each other; to be tender kind and good-Natur'd; the Man striving to do all for the Woman's good, and she Labouring as much as in her lies to

---

[74] Theophilus Cibber, *The Lives of the Poets of Great Britain and Ireland* (1753), reprint (Hildesheim, Germany: Georg Olms Verlagsbuchhandlung, 1968), p. 153.

requite his Care and Industry."[75] Although it retains a hierarchy of male dominance, the early paradigm of marriage grants to each partner an active, supportive role. By mid-century the projected separation between the sexes becomes more distinct, grounded in a discourse of "natural" difference and separate spheres. "There is a difference," Richardson's Sir Charles Grandison says, "in the *constitution*, in the *temperament*, of the two Sexes, that give to the one advantages which it denies to the other . . . Why has nature made a difference in the beauty, proportion, and symmetry, in the *persons* of the two Sexes? Why gave it delicacy, softness, grace, to that of the woman . . . strength, firmness, to men; a capacity to bear labour and fatigue; and courage, to protect the other?"[76] The earlier norm of mutuality gives way to an asymmetrical binary in which males labor to provide for and protect the family, and females offer the innate and passive virtues of beauty and ornamentation. Masculine honor becomes internalized concomitantly with a mid-century suspicion of active violence, and the shift from valiant courtier to benevolent patriarch necessitates the dependence of females. Richardson suggests that although the aestheticized construction of femininity involves less autonomy, the corresponding masculinity is also dependent. The increasingly diffuse masculine identity – renegotiated in both the public and the private realms – achieves its proper purpose only through providing for and protecting the opposite sex. Thus the paradigm changes from mutual support, where the husband holds sway, to ontological division, where the male identity is relative to the subordination of his dependents.

The dialogism between gendered discourse and literary criticism manifests a similar shift in structure. Dryden's use of gender as a critical model involves a genteel and mutually beneficial relationship between the sexes; he stresses the significance of masculine genius but also the importance of feminine regulation. As in his evaluation of Cowley, discussed in chapter 2, the characteristically feminine aspects of formal precision perfect the masculine warmth and vigor of his Pindaric odes. The masculine and feminine aspects of poetry need to balance each other in Dryden's paradigm of poetic excellence, and this is precisely the ideal of Augustan poetry brought to perfection by Pope and celebrated by his contemporary critics. The shift in literary values at mid-century

---

[75] [John Dunton,] *The Ladies Dictionary, Being a General Entertainment for the Fair Sex: A Work Never Attempted Before in English* (London, 1694), p. 327.
[76] Samuel Richardson, *The History of Sir Charles Grandison*, ed. Jocelyn Harris (Oxford: Oxford University Press, 1986), vol. VI, p. 247.

continues to appropriate the current gendered languages, and thus we find in the split between the sublime and the beautiful an analogue of the ontologically separate sexes. The sexual models of the aesthetic propose a definitive separation between the modes, but just as male superiority gains credence only in relation to his protection of domestic dependents, likewise the autonomy of the sublime can be established only in relation to the beautiful. Thus, although the sublime functions as the legislative discourse of aesthetics in mid-century criticism, it is the beautiful that limits and controls the sublime.

BEAUTY AS THE DISCOURSE OF CONTROL: EDMUND BURKE

"The true standard of the arts is in every man's power; and an easy observation of the most common, sometimes of the meanest things in nature, will give the truest lights."[77] Edmund Burke signals his participation in the mid-century literary debate over the foundation of taste with a rejection of classical models and rule-oriented mimesis in favor of rationalized sense perception. Burke's argument, like Hume's, relies upon the validity of a common standard of sensibility and judgment among men; consequently, he assumes that his judgments represent consensus. For example, to distinguish the role of beauty in lust and love he asserts, "We shall have a strong desire for a woman of no remarkable beauty; whilst the greatest beauty in men, or in other animals, though it causes love, yet excites nothing at all of desire."[78] His assertion of aesthetic consensus is clearly situated by the discourses of his subject position, namely, as a privileged male of the mid-eighteenth century. He allows for variance in taste, but only as bad or wrong taste, resulting from a lack of knowledge or practice. In response to Hume's skepticism, he confidently assumes that the standard of taste can be reached whereby all men agree.[79]

Burke's analysis focuses on the effects that the sublime and beautiful produce on the subject, and the *Enquiry*, consequently, constructs a subjectivity correspondent with Burke's gendered perspective. By universalizing Burke's perspective as constitutive of aesthetic truth, the *Enquiry* negates and silences competing points of view – the above example, for instance, occludes heterosexual female or homosexual male perspectives. Such exclusivity illustrates how the feminine (and other perspectives that conflict with the dominant authority) becomes constituted

---

[77] Burke, *Philosophical Enquiry*, p. 54.   [78] Ibid., p. 91.
[79] See Boulton's introduction, ibid., p. xxx.

outside the purview of critical judgment, as Charlotte Lennox and Clara Reeve witness.[80] Gendered subjectivity is important because the subject occupies a conspicuous place in Burke's system as the vehicle for the aesthetic. Burke's empirical–sensationalist method defines the aesthetic categories of the sublime and the beautiful by the general passions they excite; thus the sublime is constituted by anything that produces pain, and the beautiful is that which stimulates pleasure. Pain and associated ideas of danger fall under the category of feelings that work toward "self-preservation," and pleasure inspires emotions which achieve the ends of "society," including the need for procreative "generation." The former represents an aesthetic of domination and power, the latter of subordination and dependence. The assessment of "sublime" or "beautiful" actually depends upon the subject's relation to the object – "we submit to what we admire, but we love what submits to us"[81] – and the subject's relation to the aesthetic is understood through current models of difference and their implications of power. The sublime is the mode of patriarchal authority – kings, fathers, lawgivers – and beauty is the aesthetic of heterosexual desire. Gender is a primary determinant in the subject's position within each economy.

Consequently, Burke establishes the sublime as the legislative discourse in two senses: in its capacity as an aesthetic authority and as the constitutive principle of that mode. The sources of sublimity include terror, obscurity, infinity, and most importantly, power: "I know of nothing sublime, which is not some modification of power."[82] Pain, the sensation stimulated by the sublime, is always stronger than the emotion of love, and pain is a product of coercive force: "pain is always inflicted by a power in some way superior, because we never submit to pain willingly. So that strength, violence, pain, and terror, are ideas that rush in upon the mind together."[83] The qualities that mark the sublime object are consistent with Augustan criticism of the heroic: like the masculine imagination of heroic poetry, Burke's sublime is boundless; like boldness and erring genius, the sublime "abhors mediocrity."[84] And, like Dryden's concept, based in dialogism with the political discourse of late-seventeenth-century reconstituted monarchy, Burke's sublime corresponds with the character of the patriarchal ruler. Burke describes the effect of the sublime inconsistently, at times referring to the tumescent effect of imaginative identification with the sublime and at others implying an apprehension of utter devastation. Whatever raises

[80] See chapter 4, pp. 137–147 and pp. 155–163.   [81] Burke, *Philosophical Enquiry*, p. 113.
[82] Ibid., p. 64.   [83] Ibid., p. 65.   [84] Ibid., p. 81.

the self-worth of the subject "produces a sort of swelling and triumph that is extremely grateful to the human mind; and this swelling is never more perceived, nor operates with more force, than when without danger we are conversant with terrible objects, the mind always claiming to itself some part of the dignity and importance of the things which it contemplates."[85] The omnipotence of God, however, inspires an opposite reaction: "we shrink into the minuteness of our own nature, and are, in a manner, annihilated before him."[86] In either case, Burke posits the "natural" state of the subject as one of autonomy, and this is a condition of being that the sublime reaffirms either through sympathy or, more commonly, in the delight caused by the receding power of grandeur.

Beauty, in contrast, is a discourse of subordination and dependence. Thus, beauty derives from sources inferior to the subject – smallness, smoothness, gradual variation, and delicacy – a set of qualities remarkably similar to Dryden's feminine poetic of restraint. Unlike the astonishment caused by the sublime, these lesser qualities inspire love in the perceiver, or "a sense of affection and tenderness."[87] Beauty answers the ends of society by stimulating the subject toward women and sexual procreation on the one hand, and toward sympathy, imitation, and ambition among the "great society with man and all other animals" on the other.[88] Burke structures his understanding of beauty from the perspective of a male subject, and even though beauty might inhere in male and female forms, the figure of woman provides the paradigmatic effect. Hence, when he argues that smoothness is a source of beauty, Burke refers to the "smooth skins" of "fine women"; for "gradual variation," he points to "that part of a beautiful woman where she is perhaps the most beautiful, about the neck and breasts"; for the quality of delicacy, he claims that "the beauty of women is considerably owing to their weakness or delicacy, and is even enhanced by their timidity, a quality of mind analogous to it," and perhaps most infamously, to illustrate that perfection is not a cause of beauty, he asserts that the highest beauty in the female sex is always accompanied with the idea of weakness and imperfection: "Women are very sensible of this; for which reason, they learn to lisp, to totter in their walk, to counterfeit weakness, and even sickness. In all this, they are guided by nature. Beauty in distress is much the most affecting beauty."[89] Burke's observations, derived from custom, confound nature and artificiality in his discrimination of the aesthetic value of the female.

[85] Ibid., pp. 50–51.   [86] Ibid., p. 68.   [87] Ibid., p. 51.   [88] Ibid., p. 51.
[89] Ibid., pp. 114, 115, 116, 110.

The contours of the female form answer the ends of male desire as efficiently as affected lisps and limps, because that desire – whether acquisitive or contemplative – is based on the object's inferiority. Beauty in distress is most affecting because it reaffirms the subject's mastery by insinuating the object's submission to his power. Interestingly, Burke's definition of beauty resonates with Dryden's feminine poetic, but in Dryden the concepts of smoothness and sweetness function as controls against the extravagance of the masculine imagination. Burke's aesthetic categories shift the control to the mind of the subject, imputing passive traits to the beautiful object.

That beauty is an aesthetic of control appears obvious when we look at it from the perspective of the female object. While the *Enquiry* ostensibly operates within a philosophic discourse of reason and speculation, its dialogism with the social construction of gender apparently makes it suitable for the discourse of female conduct. In his *Letters to a Young Lady* John Bennett idealizes a female character retired in a garden reading the *Enquiry*, whereby she becomes "more enchanting, more *beautiful*, and more *sublime*, than the admired work of that well-known and admired author."[90] Bennett's recommendation by example illustrates the hegemonic force of Burke's descriptions of female character, but it also suggests a more sinister indoctrination of patriarchal values. By reading Burke's treatise the female subject learns to view herself from the male perspective, which is to say as an object of beauty. Bennett's idealization suggests that the highest duty of the female subject is not to become the aesthetic object but rather to internalize the male standard of judgment and so constantly to police her own objectification. Such regulation promises to yield the ultimate aestheticization – she will be more beautiful and more sublime than the *Enquiry* itself. Unlike the male subject, whose assumed superiority over things of beauty consolidates an independent subjectivity, the female reader's power is circumscribed. Because Burke recommends a beauty of smallness, defect, and dependence, the female subject paradoxically gains "control" by rendering herself incapable of autonomy.

With the masculine subject at its center, Burke's aesthetic posits the sublime as a legislative discourse and the beautiful as a discourse of dependence; however, despite his assurances to the contrary, Burke's categories do not hold. Burke considers the feelings that ensure

[90] John Bennett, *Letters to a Young Lady on a Variety of Useful and Interesting Subjects, Calculated to Improve the Heart, to Form the Manners, and Enlighten the Understanding*, ninth American edition (New York, 1827), p. 172.

self-preservation, which include pain and terror, as far more significant than those that belong to society:

Those virtues which cause admiration, and are of the sublimer kind, produce terror rather than love; such as fortitude, justice, wisdom, and the like. Never was man amiable for force of these qualities. Those which engage our hearts, which impress us with a sense of loveliness, are the softer virtues; easiness of temper, compassion, kindness, and liberality; though certainly those latter are of less immediate and momentous concern to society, and of less dignity.[91]

Burke figures the authoritative discourse in terms of the exigencies of male rule where qualities of pleasantry become immaterial; the opposing category is determined by the impression of personal attractiveness, marked by the qualifiers of feminine discourse. The former is essential for the maintenance of society, the latter unnecessary. This gendered parallel indicates the incommensurability of the categories as well as their hierarchy, and, thus, reproduces the gendered power structure that informs them. However, the aesthetic dialogism with gendered ideology incorporates certain contradictions that undermine the structure's stability. Masculine subjectivity experiences feminine beauty as neither submissive nor superfluous. Furthermore, the sublime does not function as an entirely autonomous discourse; rather, beauty acts as its dialectic antithesis, providing the grounds of possibility for the appreciation of pain as an aesthetic category.

As evidence of incommensurability of the aesthetic categories, Burke argues that the subject cannot sustain simultaneous experiences of the sublime and the beautiful because they stimulate opposite responses, one of astonishment and one of love. Despite Burke's neat binaries, though, the concepts repeatedly exceed the boundaries he establishes. In a deconstructive reading of the *Enquiry*, Frances Ferguson suggests that Burke's confident distinctions belie a fundamental fluidity in his categories. According to Ferguson, beauty, as the domesticated object, represents the customary and the habitual, whereas the sublime, in its flashes of terror, largely consists of novelty. However, Burke also claims that when the mind becomes used to an idea – even of the sublime – it no longer perceives fear. Rather than "stand on foundations so different, that it is hard . . . to think of reconciling them in the same subject," as Burke contends, Ferguson sees the sublime constantly threatening to become tamed into the beautiful.[92] The reverse is likewise apparent in

---

[91] Burke, *Philosophical Enquiry*, pp. 110–111.
[92] Ibid., p. 114; Ferguson, "The Sublime of Edmund Burke," p. 76.

the treatise; the ostensibly docile beauty represents a cunning power that Burke fears rather than loves. Ferguson explains that "the danger in beauty is that its appearance of weakness does not prevent its having an effect, which is always that of robbing us of our vigilance and recreating us in its own image."[93] Ferguson's identification of beauty as a subversive power suggests another important way in which the discourse operates as control. In this case, the love inspired by feminine beauty paradoxically threatens the autonomy of masculine subjectivity.

Within Burke's system, the apprehension of beauty purportedly raises feelings of pleasure through the perception of dominance. However, Burke describes the effects of beauty as an involuntary, physiological loss of control: "Beauty acts by relaxing the solids of the whole system."[94] Burke's susceptibility to this deceptive power is notable in his description of the smooth variation of a woman's body:

Observe that part of a beautiful woman where she is perhaps the most beautiful, about the neck and breasts; the smoothness; the softness; the easy and insensible swell; the variety of the surface, which is never for the smallest space the same; the deceitful maze, through which the unsteady eye slides giddily, without knowing where to fix or whither it is carried.[95]

Burke's account demonstrates the loosening effect, as the tone of reasonable discourse gives way to giddy anticipation of unrestricted pleasure. The fetishization of beauty produces a psychological state of confusion, leaving the viewing subject in emotional excess and without self-command. The somatic effects of beauty are perhaps more disabling: "the head reclines something on one side; the eyelids are more closed than usual, and the eyes roll gently with an inclination to the object; the mouth is a little opened . . . the whole body is composed, and the hands fall idly to the sides. All this is accompanied with an inward sense of melting and languor."[96] Although beauty is construed as a discourse of subordination and dependence, it curiously incapacitates the viewer, thereby co-opting, temporarily, the legislative power of the sublime. While the *Enquiry* never concedes the power of beauty, the heterosexual model of desire Burke appropriates incorporates this fundamental contradiction, which subsequently acts as a destabilizing potential in the aesthetic.

Ferguson's observations on the structural reversals in the aesthetic experience also have important implications for the gendered parallel in

[93] Ferguson, "The Sublime of Edmund Burke," p. 76.
[94] Burke, *Philosophical Enquiry*, pp. 149–50.   [95] Ibid., p. 115.   [96] Ibid., p. 149.

Burke's categorical separation of the two modes. Subjective similarities in the apprehension of the sublime and the beautiful suggest the necessity of a temporal distinction in the subject's relation to the aesthetic. In other words, the subject cannot experience the two sensations simultaneously, but this is not because they produce opposite emotions as Burke contends; rather, the sublime and the beautiful alternate in the way they constitute the subject. The cyclical reversal of the experiences challenges the autonomy of the sublime, which Burke repeatedly defines as independent of the beautiful. The subject cannot sustain the experience of the sublime for long, because it is an aesthetic of pain that threatens to annihilate the subject. Although Burke maintains that the sublime is pleasurable, it only causes delight in its retreat. Burke suggests that the subject seeks out beauty as a respite from the pain of the sublime; "it is rather the soft green of the soul on which we rest our eyes, that are fatigued with beholding more glaring objects."[97] A constant excitation in and by the sublime, with its obliteration of self, would destroy subjectivity, and thus the expected change in subject position from dominated to dominator becomes an essential experience for the appreciation of the sublime. Consequently, Burke implicates the beautiful in the constitution of the sublime as an aesthetic category. The effect of respite and indulgence may be inferior in dignity, but it nonetheless supplies the grounds of possibility for the subject to endure the experience of pain, and in this way the discourse of beauty acts as a control in the sense of a limiting condition for the sublime. In this light, the disabling power of beauty over the male subject represents a serious threat. In order for the aesthetic economy to function in service of male subjectivity, the dangerous deception of beauty must be suppressed.

The aesthetic of beauty, therefore, can be seen as a discourse of control in several different but intersecting ways. In the first place, the male subjectivity promoted by Burke's paradigm controls the object of beauty through discrimination and dominance. This first construction incorporates the gendered dynamic between authoritarian masculinity and contingent femininity, a domestic ideology that reproduces Burke's dynamic to establish a second form of control. As exemplified by Bennett, this discourse encourages the female subject to internalize the male standard of judgment in a paradoxical gesture that grants her self-control through affected weakness. If feminine beauty achieves its potential effect, the female object will temporarily master the viewing

<hr>

[97] Ibid., p. 111.

subject by rendering him soft, but this delusive power of feminine beauty emerges as a product of the sexual enthusiasm of Burke's text rather than as an accountable part of his aesthetic. The subject's dominance over beauty, on the other hand, becomes the condition of possibility for the aesthetic appreciation of the sublime, by granting the subject a respite from contemplating things greater than himself. The intermittent course of the sublime, then, relies upon the subject's ability to love, and hence in Burke's terms to dominate, the beautiful object.

We can understand this dialectic as a product of the changing discourses of literary value, gendered difference, and political power in the mid-century. The literary shift from heroism to sublimity involves the repudiation of the war hero and his circumscription into the realm of the sublime. As the expression of dangerous excess, the sublime necessitates an imaginative distancing, which allows the subject to endure a sense of awe in its power. The sublime becomes a way of accommodating more than the outdated virulence of the hero; it acts as a model for the subject's interaction with forms of legislative power, aestheticizing his subordination in order to render it more palatable. The beautiful, for Burke, provides the grounds of possibility for the subject's imagined (and real) subordination, by creating an alternative fiction whereby the autonomous subject enjoys sovereignty. The same functional dependence can be seen between the corresponding categories of gender, whereby the male relinquishes his violent power in civilized society but retains a sense of superior physical strength by virtue of his authority over his dependents. The feminine role of contingency (and respite and beauty) provides the grounds of possibility for the fictive autonomy of the male bourgeois subject within a political regime that asks for his voluntary subjection to rule.

PRODUCING THE IDEAL GENDERED READER: KAMES AND MORE

Burke's critical enterprise, like other mid-century literary treatises, operates under the theoretical assumption of universal human perception rationalized according to established principles into a standard of taste. However, because subjective response is conditioned by a matrix of discourses that constitute subjectivity, individual perception varies. The unknown or unpredictable behavior of the autonomous subject, consequently, raises anxiety in literary discourse and becomes the focus of intense legislation. Rather than evaluate the formal precision or classical parallels in a literary work, the purpose of criticism shifts in the mid-century to the identification of principles by which the subject learns to value literature and thereby to participate more knowledgeably in civilized culture. What is at stake is not merely the status of literary genres or modes, but rather the modern subject himself or herself.

The ontological division between the sexes apparently poses little difficulty in the assumptions of universal human nature. Discourse accommodates the "natural" differences in the perceptions of men and women by insisting upon the universality of apprehension within each sexed category. Consequently, the system of modern gendered differences underwrites the critical discourse that regulates the formation of subjectivity by designating certain modes of apprehension as masculine or as feminine. De Bolla's argument on the legislative aspect of sublimity provides a compelling theory for this function of gendered language within critical discourse. De Bolla interprets the subject as "the excess . . . that which cannot be appropriated or included within the present discursive network of control. On account of this the subject, given that it is always outside the discourses within which it is initially generated, becomes both producer and product of another set of discourses which contextualize and control subjectivity."[98] We might understand the discursive production of modern gender-codes within aesthetic discussions as one manifestation of this control. The projection and prescription of gendered subjects within the discourse embody and confine the aesthetic concepts, and, conversely, the principles of aesthetics idealize the roles of modern gendered subjects.

The formation of the male critical subject is carefully delineated in the *Elements of Criticism*, by Lord Kames. In Kames' panoramic critical vision, nothing less than the nation's future rests on the ascertainment of the principles of good taste, which necessarily raises the consequence of the critical task. Kames alludes to the political ramifications of his project in a dedication to the king: "By uniting different ranks in the same elegant pleasures, [the fine arts] promote benevolence: by cherishing love of order, they enforce submission to the government: and by inspiring delicacy of feeling, they make regular government a double blessing."[99] Far from disinterested appreciation, Kames imagines an explicitly ideological function for the arts in the promotion of benevolence, order, and delicacy. From the start, Kames' idealistic endeavor to inculcate the

---

[98] De Bolla, *Discourse of the Sublime*, p. 6.
[99] Lord Kames, Henry Home, *Elements of Criticism*, sixth edition, 2 vols. (Edinburgh, 1785), reprint (New York: Garland Publishing, 1972), vol. 1, p. v.

proper principles of criticism employs a stance of moderation between neoclassical objectives and subjective conditions, a balance uncharacteristic of the youthful extremism in Burke's aesthetic. Kames founds his critical project on a belief in moral human nature, and he recommends the cultivation of the fine arts as a means to curb the potential venality inspired by Britain's recent commercial opulence. Education in taste, therefore, will serve as a means to "retard such fatal corruption" as luxury, selfishness, and sensual gratification.[100] Thus the *Elements of Criticism* incorporates an explicit agenda for the instruction of Britain's youth – understood as male – in order to maintain political order and to regulate pleasure in a way consistent with morality. The immediate popularity of the *Elements of Criticism* and its pivotal influence on eighteenth-century aesthetics suggests the success of Kames' social program, and it indicates the process by which criticism comes to enforce hegemonic cultural views.[101]

Like Burke, Kames is anxious to establish the certainty of his aesthetic truths, and so he details the methods of criticism as a "rational science." His project is to examine "the sensitive branch of human nature" in order to distill the "genuine principles of the fine arts." He contends that the proper critic "must pierce still deeper": "he must acquire a clear perception of what objects are lofty, what low, what proper or improper, what manly, and what mean or trivial."[102] Kames posits aesthetic experience as knowledge with clearly demarcated binaries of right and wrong and "manly" or "mean." Later in his treatise, the latter two terms in binary opposition play an important role in the ascertainment of proper masculinity. Significantly, Kames removes the terms "female" or "effeminate" as comparatives to "manly," in effect measuring male behavior on a scale segregated from the female gender. "Manly" signifies the difference between exalted and ignoble rather than between man and woman, a linguistic gesture that illustrates the distinct masculine perspective of the work.

Like Burke, Kames projects the voice of consensus from his own privileged male perspective, and he consequently places the subject in relation to art in a way that parallels the Burkean power dynamic, concluding that elevated objects produce a feeling of the sublime and that "female beauty . . . shows best in distress."[103] More so than Burke,

---

[100] Ibid, p. vii.
[101] The work went through five editions during Kames' lifetime and an additional six afterward (Monk, *The Sublime*, p. 113).
[102] Kames, *Elements*, vol. I, p. 6.   [103] Ibid., p. 79.

though, Kames makes the rational understanding of male subjectivity the object of his study. He confesses at the start "that all along it has been his view, to explain the nature of man, considered as a sensitive being capable of pleasure and pain."[104] Criticism of art and the investigation of "mankind" are not at all incompatible activities, because Kames retains a mimetic paradigm for literature. Through art he comes to understand the "worth and excellence" of humanity and, consequently, by instructing youth in the correct methods of critical judgment he maintains the ethical status quo. However, the changing codes of masculinity at mid-century disrupt Kames' assumed knowledge over two key issues in the text. The aesthetic consideration of the hero and the use of the term "manly" both present a crisis of signification.

The heroic sublime, for Kames, causes a conflict between artistic appreciation and a rational criticism based in moral sentiment. Representations of grandeur and elevation conventionally earn the highest aesthetic ranking, but because the sublime stimulates a dangerous moral sympathy in the subject – swelling the heart and inciting feelings of greatness – Kames tempers the sublime with neoclassical restraint: "When the sublime is carried to its due height, and circumscribed within proper bounds, it enchants the mind, and raises the most delightful of all emotions; the reader, engrossed by a sublime object, feels himself raised as it were to a higher rank."[105] Unlike Burke's praise of the excessive, Kames enforces a limit in the sublime's "due height" and "proper bounds." Violent heroes in particular raise ethical questions for Kames because they are "universally the favourite entertainment" despite their "grossest acts of oppression and injustice."[106] The emotion of sublimity with its patently masculine model of tumescent pleasure explains why such heroes are commonly celebrated, but it nonetheless leaves Kames with an inappropriate mimetic model: "the splendour and enthusiasm of the hero transfused into the readers, elevate their minds far above the rules of justice, and render them in great measure insensible of the wrongs that are committed."[107] Such social amnesia, however fleeting, conflicts with a critical regimen designed to support moral human nature and, more ominously, to "enforce submission to the government." Able only to signal the "irregular influence of grandeur," Kames leaves these heroes precariously circumscribed in the sublime.

Kames attempts to clarify the construction of proper male subjectivity

---

[104] Ibid., p. 14.   [105] Ibid., p. 248.
[106] Ibid. Cf. De Bruyn, "'Hooking the Leviathan'," p. 206.   [107] Kames, *Elements*, vol. I, p. 248.

in his discussion of dignity. He sets the objective of the section with the following observation:

[W]ith respect to the fine arts, some performances are said to be manly, and suitable to the dignity of human nature; others are termed low, mean, trivial. Such expressions are common, though they have not always a precise meaning. With respect to the art of criticism, it must be a real acquisition to ascertain what these terms truly import.[108]

Kames identifies an uncertainty in meaning surrounding the term "manly" as used within critical discourse, but the dialogism with gendered language connects the critical ambiguity with the mid-century transition in normative masculine values. In particular, Kames' concern with "manly" involves the shift from external, aristocratic signs of status to the internalized, polite marks of civility. In this way, Kames' effort to determine the true import of "manly" is likewise constitutive of male subjectivity. Kames immediately limits the non-meaning of the term by placing it within the binary of dignity versus meanness, allotting to it an elevated position in the hierarchy. Dignity, he elaborates, is founded in man's superiority to all other beings on earth: "Man is endued with a Sense of the worth and excellence of his nature: he deems it more perfect than that of the other beings around him; and he perceives, that the perfection of his nature consists in virtue."[109] In Kames' definition, dignity becomes the defining feature of the autonomous self, a conception that bases the sovereignty of the male identity in his practice of virtue. "Further, to behave with dignity, and to refrain from all mean actions, is felt to be, not a virtue only, but a duty: it is a duty every man owes to himself." He projects an internalized form of self-regulation whereby the male subject conforms to hegemonic notions of morality as a sign of his manhood. Moreover, the normative understanding of masculinity, dramatically revised since Dryden's age, becomes the foundation of the critical use of the word "manly." Kames argues "in general, every occupation, whether of use or amusement, that corresponds to the dignity of man is termed manly."[110]

The significance of this lexicographic exercise becomes apparent when Kames returns to the problematic issue of heroism, with its potentially disturbing impact on the male subject. He disallows sublimity as an efficient cause of dignity: "If any one incline to think, that with respect to human actions, dignity coincides with grandeur ... the difference will be evident upon reflecting, that an action may be grand

---

[108] Ibid., p. 352.   [109] Ibid., p. 354.   [110] Ibid., p. 355.

without being virtuous . . . but that we never attribute dignity to any action but what is virtuous."[111] For Kames the concept of dignity provides a more socially amenable alternative to grandeur; because of its correspondence with manliness, dignity is also an aesthetic category more directly constitutive of male subjectivity than heroism or the sublime. However attractive, grandeur represents an experience beyond the bounds of propriety for the majority of men. Significantly, Kames chooses an example of male violence to illustrate the difference between warmth of passion and dignity: "Revenge . . . tho' it enflame and swell the mind, is not accompanied with dignity."[112] By raising the value of virtuous behavior over the demonstration of violence, the concept of dignity acts as a limit to the heroic. Specifically, Kames is concerned to promote an ideal of social affection that counters more primitive models of dominance and retribution, and "dignity" is key to that enterprise: "In point of dignity, the social emotions rise above the selfish, and much above those of the eye and ear: man is by his nature a social being; and to qualify him for society, it is wisely contrived, that he should value himself more for being social than selfish."[113] One of Kames' own objectives is to temper the potential excess of the autonomous self, codified as "selfishness," by rendering aesthetic experience "naturally" compatible with social virtues. His critical principles thereby enforce a corrective masculinity that corresponds to civilized moral standards.

Whereas Burke posits the beautiful as the opposite of the sublime and a respite from the dangers of the latter's obliterative power, Kames provides an antidote to the heroic sublime in the quality of dignity, which removes the beautiful from the equation and, hence, obviates the threat to male autonomy posed by the female figure of beauty. Furthermore, his concept of dignity represents correct critical judgment as a set of internalized virtues appropriate for the civilized and sovereign male subject. In this way, Kames posits the masculine privilege in criticism as commensurate with autonomous subjectivity, and this is achieved through the suppression of opposing perspectives, including the feminine. *Elements of Criticism* incorporates images of women throughout, particularly as verification of collective experience: thus Kames asserts, "a fine woman . . . raises the passion of love, which is directed to her as its object"; and "beauty, or any other good quality in a woman of rank, seldom raises love in a man greatly her inferior," and "the beauty of a mistress, which enflames the imagination, is readily communicated to a glove."[114] His

[111] Ibid., p. 353.   [112] Ibid., p. 357; *cf* p. 49.   [113] Ibid., p. 360.   [114] Ibid., pp. 43, 51, 70.

examples, however, represent women from his perspective as an object of sight or other aesthetic experience. While his treatise incorporates the female object as part of the regulated apprehension of art, the female subject is largely absent from the text. Significantly, when Hannah More educates the female reader regarding the proper realm of arts for women, she includes an understanding of the male aesthetic as well as the female to enforce the boundaries of the female sphere. The lack of female perspective in Kames' (and Burke's) aesthetic illustrates the extent to which the masculine point of view comes to represent the standard.

The implications of masculine exclusivity in Kames' treatise should not be underestimated, especially given the cultural and political goals for his project. For Kames, the reification of a recognized literary universal is an urgent responsibility. "We have," he declares in conclusion, "the same standard for ascertaining in all the fine arts, what is beautiful or ugly, high or low, proper or improper, proportioned or disproportioned: and here, as in morals, we justly condemn every taste that deviates from what is thus ascertained by the common standard."[115] Kames participates in the unifying discourse of criticism, erecting authoritative structures through the definition of "right" principles and the eradication of contradictory views. Kames' treatise does not overtly concern itself with the feminine perspective; rather, Kames confronts and controls the political fear of excess, which appears to be a greater danger in the mid-century literary discourse. The negotiation of literary authority in *Elements of Criticism* adopts gendered language and paradigms to mediate certain cultural conflicts, but it focuses on male concerns from a masculine perspective and hence projects an ideal of the male reading subject.

Though on a much humbler scale, Hannah More's *Essays on Various Subjects* accomplishes an analogous projection of the ideal female reader. As part of the literature on female conduct, More's text is an overtly didactic work designed to indoctrinate a standard of morals and manners in young women. Consequently, the regulation of subjective behavior is the primary end of *Essays*, where it is a consequence of the legislation of aesthetic criticism in *Elements*. Interestingly, More uses a universal standard of taste, stratified by the categories of sex, as a model of internal law to regulate the formation of female subjectivity. Like Kames, More justifies her project as a service to greater society:

The prevailing manners of an age depend more than we are aware, or are willing to allow, on the conduct of the women; this is one of the principal hinges

---

[115] Ibid., vol. II, pp. 496–497.

on which the great machine of human society turns. Those who allow the influence which female graces have, in contributing to polish the manners of men, would do well to reflect how great an influence female morals must also have on their conduct.[116]

Without the sentiment of Fordyce or Bennett, More imputes a great measure of importance to women's cultural role, and she is invested in widening the scope of female responsibility to incorporate morals. She recognizes the reigning notion of female aesthetic value – those "female graces" – but she desires to increase the significance of that value by adding the more substantial practice of virtue. In either case, More respects the contingent status of female worth, implying that it is only through an impact on men that female behavior matters. More's concession to the existing influence of "female graces" underscores the culture's aestheticization of women as beautiful objects; rather than question this discursive practice, she resignifies the aestheticized female subject and grants her a more active part in society than normative aesthetics, exemplified by Kames.

Written during a phase in More's life when she was more involved in literary pursuits than in religious duties, this didactic work has a purposeful dialogism with the discourse of aesthetics.[117] In fact, she opens and closes the work with a digression on the topic; the introduction distinguishes the tastes of men and women, and the final essay discusses "Genius, Taste, and Good Sense." On the one hand, More's appropriation of aesthetic discourse in her construction of proper gendered behavior testifies to the consistency between the two discourses in their respective views of human "nature." On the other hand, More posits the aesthetic discourse as a fixed measure of internalized standards to regulate the mind and, hence, behavior; the female subject's external correspondence with these gendered codes of taste manifest propriety, the visual emblem of inner virtue.

More's behavioral prescriptions depend upon a schematic division of physical and mental space into distinctly gendered components, and it is worth emphasizing that the discourse of the sublime and the beautiful fully reproduces the ideology of separate spheres and domesticity she aims to engender. More's urgent assertion of sexual division both signals the ontological understanding of sexual categories and registers the

---

[116] Hannah More, *Essays on Various Subjects, Principally Designed for Young Ladies*, in *The Works of Hannah More*, 2 vols. (New York: Harper and Brothers, 1836), vol. II, p. 552.

[117] *DNB*, ed. Leslie Stephen and Sydney Lee (Oxford: Oxford University Press, 1921–1922); vol. XIII, pp. 861–867; M. G. Jones, *Hannah More* (Cambridge: Cambridge University Press, 1952), chapter 2.

importance of social custom in their interpretation: "These distinctions cannot be too nicely maintained, for besides those important qualities common to both, each sex has its respective, appropriated qualifications, which would cease to be meritorious the instant they ceased to be appropriated. Nature, propriety, and custom, have prescribed certain bounds to each; bounds which the prudent and the candid will never attempt to break down."[118] The gendered roles are only in part naturalized; they require supervision, which suggests the need for internal scrutiny. More does not view the violation of gendered codes as monstrous so much as productive of social discord. Furthermore, she supposes only the imprudent or uncandid would challenge the established divisions, reading gender deviation as a sign of immorality.

More defines the private realm as singularly appropriate for women because it is in this context that their domestic virtues – moral and aesthetic – gain intelligibility. She compares women to "the costliest vases" placed "remote from any probability of accident or destruction," because, like these fine objects of decor, they "find their protection in their weakness, and their safety in their delicacy."[119] More encourages an aesthetic self-objectification for women, but unlike Bennett, for instance, she does not emphasize beauty as a satisfaction for male desire. Rather, she insinuates "that where there is more beauty and more weakness, there should be greater circumspection and superior prudence."[120] Hence the aesthetic value of women necessitates their moral regulation. Significantly, Burke's formulation of feminine beauty as weakness operates within More's treatise as a cultural fact. Men, by contrast, illustrate qualities of strength and power; they resemble objects "formed for the more public exhibitions on the great theatre of human life. Like the stronger and more substantial wares, they derive no injury, and lose no polish, by being always exposed, and engaged in the constant commerce of the world."[121] More opposes the fragility of the feminine object with the coarser stuff of masculinity, suggesting through a curious blend of literary and commercial metaphor that masculine subjectivity thrives in active play with its environment. Naturalizing the aesthetic function of men as sublime agents, she claims, "They were intended by Providence for the bustling scenes of life; to appear terrible in arms, useful in commerce, shining in councils."[122] More imputes a diversity of characteristics to the figure of man, from violent heroism and bourgeois civility to political rhetoric. Her division of gender roles and spaces uses

[118] More, *Essays*, vol. II, p. 550.   [119] Ibid.   [120] Ibid., p. 551.   [121] Ibid.   [122] Ibid.

the aesthetic principles of beauty and sublimity to characterize the feminine and masculine subjects as respectively passive and active.

More's aesthetic binaries then authorize her demarcation of the mental capacities of the sexes. More claims "that the female mind, in general, does not appear capable of attaining so high a degree of perfection in science as the male."[123] As part of the regulation of female subjectivity, More repeatedly delimits the scope of female ambition through iterations of custom or nature that enforce female inferiority. Her use of literary taste in this respect is exemplary. The "sex," she allows, "have lively imaginations, and those exquisite perceptions of the beautiful and the defective," or the faculty of taste, which she defines later as an intuitive apprehension in absence of judgment. Philosophic discrimination, or "the abstruser walks of literature," she presumes, women "will readily relinquish."[124] More's assumptions indicate that the dialogic construction of aesthetics *vis-à-vis* gender has had the reciprocal effect of enforcing gendered scripts. Where Burke adopts the gendered characteristics of aesthetic objects to differentiate the sublime and the beautiful, More appropriates Burkean distinctions of aesthetics to legislate and limit female subjectivity.

Subsequently, More uses the aesthetic standards codified by gender as prescriptive codes for female writing. She describes a literary landscape navigated by gendered markers: "There are green pastures, and pleasant valleys, where [women] may wander with safety to themselves and delight to others. They may cultivate the roses of imagination, and the valuable fruits of morals and criticism; but the steeps of Parnassus, few, comparatively, have attempted to scale with success."[125] More projects a universal aesthetic apprehension among women, allowing them a flat and low space, whose geographic features represent women's artistic range. Her imagery connotes a feminine aesthetic of regulated movement and practical or harmless occupation. In contrast, the elevated mountain of difficult access denotes the sublime qualities of poetic excellence, a common image that More draws in strict opposition to the feminine space. She attributes the difference in male and female writing to the degree of learning each acquires, an insight Aphra Behn forcefully articulated more than one hundred years earlier. In a capitulation that sharply contrasts Behn's satire, More allows that the need for "many languages and many sciences" explains the relative failure of female poets: "The lofty epic, the pointed satire, and the more

[123] Ibid.   [124] Ibid.   [125] Ibid.

daring and successful flights of the tragic muse, seem reserved for the bold adventures of the other sex."[126] More adopts the language of Dryden's masculine heroic to insinuate that the masculine aesthetic of agency and motion conflicts with the internalized feminine standard of taste. The modifiers – lofty, pointed, daring, and bold – indicate an independent or unregulated behavior that clashes with the domestic, subordinate femininity she wants to promote.

Like Hume and Kames before her, More represents taste as a function of moral human nature, and consequently indicative of a transcendent "truth" to be honored throughout time. However, her understanding of the female role within the larger gendered system differs from her male contemporaries, and – while I make no claims for More as a proto-feminist – she challenges ever so slightly the hegemony of male-authored "truth." In the first place, More grants the female perspective credence – unlike Burke or Kames – by claiming certain aesthetic modes as appropriate for the female subject. For instance, More grants women access to imagination, one of the definitive literary qualities, and although she clearly protects judgment as a masculine prerogative, she nonetheless stakes a creative space for her sex. Moreover, she insists on the importance of the female role in society: "considerable advantages are reaped from a select society of both sexes. The rough angles and asperities of male manners are imperceptibly filed, and gradually worn smooth, by the polishing of female conversations, and the refining of female taste; while the ideas of women acquire strength and solidity, by their associating with sensible, intelligent and judicious men."[127] More concedes the aesthetic function of women, but she translates it into a civilizing force whereby female subjects can exert a moral influence. Her model recalls Dryden's Augustan paradigm of literary balance, where the feminine style of precision and ornament smoothes the rougher expression of masculine boldness, except that she enjoins the aesthetic to a higher social purpose.

Her closing essay "Miscellaneous Observations on Genius, Taste, Good Sense, &c." is consistent in retaining a sense of balance between masculine and feminine modes of the aesthetic. She specifically compares "good sense," a term denoting feminine restraint, with "genius," a word describing poetic excess: "It is the peculiar property of genius to strike out great or beautiful things: it is the felicity of good sense not to do absurd ones. Genius breaks out in splendid sentiments and elevated

---

[126] Ibid.   [127] Ibid., p. 552.

ideas; good sense confines its more circumscribed, but perhaps more useful walk, within the limits of prudence and propriety."[128] The movement and agency of genius resonates with More's earlier description of masculine activity, while the circumscribed prudence of good sense parallels the standard of feminine taste. More's description of the interaction between genius and good sense reiterates the fundamental importance of the feminine: "The vast conceptions which enable a true genius to ascend the sublimest heights, may be so connected with the stronger passions, as to give it a natural tendency to fly off from the straight line of regularity; till good sense, acting on fancy, makes it gravitate powerfully towards that virtue which is its proper centre."[129] Just as feminine conversation and taste soften the rough edges of masculine conduct, the propriety of good sense serves to keep genius on its proper course. More's reference to regularity indicates an anxiety about the sublime similar to that manifest in Warton, Hume, and Kames. While Smith translates Longinus in praise of "brave irregularities," Kames cautions his reader against the "irregular influences of grandeur," finding it necessary to circumscribe the sublime within due height and proper bounds. The self-indulgent and antisocial impulse of the sublime is counter to Kames' ideal of moral human nature, and More operates by a similar principle. Her line of regularity is an aesthetic manifestation of hegemonic values, and good sense serves as the compass to draw genius back to its moral center. However, where Kames locates the limiting control over the sublime in the masculine quality of dignity, thereby removing feminine influence from the aesthetic, More insists on a moral guide consistent with and suited to the female subject. Her aesthetic essay, designed for "exciting a taste for literature in young ladies," aligns a feminine model for subjectivity with the moral qualities of good sense. In this way, what might appear to be an anachronistic embrace of the Augustan paradigm of gendered balance serves as resistance to a trend in aesthetics that diminishes the impact of the feminine.

More's *Essays* represents an important cross-section in the discourses of literary and gendered values, where the formation of gendered subjectivity explicitly appropriates the legislative discourses of criticism. The literary criticism in this chapter reciprocally illustrates a strong and explicit concern with the cultural constructions of gendered behavior. When we compare More's description of the ideal female reader with Kames' projection of male subjectivity, the differences indicate the

[128] Ibid., p. 572.   [129] Ibid., p. 573.

pervasive social effects of literary constructions of truth. By the 1770s the aesthetic dependent upon feminine constructions of language dictates a corresponding subjectivity of contingency, weakness, moral purity, and ornamental beauty. In contrast, the aesthetic consistent with changing codes of masculinity represents male subjectivity as autonomous, civilized, transcendent and authoritarian. The conflation of gender and aesthetics indicates how the discriminations of gender and literary value work in conjunction to establish cultural norms of behavior consistent with the developing capitalist society. But the asymmetrical formulation of the masculine within the realm of the aesthetic and the feminine outside that territory – as a commodity, ornament, or moral influence – posits an illegitimate designation of literary authority which seriously limits the female subject.

The comparison between More and Kames yields another important insight regarding the foundation of aesthetic truths. I entitle this chapter "Returning to the beautiful" to suggest the need for an ideological critique of the aesthetic that does not diminish the role of beauty. Even though much creditable scholarship has recognized the gendered models operating within aesthetic discourse, little has been said about the implications, particularly for the female subject. In part this is because the dominant aesthetic of the eighteenth century, the sublime, assumes a universal and transcendent perspective that silences competing points of view. Works by De Bolla and Eagleton criticize that assumption by situating the sublime in its historical and political contexts. However, these ideological readings confirm the aesthetic as a masculine discourse concerned with the negotiation of male subjectivity in the political hegemony of the era. Poovey's article on Burke's commodification of female beauty suggests some problems with the gendered asymmetry in the discourse, but much of the critical work risks obscuring the feminine perspective. Such a focus ignores the dialectical relationship between the sublime and the beautiful, in which the latter operates as a limiting condition for the aesthetic category. Similarly, the acceptance of a critical perspective as masculine – the founding gesture of a truth based in universal human nature – dismisses the relevance of a feminine point of view. The comparison between Kames and More illustrates the difference. Kames' critical ideal assumes a scientific rationale that appears to transcend matters of gender (however, his concern over the term "manly" indicates that the *Elements* actually simplifies gender by denying the feminine). More, on the other hand, exposes the aesthetic system as informed by both genders and affecting both categories of sexed subjects. Although she maintains the gendered hierarchy and the circumscribed role of female dependence, and although she reproduces the discursive practice of the aesthetic objectification of women, her *Essays* returns to beauty a significance that literary discourse is wont to suppress. I do not want to overread her femino-centrism, but her difference with Kames suggests the potential exploration of beauty as an alternative register of literary quality, especially for female writers of her era.

The history of the discursive change in aesthetic and gendered values posited in this chapter is obviously partial, but the examples suggest a number of key points. Most importantly, the widespread change in literary taste from Augustan to Romantic or from Ancient to Modern incorporates a politics of gender perceived primarily as a binary system of ontological difference. By appropriating the concept of moral human nature, the discourse of aesthetics universalizes a standard of taste consistent with the collective experience of diverse subjects. Through the language of gender, mid-century critics employ the standard of taste to mediate social conflicts like those raised by the heroic and the female author. Consequently, literary taste comes to represent moral and social standards with didactic implications for the bourgeois reading subject, and these norms are purveyed in strictly dichotomous terms of gender. Masculine values divide into the public expectations for affective sociability and economic autonomy and the private authority meted out through benevolence and paternal care. Feminine values include a corresponding domestic contingency, weakness, beauty, and goodness. Literary discourse interprets male and female subjects in distinctive aesthetic realms; conversely, the discourse on conduct adopts the "truths" established by aesthetics to justify and regulate its constructions of gendered subjectivity. The universal voice of rationalized sense perception is articulated from the male perspective, and literary discourse consequently adopts the dominant construction of bourgeois masculinity as the standard of critical "truth," a bias that diminishes or erases competing interpretations. Thus as critical activity acquires responsibility for civilizing Britain's youth, the discourse consolidates and promotes a critical authority consistent with the characteristics of the autonomous male subject. The female subject, ascribed to the status of aestheticized object at worst and domestic moral compass at best, is increasingly denied the right to practice judgment or reason, although she is allowed circumscribed movement within the imaginative fields of the beautiful.

Polemical postscript[1]

If we accept Hannah More's vision of the gendered literary landscape as normative, then the contest for Mount Parnassus by the end of the eighteenth century is, on one level, clearly decided. Women are welcome to amble in the low valley, but the elevated realm of literary achievement belongs to men. Despite the changing codes of gender that inform the negotiation of literary value, this patriarchal organization reigns throughout the years 1660–1790. The deceptively simple fact that emerges from the preceding chapters is that eighteenth-century British writers, both men and women, rely on the historically situated gendered hierarchy to justify and classify literature. Or, in less neutral terms, literary criticism encodes and reproduces the discursively constructed values of male authority and female contingency as transcendent aesthetic truths. By demonstrating how literary languages preserve and elevate an ideal consistent with masculine privilege in culture, even in the putatively feminine genre of the novel, this study dismisses the already suspect notion that literary form is politically neutral.

On another level, however, the contest for Mount Parnassus is still unsettled. The model of history incorporated here insists that local articulations have the potential to challenge or change hegemonic structures in discourse. The history of change in the dialogic interaction between gendered discourse and the language of literary criticism testifies to that possibility. The gendered models that inform a governing poetics – in retrospect, what determines a category known as the "Literary" – shift from the time of Dryden's mutually ameliorative categories of style to Burke's ontologically divided sublime and beautiful. Each model articulates a distinct feminine and masculine aesthetic, but they differ with regard both to the relationship between the genders and to their respective modes of identification with gendered subjects in discourse.

[1] Apologies to Northrop Frye.

211

In the former, the masculine emphasis on heightened imagination, bold expression, speed, and strength is tempered by the feminine qualities of softness, smoothness, and sweetness, in order to produce the Augustan ideal. Consequently, male writers are frequently described in both masculine and feminine terms. The semiotic conception of gendered constructions allows for a greater range of play between the subjects in discourse and the assertions of gendered value in criticism, as the writings of Dryden and Behn both witness. Although the feminine plays a subordinate role in the overall determination of literary excellence, nonetheless it participates in the constitution of the "Literary," or that which culture accepts as a bona fide literary ideal. In this way, the earlier model of gendered dialogism, which More adopts as late as 1777, proposes a more instrumental part for the feminine and, hence, for the feminine subject for whom it operates as a behavioral analogue. Instead of relegating the feminine to an alternative space outside of the "Literary," as the later aesthetic will do, a model of mutual amelioration assures the feminine of at least a minor purpose.

One effect of the intersection between the mid-century codes of gender and criticism, an effect which continues through Romanticism, is that the construction of ontological difference between the sexes informs the assymetry and separation between the literary ideals marked by masculine and feminine language. As the masculine perspective begins to define a theoretically universal, moral human nature, the masculine aesthetic likewise comes to represent universal standards based on that philosophy, and, thus, critical categories associated with the masculine become solely constitutive of literary value. When considered in literary discourse, the language of the feminine appears incommensurate with excellence; rather, it signifies the trivial, the poorly executed, the useful or didactic, the particular, or the derivative.[2] Instead of characterizing a set of important but inferior literary qualities, the feminine comes to denominate an alternative to the authorized "Literary," a compensation illustrated by such categories as "women's literature." The injustice of the literary discrimination is obscured both by the authoritative discourse of human nature that regulates ontological division and by the entrenched rhetorical codes of gallantry that "soften" women's "slavish dependence" on men.

It is important to stress that these conclusions reflect the ideals expressed by the language of literary criticism; they indicate the unifying

[2] For a fuller history of this aspect of the aesthetic, see Naomi Schor, *Reading in Detail: Aesthetics and the Feminine* (New York: Routledge, 1989).

force of hegemonic discourse, but they do not necessarily describe the historical experience of individual subjects in that discourse. Some eighteenth-century female writers compose in the sublime mode, and some, indeed, scale the heights of Parnassus, but they do so within a discursive context that legislates against those appropriations of gendered privilege. Because eighteenth-century literature itself is produced through historically situated aesthetics, recognition of complex gendered codes in literary criticism facilitates a fuller interpretation of those texts, whether canonical or otherwise. In particular, the articulation of feminine literary language within a given historical era may provide a set of formal criteria better suited to evaluate the literature by women than has been the case thus far. There is no predetermined or foreclosed relationship between the female author and the gendered literary ideals of her culture; however, the identification of dialogism between the regulatory languages of gender and the aesthetic may allow us to assess the literary quality of texts by women in a way that is neither condescending nor based primarily on extra-literary discourses.

While critical dialogism with gender provides a useful vocabulary with which to analyze the formal attributes of literature by female authors, it also sheds light on several of our long-standing critical preoccupations. Through attention to the gendered valences of critical language, for instance, the prestige of the heroic is understood not only as a nationalistic premise but also as a discursive effort to consolidate masculine authority; the subsequent decline of the heroic in the succeeding century corresponds with the historical reconstitution of masculinity in the matrix of discourses shaping the economic, political, and philosophical transition to modern subjectivity. Consequently, the poetic shift to values of interiority and sublimity reflect less a valorization of the feminine than a reformulated masculine, capable of sentiment and reason. The historical development of the novel can also be situated within the cultural matrix of gendered critical values, where the exaggerated markers of femininity are understood to be the formal, generic designations of alterity or inferiority. At the same time, criticism of the novel maintains an uneasy relationship to the Ancients, at once establishing the novel's "newness" and appropriating the masculine authority through assertions of classical paternity.

Moreover, this study illustrates several places where the critical discourse exposes a gap between the construct of universal human nature and feminine epistemology. Championed by mid-century as the definitive feature of literary excellence, human nature is touted as

Shakespeare's finest knowledge, despite Charlotte Lennox's insistence that his female characters are unnatural. Additionally, Clara Reeve's claim to a feminine moral authority and attempts by critics of the novel to valorize feminine experience all point to ways in which critical discourse separates the feminine from that which concerns the "Literary." These fissures corroborate the feminist contention that .discourses of Western humanism posit the masculine perspective as universal, and, thus, they complicate the discursive context that precipitates the development of disinterested aesthetics in the nineteenth century.

Much recent literary criticism, including this study, begins with the assumption that the authoritative discourse of "nature," along with Woolf's "incandescence" or the unproblematic notion of objectivity is impossibly compromised by the ideological contingency of linguistic systems. Questions about the historicity of the aesthetic posed by Terry Eagleton and Martha Woodmansee, for example, focus on the complicity between artistic values and political structures of power. Other critics argue that the literary theories of the Restoration and the eighteenth century reflect the nationalistic character of growing imperialism as well as the bourgeois values of an aggressive market economy. My work contributes to the demystification of the "Literary" by demonstrating how this literary criticism also relies on patriarchal languages to define and stratify its values.

But the investigation ought not to be abandoned at this point. To be conscious of the political implications of literature so that we do not reproduce or reinforce unethical paradigms leaves the contemporary critic and teacher in a potentially untenable position, where we approach literature as a suspect on trial, or we focus so intently on politics we leave ourselves with no authority to make aesthetic judgments. George Levine in *Aesthetics and Ideology* addresses such critical paralysis in an attempt to negotiate between the possibilities of serious ideological criticism and the preservation of an aesthetic "that operates differently from [other modes] and contributes in distinctive ways to the possibilities of human fulfillment and connection."[3] His concern for the category of the "Literary" raises doubts about the type of demystification of literary values in this work.

Ultimately I argue that the universal and transcendent literary values in the eighteenth century are historically constructed and dependent upon contemporaneous discourses of gendered difference. Consequently,

---

[3] George Levine (ed.), *Aesthetics and Ideology* (New Brunswick: Rutgers University Press, 1994), p. 3.

the expression of value that is justified under those pretenses is not universal or transcendent but historically situated. This conclusion does not, therefore, negate the possibility of literary value. Both the conception of partial agency and discourse in flux, which inform my model of history, posit the notion that all knowledge is situated, that is, constituted through the discourses of a specific historical, cultural matrix. The only objective "truth" one can achieve in this understanding is through a recognition of the partiality of knowledge.

The point of my historical investigation is not to demonize eighteenth-century critics as hopelessly sexist. By investigating the gendered values and language of that specific literary discourse we can represent them as historically located. We cannot simply excise the gendered constructions in critical work because they signify a world-view which shapes the entire critical discourse under question. Instead, by placing the gendered language within its historical context, we receive the meaning as something other than the inevitable product of eternal and universal categories of gender. This inquiry consequently opens up the possibility for interpreting the text and its negotiation of gendered values. We might, like Lord Kames writing at a historical moment of linguistic instability, be concerned as to what these gendered terms import, and we might find that they mean different things for different readers. If the partiality and location of situated knowledge is scrupulously examined, questioned, and possibly shared, this investigation does not have to result in meaningless relativism.[4] Ultimately, our critical and pedagogical activity might engage with the meaning of eighteenth-century texts without an insistence that the "Literary" constitutes value for all time and all people.

---

[4] See Donna Haraway for a discussion of "embodied objectivism," one strategy to avoid relativism, in "Situated Knowledges: The Science Question in Feminism and the Privilege of Partial Perspective" in *Simians, Cyborgs, and Women: The Reinvention of Nature* (New York: Routledge, 1991), 183–201; alternatively, Judith Butler posits the need for a cultural translation of radically contingent knowledges in Butler, Seyla Benhabib, Drucilla Cornell, Nancy Fraser, *Feminist Contentions: A Philosophical Exchange*, intro. by Linda Nicholson (New York and London: Routledge, 1995), pp. 35–57.

Bibliography

PRIMARY WORKS

Addison, Joseph, and Richard Steele, *The Spectator*, ed. Donald F. Bond, 5 vols. (Oxford: Clarendon Press, 1965).

Allestree, Richard, *The Ladies Calling. The Second Part of the Works of the Learned and Pious* (Oxford, 1687).

Anon. (trans.), *An Essay on the Sublime: Translated from the Greek* (Oxford, 1698).

Anon., *The Whore's Rhetorick, calculated to the meridian of London and conformed to the rules of Art* (London, 1683).

Arieti, James A., and John M. Crossett (trans.), *Longinus: On the Sublime*, Texts and Studies in Religion 21 (New York: Edwin Mellen Press, 1985).

Astell, Mary, *The First Feminist: "Reflections Upon Marriage" and Other Writings by Mary Astell*, ed. Bridget Hill (Aldershot: Gower/Maurice Temple Smith, 1986).

Barbauld, Anna Letitia, *The British Novelists*, new edition, vol. 1 (London, 1820).

Barker, Jane, *A Patchwork Screen* (London, 1723).

Behn, Aphra, *The History of the Nun: or, The Fair Vow-Breaker* (London, 1689), reprint, in Charles C. Mish, ed., *Restoration Prose Fiction 1666–1700: An Anthology of Representative Pieces* (Lincoln: University of Nebraska Press, 1970).

The Works of Aphra Behn, ed. Janet Todd, 7 vols. (Columbus: Ohio State University Press, 1992–1996).

The Works of Aphra Behn, ed. Montague Summers, second edition, 6 vols. (New York: Blom, 1967).

[Bellon, Peter,] *The Reviv'd Fugitive: A Gallant Historical Novel* (London, 1690).

Bennett, John, *Letters to a Young Lady on a Variety of Useful and Interesting Subjects, Calculated to Improve the Heart, to Form the Manners, and Enlighten the Understanding*, ninth American edition (New York, 1827).

Blackamore, Arthur, *Luck at Last; or, The Happy Unfortunate*, reprint, in William H. McBurney, ed., *Four Before Richardson* (Lincoln: University of Nebraska Press, 1963).

Blackstone, William, *Commentaries on the Laws of England*, reprint, vol. 1, London, 1765; (London: Dawsons, 1966).

Boswell, James, *The Life of Samuel Johnson*, introduction by Claude Rawson (New York: Alfred A. Knopf, 1906, 1992).

Boyle, Robert, preface to *Martyrdom of Theodora and of Didymus* (London, 1687), intro. Charles Davies, Augustan Reprint Society 42 (Los Angeles: University of California Press, 1953).

Boyle, Roger, preface to *Parthenissa* (London, 1655), intro. Charles Davies, Augustan Reprint Society 42 (Los Angeles: University of California Press, 1953).

Burke, Edmund, *A Philosophical Enquiry into the Origin of our Ideas of the Sublime and Beautiful*, ed. J. T. Boulton (London: Routledge, 1958).

Calprenède, Gauthier de Costes de la, translator's preface to *Cassandre* (1644–1650), trans. (London, 1703) in Ioan Williams, ed., *The Novel and Romance: 1700–1800; A Documentary Record* (New York: Barnes and Noble, 1970).

[Chapelle, Jean, de la], *The Unequal Match or, The Life of Mary of Anjou, Queen of Majorca* (London, 1681).

Chudleigh, Lady Mary, "To the Ladies," in *The Norton Anthology of Literature by Women, The Tradition in English*, ed. Sandra M. Gilbert and Susan Gubar (New York: W.W. Norton, 1985).

Cibber, Theophilus, *The Lives of the Poets of Great Britain and Ireland* reprint (Hildesheim, Germany: Georg Olms Verlagsbuchhandlung, 1968).

Cobbett, William, *The Parliamentary History of England, from the Earliest Period to the Year 1803*, vol. xv (London, 1813).

Cogan, Henry, preface to *Ibrahim*, ed. and intro. by Benjamin Boyce, Augustan Reprint Society 32 (Los Angeles: University of California Press, 1952).

Collier, Jeremy, *A Short View of the Immorality and Profaneness of the English Stage* (1698), facsimile, preface Arthur Freeman (New York: Garland Publishing, Inc., 1972).

Congreve, William, preface to *Incognita* (1692), in Paul Salzman, ed., *An Anthology of Seventeenth-Century Fiction* (Oxford: Oxford University Press, 1991).

Critical Review, second series, vol. 5 (1792).

Croxall, Samuel, preface to *A Select Collection of Novels* (1720), in Ioan Williams, ed., *The Novel and Romance: 1700–1800; A Documentary Record* (New York: Barnes and Noble, 1970).

Davys, Mary, preface to *The Works of Mrs. Davys . . . in Two Volumes*, in William H. McBurney, ed., *Four Before Richardson* (Lincoln: University of Nebraska Press, 1963).

The Reform'd Coquet, ed. Michael F. Shugrue, intro. Josephine Grieder, reprint, *Foundations of the Novel* (New York: Garland Publishing, 1973).

Dennis, John, *The Critical Works of John Dennis*, ed. Edward Niles Hooker, 2 vols. (Baltimore: Johns Hopkins Press, 1939–1943).

Dryden, John, *John Dryden: Of Dramatic Poesy and Other Critical Essays*, ed. George Watson, second edition, 2 vols. (London: Dent and New York: Dutton, 1968).

The Poems of John Dryden, ed. James Kinsley, 4 vols. (Oxford: Clarendon Press, 1958).

[Dunton, John,] *The Ladies Dictionary, Being a General Entertainment for the Fair Sex: A Work Never Attempted Before in English* (London, 1694).

Elledge, Scott, ed., *Eighteenth-Century Critical Essays*, 2 vols. (Ithaca: Cornell University Press, 1961).

Fielding, Henry, "An Essay on the Knowledge of the Characters of Men," in *The Complete Works of Henry Fielding, Esq.*, ed. William Ernest Henley, 16 vols. (New York: Croscup and Sterling Co., 1902).

Joseph Andrews, ed. Martin C. Battestin (Middleton: Wesleyan University Press, 1967).

Fielding, Sarah, *Remarks on Clarissa*, intro. Peter Sabor, Augustan Reprint Society 231–232 (Los Angeles: William Andrews Clark Memorial Library, 1985).

Finch, Anne, *Selected Poems of Anne Finch Countess of Winchilsea*, ed. Katherine M. Rogers (New York: Frederick Ungar Publishing Co., 1979).

Fordyce, John, *Sermons to Young Women: In Two Volumes*, new edition (Boston, 1767).

Gentleman's Magazine; or Monthly Intelligencer, vol. 23 (1753); vol. 24 (1754).

Griffith, Elizabeth, *The Morality of Shakespeare's Drama Illustrated*, 1775; reprint (New York: AMS Press, 1971).

Hall, John, trans., *Peri Hupsous, or Dionysius Longinus of the Height of Eloquence. Rendred Out of the Originall* (London, 1652).

Haywood, Eliza, Dedication of *Lasselia; or the Self Abandon'd. A Novel* (1723), in Ioan Williams, ed., *Novel and Romance: 1700–1800; A Documentary Record* (New York: Barnes and Noble, 1970).

from "The Tea-Table, or a Conversation between some Polite Persons of both sexes at a Lady's Visiting Day" (1725), in Ioan Williams, ed. *Novel and Romance: 1700–1800; A Documentary Record* (New York: Barnes and Noble, 1970).

Hill, Bridget, ed., *Eighteenth-Century Women: An Anthology* (London: Allen & Unwin, 1984).

Hopkins, Gerard Manley, *The Letters of Gerard Manley Hopkins to Robert Bridges*, ed. and intro. Claude Colleer Abott (Oxford: Oxford University Press, 1955).

Huet, Pierre Daniel, Bishop of Avranches, *Sur l'Origine des Romans* (1670), trans. Stephen Lewis as *The History of Romances* (London, 1715), in Ioan Williams, ed., *The Novel and Romance 1700–1800: A Documentary Record* (New York: Barnes and Noble, 1970).

Hurd, Richard, "A Dissertation on the Idea of Universal Poetry," in Scott Elledge, ed., *Eighteenth-Century Critical Essays*, 2 vols. (Ithaca: Cornell University Press, 1961).

Johnson, Samuel, *A Dictionary of the English Language: in which the words are deduced from their originals, and Illustrated in their different significations by examples from the best writers . . . In two Volumes* (London, 1755).

The Letters of Samuel Johnson ed. Bruce Redford, 5 vols. (Princeton: Princeton University Press, 1992–1994).

The Six Chief Lives from Johnson's Lives of the Poets with Macaulay's Life of Johnson, ed. Matthew Arnold, reprint (New York: Russell and Russell, 1968).

The Yale Edition of the Works of Samuel Johnson, 16 vols. (New Haven: Yale University Press, 1958–).

Kames, Lord, Henry Home, *Elements of Criticism*, 2 vols. (Edinburgh, 1785), sixth edition, reprint (New York: Garland Publishing, 1972).

Kant, Immanuel, *Observations on the Feeling of the Beautiful and the Sublime*, trans. John T. Goldthwait (Berkeley: University of California Press, 1960).

Kepple, Joseph, *Maiden-Head Lost by Moon-light*, reprint, ed. Charles C. Mish, in *Restoration Prose Fiction* (Lincoln: University of Nebraska Press, 1970).

Lennox, Charlotte, *Shakespear Illustrated: Or the Novels and Histories on which the Plays of Shakespear are Founded*, vols. I and II (London, 1753), vol. III (London, 1754).

Locke, John, *Some Thoughts Concerning Education*, in *English Philosophers of the Seventeenth and Eighteenth Centuries: Locke, Berkeley, Hume*, Harvard Classics, ed. Charles W. Eliot, 50 vols. (New York: P.F. Collier and Son, 1910), vol. XXXVII, pp. 3–195.

Mackenzie, Sir George, preface to *Aretina; Or the Serious Romance* (London, 1660) intro. Charles Davies, Augustan Reprint Society 42 (Los Angeles: University of California Press, 1953).

Manley, Mary Delarivière, preface to *The Secret History of Queen Zarah* (1705) ed. and intro. by Benjamin Boyce, Augustan Reprint Society 32 (Los Angeles: University of California Press, 1952).

Marvell, Andrew, *The Poems and Letters of Andrew Marvell*, ed. H. M. Margoliouth, third edition, rev. by Pierre Legouis, 2 vols. (Oxford: Clarendon Press, 1971).

McBurney, William, ed., *Four Before Richardson: Selected English Novels, 1720–1727* (Lincoln: University of Nebraska Press, 1963).

Milton, John, *Complete Poems and Major Prose*, ed. Merritt Y. Hughes (New York: Macmillan, 1957).

Mish, Charles C., ed. *Restoration Prose Fiction 1666–1700: An Anthology of Representative Pieces* (Lincoln: University of Nebraska Press, 1970).

Monthly Review, vol. 9 (August 1753); vol. 10 (April 1754).

More, Hannah, *Essays on Various Subjects, Principally Designed for Young Ladies* in *The Works of Hannah More*, 2 vols. (New York: Harper and Brothers, 1836), vol. II, pp. 550–576.

Nightwalker: or, Evening Rambles in search after Lewd Women, with the Conferences Held with them, etc. (London, 1696).

Obliging Mistress: Or the Fashionable Gallant (London, 1678).

Philips, Katherine, *Poems* (1667), facsimile reproduction, intro. Travis Dupriest (Delmar, New York: Scholars' Facsimiles & Reprints, 1992).

Pix, Mary, *The Inhumane Cardinal; or, Innocence Betray'd* (London, 1696) facsimile reproduction, intro. Constance Clark (Delmar, New York: Scholars' Facsimiles & Reprints, 1984).

Pope, Alexander, trans., *The Iliad of Homer*, ed. Maynard Mack, in *The Twickenham Edition of the Poems of Alexander Pope*, vols. VII and VIII (London: Methuen, 1967).

The Twickenham Edition of the Poems of Alexander Pope, 10 vols., *The Rape of the Lock and Other Poems*, vol. II, ed. Geoffrey Tillotson (London: Methuen and Co., 1940).

Reeve, Clara, *The Progress of Romance and The History of Charoba, Queen of Aegypt* (1785), bibliographical note by Esther M. McGill (New York: Facsimile

Text Society, 1930).

Richardson, Samuel, *The History of Sir Charles Grandison*, ed. Jocelyn Harris (Oxford: Oxford University Press, 1986).

    Pamela; Or, Virtue Rewarded, ed. Peter Sabor, intro. Margaret Doody (London: Penguin, 1980).

Rochester, John Wilmot, Earl of, *Complete Poems of John Wilmot, Earl of Rochester*, ed. David M. Vieth (New Haven: Yale University Press, 1968).

Salzman, Paul, ed. and intro., *An Anthology of Seventeenth-Century Fiction* (Oxford: Oxford University Press, 1991).

Scott, Sir Walter, *The Life of Dryden*, ed. Bernard Kreissman (Lincoln: University of Nebraska Press, 1963).

Scudéry, [Madeleine], de, preface to *Artamène*, from 1691 edition, in Ioan Williams, ed., *The Novel and Romance 1700–1800: A Documentary Record* (New York: Barnes and Noble, 1970).

    Clelia, trans. (London, 1655).

    Preface to *Ibrahim*, in Benjamin Boyce, ed. and intro., Augustan Reprint Society 32 (Los Angeles: University of California Press, 1952).

Shadwell, Thomas, "Preface to *The Humorists*," in J. E. Spingarn, ed., *Critical Essays of the Seventeenth Century*, second edition, 3 vols. (Bloomington: Indiana University Press, 1963).

Shaftesbury, Anthony Ashley Cooper, Earl of, *Second Characters: Or, the Language of Form*, ed. Benjamin Rand (Cambridge: Cambridge University Press, 1914).

Smith, William, trans., *Dionysius Longinus on the Sublime: Translated from the Greek, with Notes and Observations, and Some Account of the Life, Writings and Character of the Author*, second edition (London, 1742).

Sprat, Thomas, "An account of the Life and Writing of Mr. Abraham Cowley: Written to Mr. M. Clifford" (1668), in J. E. Spingarn, ed., *Critical Essays of the Seventeenth Century*, second edition, 3 vols. (Bloomington: Indiana University Press, 1963).

Swift, Jonathan, *The Poems of Jonathan Swift*, ed. Harold Williams, second edition, 3 vols. (Oxford: Clarendon Press, 1958).

    The Prose Works of Jonathan Swift, D.D. ed. Temple Scott, 12 vols. (London: G. Bell and Sons, Ltd., 1919).

Urfé, Honoré d', *Astrea*, trans. J.D. (London, 1657).

Waller, Edmund, "Instructions to a Painter" in *Poems on Affairs of State: Augustan Satirical Verse, 1660–1714*, ed. George deF Lord, 7 vols. (New Haven: Yale University Press, 1963), vol. II.

Warton, Joseph, *An Essay on the Writings and Genius of Pope* (London, 1756).

Welsted, Leonard, trans., *The Works of Dionysius Longinus, On the Sublime: Or a Treatise Concerning the Sovereign Perfection of Writing, Translated from the Greek* (London, 1712).

Williams, Ioan, ed., *Novel and Romance: 1700–1800; A Documentary Record*, (New York: Barnes and Noble, 1970).

Wollstonecraft, Mary, *The Works of Mary Wollstonecraft*, ed. Janet Todd and

Marilyn Butler, 7 vols. (New York: New York University Press, 1989).

Woolf, Virginia, *A Room of One's Own* (San Diego, New York, and London: Harvest/HBJ, 1929).

Wycherley, William, *The Country Wife*, in *Restoration Plays*, intro. Brice Harris (New York: Modern Library, 1953).

SECONDARY WORKS

Abrams, M.H., *The Mirror and the Lamp: Romantic Theory and the Critical Tradition* (Oxford: Oxford University Press, 1953).

Adams, Hazard, *Critical Theory Since Plato* (Fort Worth: Harcourt Brace Jovanovich, 1971, revised 1992).

Adburgham, Alison, *Women in Print: Writing Women and Women's Magazines from the Restoration to the Accession of Victoria* (London: Allen and Unwin, 1972).

Aden, John M., "Dryden and the Imagination: The First Phase," *PMLA* 74 (1959), 28–40.

Alcoff, Linda, "Cultural Feminism versus Post-Structuralism: The Identity Crisis in Feminist Theory," *Signs: Journal of Women in Culture and Society*, 13.3 (Spring 1988), 405–436.

Argyos, Ellen, "Intruding Herself into the Chair of Criticism" in Frederick M. Keener and Susan E. Lorsch, eds., *Eighteenth-Century Women and the Arts* (New York: Greenwood Press, 1988), pp. 283–289.

Armstrong, Nancy, *Desire and Domestic Fiction: A Political History of the Novel* (Oxford: Oxford University Press, 1987).

Armstrong, Nancy and Tennenhouse, Leonard, eds., *The Ideology of Conduct: Essays on Literature and the History of Sexuality* (New York: Methuen, 1987), 1–24.

Atkins, J.W.H., *English Literary Criticism of the Seventeenth and Eighteenth Centuries* (London: Methuen, 1951).

Bakhtin, Mikhail M., *The Dialogic Imagination: Four Essays*, ed. Michael Holquist, trans. Caryl Emerson and Michael Holquist (Austin: University of Texas Press, 1981).

Ballaster, Ros, *Seductive Forms: Women's Amatory Fiction from 1684 to 1740* (Oxford: Clarendon Press, 1992).

"Romancing the Novel: Gender and Genre in Early Theories of Narrative," in Dale Spender, ed., *Living By the Pen; Early British Women Writers* (New York: Teachers College Press, 1992), pp. 188–200.

Barrell, John, "'The Dangerous Goddess': Masculinity, Prestige, and the Aesthetic in Early Eighteenth-Century Britain," *Cultural Critique* 12 (Spring 1989), 101–131.

Barrett, Michele, "Ideology and the Cultural Production of Gender," in Judith Newton and Deborah Rosenfelt, eds., *Feminist Criticism and Social Change* (London: Methuen, 1985).

Bates, Catherine, "'Of Court it seemes': A Semantic Analysis of *Courtship* and *To Court*," *Journal of Medieval and Renaissance Studies* 20.1 (Spring 1990), 21–57.

Beatty, Richmond Croom, "Criticism in Fielding's Narratives and His Estimate of Critics," *PMLA* 49 (1934), 1087–1102.

Belsey, Catherine, "Constructing the Subject: Deconstructing the Text," in Judith Newton and Deborah Rosenfelt, eds., *Feminist Criticism and Social Change: Sex, Class, and Race in Literature and Culture* (New York, Methuen, 1985), 45–64.

Bennett, Shelley M., "Changing Images of Women in Late-Eighteenth-Century England: the 'Lady's Magazine,' 1770–1810," *Arts Magazine* 55 (May 1981), 138–141.

Blanchard, Rae, "Richard Steele and the Status of Women," *Studies in Philology* 26 (1929), 325–355.

Bloch, Ruth H., "Untangling the Roots of Modern Sex Roles: A Survey of Four Centuries of Change," *Signs* 4.2 (1978), 237–252.

Burke, John J., "History without History: Henry Fielding's Theory of Fiction," in *A Provision of Human Nature: Essays on Fielding and Others in Honor of Miriam Austin Locke*, ed. Donald Kay (University of Alabama Press, 1977), 45–63.

Butler, Judith, *Bodies That Matter: On the Discursive Limits of "Sex"* (New York: Routledge, 1993).

"Contingent Foundations: Feminism and the Question of Postmodernism" in Butler, Seyla Benhabib, Drucilla Cornell, Nancy Fraser, *Feminist Contentions: A Philosophical Exchange*, intro. by Linda Nicholson (New York: Routledge Press, 1995), 35–57.

Cantrell, Carol H., "Analogy as Destiny: Cartesian Man and the Woman Reader" in Hilde Hein and Carolyn Korsmeyer, eds., *Aesthetics in Feminist Perspective* (Bloomington: Indiana University Press, 1993), 218–228.

Castle, Terry, "Sublimely Bad – Review of *Secresy*," *The London Review of Books* (Feb. 23, 1995), 18–19.

Clark, Constance, "Critical Remarks on the Four Taking Plays of This Season by Corinna, a Country Parson's Wife," in Mary Anne Schofield and Cecilia Macheski, eds., *Curtain Calls: British and American Women and the Theater 1660–1820* (Athens: Ohio University Press, 1991), 291–308.

Clingham, Greg, "Another and the Same: Johnson's Dryden," in Jennifer Brady and Earl Miner, eds., *Literary Transmission and Authority: Dryden and Other Writers*, Cambridge Studies in Eighteenth-Century English Literature and Thought (Cambridge: Cambridge University Press, 1993), pp. 121–159.

Crawford, Patricia, "Women's Published Writings 1600–1700," M. Prior, ed., *Women in English Society 1500–1800* (London: Methuen, 1985), 211–282.

Davis, Lennard, *Factual Fictions: The Origins of the English Novel* (New York: Columbia University Press, 1983).

Davis, Robert Con, and Laurie Finke, eds., *Literary Criticism and Theory: The Greeks to the Present* (New York: Longman, 1989).

De Bolla, Peter, *The Discourse of the Sublime: Readings in History, Aesthetics, and the Subject* (Oxford: Basil Blackwell, 1989).

De Bruyn, Frans, " 'Hooking the Leviathan': The Eclipse of the Heroic and the Emergence of the Sublime in Eighteenth-Century British Literature," *The Eighteenth-Century: A Journal of Theory and Interpretation* 28.3 (1987), 195–215.

Diamond, Irene, and Lee Quinby, eds., *Feminism and Foucault: Reflections on Resistance* (Boston: Northeastern University Press, 1988).

Dickie, George, *Aesthetics: An Introduction* (New York: Pegasus, 1971).

DNB, eds. Leslie Stephen and Sidney Lee, 22 vols. (Oxford: Oxford University Press, 1921–1922, reprint 1967–1968).

Donovan, Josephine, "Everyday Use and Moments of Being: Toward a Nondominative Aesthetic," in Hilde Hein and Carolyn Korsmeyer, eds., *Aesthetics in Feminist Perspective* (Bloomington: Indiana University Press, 1993), 53–67.

Doody, Margaret Ann, "Shakespeare's Novels: Charlotte Lennox Illustrated," *Studies in the Novel* 19 (Fall 1987), 296–307.

Duffy, Maureen, *The Passionate Shepherdess: Aphra Behn 1640–89*, reprint (London: Methuen, 1989).

Eagleton, Terry, *The Function of Criticism from the Spectator to Post-Structuralism* (London: Verso, 1984).

The Ideology of the Aesthetic (Oxford: Basil Blackwell, 1990).

Emerson, O. F., "John Dryden and a British Academy," *Proceedings of the British Academy* 10 (1921–1923), 45–58.

Engell, James, *Forming the Critical Mind: Dryden to Coleridge* (Cambridge: Harvard University Press, 1989).

Ferguson, Frances, "The Sublime of Edmund Burke, or the Bathos of Experience," *Glyph* 8 (Baltimore: The Johns Hopkins University Press, 1981), 62–78.

Ferguson, Moira, ed., *First Feminists, British Women Writers 1578–1799* (Bloomington: Indiana University Press, 1985).

Finke, Laurie, *Feminist Theory, Women's Writing*, Reading Women Writing Series (Ithaca: Cornell University Press, 1992).

"Aphra Behn and the Ideological Construction of Restoration Literary Theory," Heidi Hutner, ed., *Rereading Aphra Behn: History, Theory, and Criticism* (Charlottesville: University Press of Virginia, 1993), 17–43.

Folger Collective on Early Women Writers, eds., *Women Critics, 1660–1820: An Anthology* (Bloomington: Indiana University Press, 1995).

Forster, Antonia, *Index to Book Reviews in England, 1749–1774* (Carbondale: Southern Illinois University Press, 1990).

Foucault, Michel, *The History of Sexuality*, trans. Robert Hurley, 3 vols. (New York: Vintage Books, 1980).

Power/Knowledge: Selected Interviews and Other Writings, 1972–77, ed. Colin Gordon (New York: Pantheon, 1980).

"The Order of Discourse," trans. Ian Mcleod, in Robert Young, ed., *Untying the Text, A Post-Structuralist Reader* (London: Routledge and Kegan Paul, 1981), 48–78.

Fox-Genovese, Elizabeth, "The Feminist Challenge to the Canon," *National Forum* 69.3 (Summer 1989), 32–34.

Franklin, Colin, *Shakespeare Domesticated: The Eighteenth Century Editions* (Scolar Press, 1991).

Fraser, Antonia, *The Weaker Vessel* (New York: Vintage Books, 1984).

Frye, Northrop, *Anatomy of Criticism* (Princeton: Princeton University Press, 1957).

Gallagher, Catherine, *Nobody's Story: The Vanishing Acts of Women Writers in the Marketplace, 1670–1820* (Berkeley: University of California Press, 1994).

Gilbert, Sandra M. and Susan Gubar, *The Madwoman in the Attic: The Woman Writer and the Nineteenth-Century Literary Imagination* (New Haven: Yale University Press, 1979).

Goreau, Angeline, ed., *The Whole Duty of a Woman, Female Writers in Seventeenth-Century England* (Garden City: Dial Press, 1985).

Green, Susan, "A Cultural Reading of Charlotte Lennox's *Shakespear Illustrated*" in J. Douglas Canfield and Deborah C. Payne, eds., *Cultural Reading of Restoration and Eighteenth-Century English Theater* (Athens: University of Georgia Press, 1995), 228–257.

Griffin, Dustin, *Satire: A Critical Reintroduction* (Lexington: University Press of Kentucky, 1994).

Haraway, Donna J., *Primate Visions: Gender, Race, and Nature in the World of Modern Science* (London: Routledge, 1989).

Simians, Cyborgs, and Women: The Reinvention of Nature (New York: Routledge, 1991).

Hartsock, Nancy, "Foucault on Power: A Theory for Women?" in Linda J. Nicholson, ed., *Feminism / Postmodernism* (New York: Routledge, 1990), 157–175.

Hinnant, Charles H., *The Poetry of Anne Finch: An Essay in Interpretation* (Newark: University of Delaware Press, 1994).

Hipple, Walter J., Jr. *The Beautiful, the Sublime and the Picturesque in Eighteenth-Century British Aesthetic Theory* (Carbondale: Southern Illinois University Press, 1957).

"Philosophical Language and the Theory of Beauty in the Eighteenth Century," in Howard Anderson and John S. Shea, eds., *Studies in Criticism and Aesthetics 1660–1800: Essays in Honor of Samuel Holt Monk* (Minneapolis: University of Minnesota Press, 1967), 213–231.

Hope, A.D., "Anne Killigrew, or the Art of Modulating," *Southern Review* 1 (1963), 4–14.

Hume, Robert D., *Dryden's Criticism* (Ithaca: Cornell University Press, 1978).

"Dryden on Creation: 'Imagination' in the Later Criticism," *Review of English Studies*, ns, 21.83 (1970), 295–314.

Hunter, Jean, "The 18th-Century Englishwoman: According to the *Gentleman's Magazine*," Paul Fritz and Richard Morton, eds., *Woman in the 18th Century and Other Essays* (Toronto: Samuel Steves Hakkert & Co., 1976).

Hunter, J. Paul, *Before Novels: The Cultural Contexts of Eighteenth-Century English Fiction* (New York: W.W. Norton & Co., 1990).

Jardine, Alice, *Gynesis: Configurations of Woman and Modernity* (Ithaca: Cornell University Press, 1985).

Jensen, H. James, *A Glossary of John Dryden's Critical Terms* (Minneapolis: University of Minnesota Press, 1969).

Jones, M. G., *Hannah More* (Cambridge: Cambridge University Press, 1952).

Kelly, Joan, *Women, History and Theory: The Essays of Joan Kelly* (Chicago: University of Chicago Press, 1984).

Kernan, Alvin, *The Cankered Muse* (New Haven: Yale University Press, 1959).

Kinsley, James and Helen, eds., *Dryden: The Critical Heritage* (New York: Barnes and Noble, 1971).

Kowaleski-Wallace, Beth, "Milton's Daughters: The Education of Eighteenth-Century Women Writers," *Feminist Studies* 12.2 (Summer 1986), 275–293.

Langbauer, Laurie, *Women and Romance: The Consolations of Gender in the English Novel* (Ithaca: Cornell University Press, 1990).

Laqueur, Thomas, *Making Sex: Bodies and Gender from the Greeks to Freud* (Cambridge: Harvard University Press, 1990).

Leranbaum, Miriam, " 'Mistresses of Orthodoxy': Education in the Lives and Writings of Late Eighteenth-Century English Women Writers," *Proceedings of the American Philosophical Society*, 121.4 (August 1977), 281–301.

Levine, George, ed., *Aesthetics and Ideology* (New Brunswick: Rutgers University Press, 1994).

Lipking, Joanna, "Fair Originals: Women Poets in Male Commendatory Poems," *Eighteenth-Century Life* 12 (May 1988), 58–72.

Lipking, Lawrence, "Aristotle's Sister: A Poetics of Abandonment," *Critical Inquiry* 10 (September 1983), 61–81.

Loundsbury, Thomas R., *Shakespeare as a Dramatic Artist with an Account of his Reputation at Various Periods* (New York: Charles Scribner's Sons, 1901).

Lowenthal, Cynthia, *Lady Mary Wortley Montagu and the Eighteenth-Century Familiar Letter* (Athens: University of Georgia Press, 1994).

Maurer, Shawn Lisa, "Reforming Men: Chaste Heterosexuality in the Early English Periodical," *Restoration* 16.1 (1992), 38–55.

McKeon, Michael, *The Origins of the English Novel 1600–1740* (Baltimore: The Johns Hopkins University Press, 1987).

"Historicizing Patriarchy: The Emergence of Gender Difference in England, 1660–1760," *Eighteenth-Century Studies*, 28.3 (1995), 295–322.

Medoff, Jeslyn, "The Daughters of Behn and the Problem of Reputation," in Isobel Grundy and Susan Wiseman, eds., *Women, Writing, History 1640–1740* (London: B.T. Batsford Ltd., 1992), 33–54.

Mermin, Dorothy, "Women Becoming Poets: Katherine Philips, Aphra Behn, Anne Finch," *ELH* 57.2 (1990), 335–356.

Messenger, Ann, *His and Hers: Essays in Restoration and Eighteenth-Century Literature* (Lexington: University Press of Kentucky, 1986).

Messer-Davidow, Ellen, " 'For Softness She': Gender Ideology and Aesthetics in Eighteenth-Century England," in Frederick M. Keener and Susan E. Lorsch, eds., *Eighteenth-Century Women and the Arts*, Contributions to Women's Studies No. 98 (New York: Greenwood Press, 1988), 45–56.

Miller, Peter John, "Eighteenth-Century Periodicals for Women," *History and Education Quarterly* 11.3 (1971), 279–286.

Miner, Earl, *Dryden's Poetry* (Bloomington: Indiana University Press, 1967).

Miner, Earl and Jennifer Brady, eds., *Literary Transmission and Authority: Dryden and Other Writers*, Cambridge Studies in Eighteenth-Century Literature and Thought (Cambridge: Cambridge University Press, 1993).

Mitchell, W. J. T., *Iconology: Image, Text, Ideology* (Chicago: University of Chicago Press, 1986).

Moers, Ellen, *Literary Women* (London: The Women's Press, 1978).

Monk, Samuel H., *The Sublime: A Study of Critical Theories in XVIII-Century England*, second edition (Ann Arbor: University of Michigan Press, 1960).

Moore, Catherine E., " 'Ladies . . . Taking the Pen in Hand', Mrs. Barbauld's Criticism of Eighteenth-Century Women Novelists," in Mary Anne Schofield and Cecilia Macheski, eds., *Fetter'd or Free? British Women Novelists, 1670–1815* (Athens: Ohio University Press, 1986), 383–397.

Myers, Sylvia, "Learning, Virtue and the Term 'Bluestocking'," *Studies in Eighteenth-Century Culture* 15 (1986), 279–288.

Nicolson, Marjorie Hope, *Mountain Gloom and Mountain Glory: The Development of the Aesthetics of the Infinite* (Ithaca: Cornell University Press, 1959).

Nussbaum, Felicity, *The Autobiographical Subject: Gender and Ideology in Eighteenth-Century England* (Baltimore: The Johns Hopkins University Press, 1989).

O'Donnell, Mary Ann, *Aphra Behn: An Annotated Bibliography of Primary and Secondary Sources* (New York: Garland, 1986).

O'Donnell, Sheryl, "Mr. Locke and the Ladies: The Indelible Words on the Tabula Rasa," *Studies in Eighteenth-Century Culture* 8 (1979), 151–164.

Okin, Susan Moller, "Women and the Making of the Sentimental Family," *Philosophy and Public Affairs* 11.1 (1982), 65–88.

Pearson, Jacqueline, *The Prostituted Muse: Images of Women & Women Dramatists 1642–1737* (New York: Harvester-Wheatsheaf, 1988).

Perry, Ruth, *Women, Letters, and the Novel* (New York: AMS Press, 1980).

Pohli, Virginia, "Formal and Informal Space in Dryden's Ode, 'To the Pious Memory of . . . Anne Killigrew'," *Restoration* 15.1 (Spring 1991), 27–40.

Pollak, Ellen, *The Poetics of Sexual Myth, Gender Ideology in the Verse of Swift and Pope* (Chicago: University of Chicago Press, 1985).

Poovey, Mary, *The Proper Lady and the Woman Writer: Ideology as Style in the Works of Mary Wollstonecraft, Mary Shelley, and Jane Austen* (Chicago: University of Chicago Press, 1984).

"Aesthetics and Political Economy in the Eighteenth Century: The Place of Gender in the Social Constitution of Knowledge," in George Levine, ed., *Aesthetics and Ideology* (New Brunswick: Rutgers University Press, 1994), 79–105.

Porter, Roy, "Mixed Feelings: The Enlightenment and Sexuality in Eighteenth-Century Britain," in Paul-Gabriel Bouce, ed., *Sexuality in Eighteenth-Century Britain* (Manchester: Manchester University Press, 1982), 1–27.

Reynolds, Myra, *The Learned Lady in England 1650–1760* (Boston: Houghton Mifflin, 1920).

Richter, David H., *The Critical Tradition: Classic Texts and Contemporary Trends* (New York: St. Martin's Press, 1989).

Roberts, David, *The Ladies: Female Patronage of Restoration Drama 1660–1700* (Oxford: Clarendon Press, 1989).

Robinson, Herbert Spencer, *English Shakesperian Criticism in the Eighteenth Century*, second edition (New York: Gordian Press, 1968).

Rogers, Katharine M., "Britian's First Woman Drama Critic: Elizabeth Inchbald," in Mary Anne Schofield and Cecilia Macheski, eds., *Curtain Calls: British and American Women and the Theater 1660–1820* (Athens: Ohio University Press, 1991), 277–290.

Sale, William Merritt, *Samuel Richardson: A Bibliographical Record of His Literary Career with Historical Notes* (New Haven: Yale University Press, 1936).

Schofield, Mary Anne and Cecilia Macheski, eds., *Curtain Calls: British and American Women and the Theater, 1660–1820* (Athens: Ohio University Press, 1991).

Schor, Naomi, *Reading in Detail: Aesthetics and the Feminine* (New York: Routledge, 1989).

Scott, Joan W., "Gender: A Useful Category of Historical Analysis," *American Historical Review* 91 (December 1986), 1053–1075.

Shevelow, Kathryn, *Women and Print Culture: The Construction of Femininity in the Early Periodical* (London: Routledge, 1989).

Showalter, Elaine, *A Literature of Their Own: British Women Novelists from Brontë to Lessing* (London: Virago, 1978).

Silber, C. Anderson, "Nymphs and Satyrs: Poet, Readers and Irony in Dryden's Ode to Anne Killigrew," *Studies in Eighteenth-Century Culture*, 14 (1985), 193–212.

Simpson, David, "Commentary: Updating the Sublime," *Studies in Romanticism* 26.2 (Summer 1987), 245–258.

Sitter, John, *Literary Loneliness in Mid-Eighteenth-Century England* (Ithaca: Cornell University Press, 1982).

Sklar, Elizabeth S., "So Male a Speech: Linguistic Adequacy in Eighteenth-Century England," *American Speech* 64.4 (1989), 372–379.

Small, Miriam Rossiter, *Charlotte Ramsay Lennox: An Eighteenth Century Lady of Letters* (New Haven: Yale University Press, 1935).

Smith, Hilda L., *Reason's Disciples: Seventeenth-Century English Feminists* (Urbana: University of Illinois Press, 1982).

Spencer, Jane, *The Rise of the Woman Novelist: From Aphra Behn to Jane Austen* (Oxford: Basil Blackwell, 1986).

Spender, Dale, *Mothers of the Novel: 100 Good Women Writers before Jane Austen* (London: Pandora Press, 1986).

Spender, Dale, ed., *Living By the Pen: Early British Women Writers* (New York: Teachers College Press, 1992).

Stanton, Judith Phillips, "'This New-Found Path Attempting': Women Dramatists in England, 1660–1800," in Mary Anne Schofield and Cecilia Macheski, eds., *Curtain Calls: British and American Women and the Theater, 1660–1820* (Athens: Ohio University Press, 1991), 325–354.

Staves, Susan, *Player's Scepters: Fictions of Authority in the Restoration* (Lincoln: University of Nebraska Press, 1979).

Stone, Lawrence, *The Family, Sex and Marriage in England 1500–1800*, abridged edition (New York: Harper and Row, 1977).

Straub, Kristina, "Women, Gender and Criticism," in Robert Con Davis and Laurie Finke, eds., *Literary Criticism and Theory: The Greeks to the Present* (New York: Longman, 1989), 855–876.

Sutherland, James, "The Background of the Age," *English Literature of the Late Seventeenth Century* (Oxford: Clarendon Press, 1969).

Sutton, John L., "The Source of Mrs. Manley's Preface to *Queen Zarah*," *Modern Philology* (November 1984), 167–172.

Todd, Janet, *The Sign of Angellica: Women, Writing and Fiction 1660–1800* (New York: Columbia University Press, 1989).

Tuchman, Gaye and Nine E. Fortin, *Edging Women Out: Victorian Novelists, Publishers, and Social Change* (New Haven: Yale University Press, 1989).

Turner, James Grantham, " 'Illustrious Depravity' and the Erotic Sublime," in Paul J. Korshin, ed., *The Age of Johnson 2* (New York: AMS, 1989), 1–38.

"The Libertine Sublime: Love and Death in Restoration England," *Studies in Eighteenth-Century Culture* 19 (1989), 99–115.

Van Doren, Mark, *John Dryden: A Study of His Poetry*, third edition (Bloomington: Indiana University Press, 1960).

Vickers, Brian, ed., *Shakespeare: The Critical Heritage*, 6 vols. (London and Boston: Routledge, 1976).

Vieth, David, "Irony in Dryden's Ode to Anne Killigrew," *Studies in Philology* 63 (1965), 91–100.

Walkowitz, Judith, Myra Jehlen, and Bell Chevigny, "Patrolling the Borders: Feminist Historiography and the New Historicism," *Radical History Review* 43 (Winter 1989), 23–43.

Wasserman, Earl, "Johnson's *Rasselas*: Implicit Contexts," *Journal of English and Germanic Philology*, 74 (1975), 1–25.

Watt, Ian, *The Rise of the Novel: Studies in Defoe, Richardson and Fielding* (Berkeley: University of California Press, 1957).

Weiskel, Thomas, *The Romantic Sublime: Studies in the Structure and Psychology of Transcendence* (Baltimore: The Johns Hopkins University Press, 1976).

Williams, Carolyn D., *Pope, Homer and Manliness: Some Aspects of Eighteenth-Century Classical Learning* (London: Routledge, 1993).

Winn, James A., *John Dryden and His World* (New Haven: Yale University Press, 1987).

"When Beauty Fires the Blood": Love and the Arts in the Age of Dryden (Ann Arbor: University of Michigan Press, 1992).

Woodbridge, Linda, "A Strange, Eventful History: Notes on Feminism, Historicism, and Literary Study," *Exemplaria: A Journal of Theory in Medieval and Renaissance Studies* 2.2 (Fall 1990), 692–696.

Woodmansee, Martha, *The Author, Art, and the Market: Rereading the History of Aesthetics* (New York: Columbia University Press, 1994).

Young, Karl, "Samuel Johnson on Shakespeare: One Aspect," *University of Wisconsin Studies in Language and Literature* 18 (1923), 146–226.

Zomchick, John P., " 'A Penetration which nothing can deceive': Gender and the Juridical Discourse in some Eighteenth-Century Narratives," *Studies in English Literature* 29. 3 (1989), 535–561.

Index

Adburgham, Alison 88 n.
Addison, Joseph 4, 7–8, 11, 31–32, 33, 36, 51, 111, 128, 157, 168
  Spectator 4, 7–8, 11, 31–32, 87, 168
aesthetics
  birth of 85–86, 163, 166, 168, 168–210 *passim*
  ideological criticism of 169–173, 168–210 *passim*, 211–215
Allestree, Richard 52–53, 75
Ancients vs. Moderns, 1–3, 24–28, 63–64, 108–117, 140–143, 213–214
Aristotle, 31, 33, 83, 90, 106, 108 and n. 81, 112, 116, 117, 124, 153
Armstrong, Nancy 20 n. 50, 53 n. 41, 81–83, 97, 117, 119
Astell, Mary 23
Atkins, J. W. H. 42

Bakhtin, M. M. 6–7, 14–16, 37, 80
  authoritative discourse 6–7
  dialogism 15, 17
  heteroglossia 15
  unitary language 15–16
Ballaster, Ros 88 n. 23, 97 n. 52, 156
Barbauld, Anna Letiticia 83–4
Barker, Jane 36
Barrell, John 69 n. 96, 186
Barrett, Michele 85
Bates, Catherine 19–20
beauty
  of women 20–23, 53–4, 92, 100–102, 103, 146, 168, 171–172, 186, 187–189, 192–193, 195, 199, 202–203, 204–206, 209
  in contrast to the sublime 168–210 *passim*
  as a quality of language 46, 57–60, 91, 94–95, 110, 142, 168–210 *passim*
Behn, Aphra 20, 30–31, 36, 71, 93, 95, 97, 99, 102–103, 127, 128–137, 158–159, 164, 166, 206, 212
  on Dryden 130–131

History of the Nun 93, 102–103
  Preface to *The Dutch Lover* 130–134
  Preface to *The Luckey Chance* 30–31, 135–136
  Preface to *Sir Patient Fancy* 134–135
  on Shadwell 130–131, 134
Bellon, Peter 93
Bennett, John 3, 193, 196, 204, 205
Blackamore, Arthur 113
Blackstone, William 187
Boileau, Nicholas 178
Boyle, Robert 90
Boyle, Roger 90, 108–109
Budgell, Eustace 87
Burke, Edmund 3, 29, 153, 169, 170–172, 184, 186, 190–197, 199–200, 202–203, 205–206, 211
  Philosophical Enquiry 3, 29, 170, 190–197
Butler, Judith 13, 215 n. 4

Calprenéde: *Cassandre* 94
Carter, Elizabeth 32
Castle, Terry 118–119
Cavendish Margaret, Duchess of Newcastle 45, 158
Chapelle, Jean de la 93
Charles II 50, 54, 73, 98, 102
Chevigny, Bell, with Myra Jehlen and Judith Walkowitz 13
Chudleigh, Lady Mary 23
Cibber, Theophilus 29–30, 188
classical languages 94, 130, 148, 152, 175
classicism; neoclassicism 3, 24–25, 35–36, 55, 72, 91, 106–117, 119–120, 132–133, 138, 140–147, 168, 174–176, 182–184, 190, 197–198, 199, 200, 213
classics: study of 31–34, 94, 148, 206
Cobb, Samuel 4
Cogan, Henry 94, 109
Collier, Jeremy 68, 69, 70, 95
Congreve, William 35, 43, 109–111, 112

229